# Ancient China: Villages

## 108 Ancient Chinese Villages

Ancient China: Villages

Idyllic river and mountain villages
Festivals and ethnic cullture
Villages from Chinese ink paintings
High speed rail
Directions from major tourist hubs

# Top Ten Ancient Chinese Villages

Selected by China Rail and the editorial team of this book sozhen.com.

1

## Hong Village 宏村 p2

【 Yixian County, Anhui Province 】

*The Village from a Chinese Ink Painting*

Flanked by the Yellow Mountain, on sunny days, Hong Village offers sublime views that unveil like a slow-spreading landscape scroll, in which the surrounding mountains, white walls and black tiles are reflected on the lake. The village also has more than 140 well-preserved ancient houses dating back to the Ming and Qing Dynasties.

***Attractions:*** Chengzhi Hall, South Lake, Moon Lake, South Lake College, Jade Garden.

2

## Tangyue Village 棠樾古村 p20

【 Shexian County, Anhui Province 】

*The Village of Memorial Arches*

Tangyue Village's memorial arches, ancient temples and residences are known as the "Three Wonders of Huizhou Ancient Architecture". There are seven Ming and Qing Dynasty memorial arches inside the village representing loyalty, falial piety, integrity, and righteousness.

***Attractions:*** Memorial Arches, Temple for Men, Temple for Women, Bao's Family Garden.

## Xiwan Village 西湾古村 p37

【 Linxian County, Shanxi Province 】

*The Village of Cave Dwellings and Mansions*

Sheltered by a hill beside the tranquil Qiushui River, Xiwan Village contains groups of fortress-style ancient residences. Simply from the luxuriousness of the structures, it is clear that the residences in Xiwan Village were owned by the wealthy and powerful.

***Attractions:*** Houses of Chen Normal School, Sixiao Hall, Chen Family Ancestral Hall.

3

## Huangcheng Village 皇城古村 p57

【 Yangcheng County, Shanxi Province 】

*The Prime Minister's Village*

Huangcheng Village's unique complex of official mansions and residences is regarded as an epitome of Chinese civilisation. Chen Jingting, a former tutor to Qing Emperor Kangxi, occupied the Prime Minister's Mansion, which boasts 9 gagtes, 1700 metres of walls and 19 large courtyards.

***Attractions:*** Tower of Imperial Inscription, Tower of Rivers and Mountains, Villa of the Golden Mean, Yushu Pavilion

4

5

## Peitian Village 培田古村 p74

【 Liancheng County, Fujian Province 】

*The Hakka Village of Eighteen Wells*

Peitian Village is encirced by three streams and five mountains, and the village is said to be embraced by "three dragons and five tigers". Due to the rainy weather of the south, the residences in Peitian Village were built by the Hakka people in the formation of "nine halls and 18 wells".

***Attractions:*** Official Hall, Jijin Hall, Yanqing Hall, Nanshan College.

## Guodong Village 郭洞古村 p98

**【Wuyi County, Zhejiang Province】**

*The Feng Shui Village*

Guodong Village was designed according to the Taoist "Inner Landscape Diagram" preserved in Beijing's White Cloud Temple. Beside the village, two streams converge before meeting the green mountains in the distance. It is said that Guodong Village's water gate is a barrier at the entrance of the village to prevent invading enemies.

***Attractions:*** He Family Ancestral Hall, Xinwu Li Residence, Huilong Bridge, Transporting Bamboo on Water .

6

7

## Daqitou Village 大旗头古村 p114

**【Foshan City, Guangdong Province】**

*The Village of "Wok-Ear" Residences*

While the style would eventually be widespread, Daqitou was the first Chinese village to feature "wok-ear" residences. The top of the walls are tall in the middle and low at the sides, resembling the "ears" of a traditional official's hat. In ancient times, such residences were reserved solely for government officials.

***Attractions:*** Comb-like Layout, Wok-ear Residences, the Four Treasures of the Study Zheng Family Ancestral Hall

## Zhaoxingzhai Village 肇兴寨 p218

**【Liping County, Guizhou Province】**

*The Dong Ethnic Village*

Zhaoxingzhai Village is the largest and oldest Dong ethnic village in China. Inside the village there are rows upon rows of timber "diaojiaolous" ("hanging foot" dwellings) and five drum towers sitting like lotuses, a perfect complement to the beautiful flower bridges.

***Attractions:*** Drum Towers, Flower Bridges, Dong song and dance perforamnces

8

## Zhang Guying Village 张谷英古村 p168

**【Yueyang City, Hunan Province】**

*The Village of Dragons*

The Dragon Pearl Stone lies before the magnificent Dangdamen residence and is regarded as the mouth of the dragon of Longxing Mountain. Two big ponds on the right and left sides of the village gates are used as fireproofing mechanisms and are known as the "eyes of the dragon".

***Attractions:*** Door with Big Drum Stones, Wang Family House, Shangxin Wu Residence, Three Bridges Within 100 Steps.

9

## Zhu Jiayu Village 朱家峪古村 p201

**【Zhangqiu City, Shandong Province】**

*The Village of the Holy Spring*

Surrounded by mountains, Zhu Jiayu Village boasts temples, pavilions, stone bridges, old roads and ancient springs, allowing visitors to unravel the mysteries of the past, all while enjoying the magnificent scenery the village has to offer.

***Attractions:*** Holy Springs, Kangxi Twin Bridges, Wenchang Pavilion, Seven Bridges

10

# Location of Ancient Chinese Villages

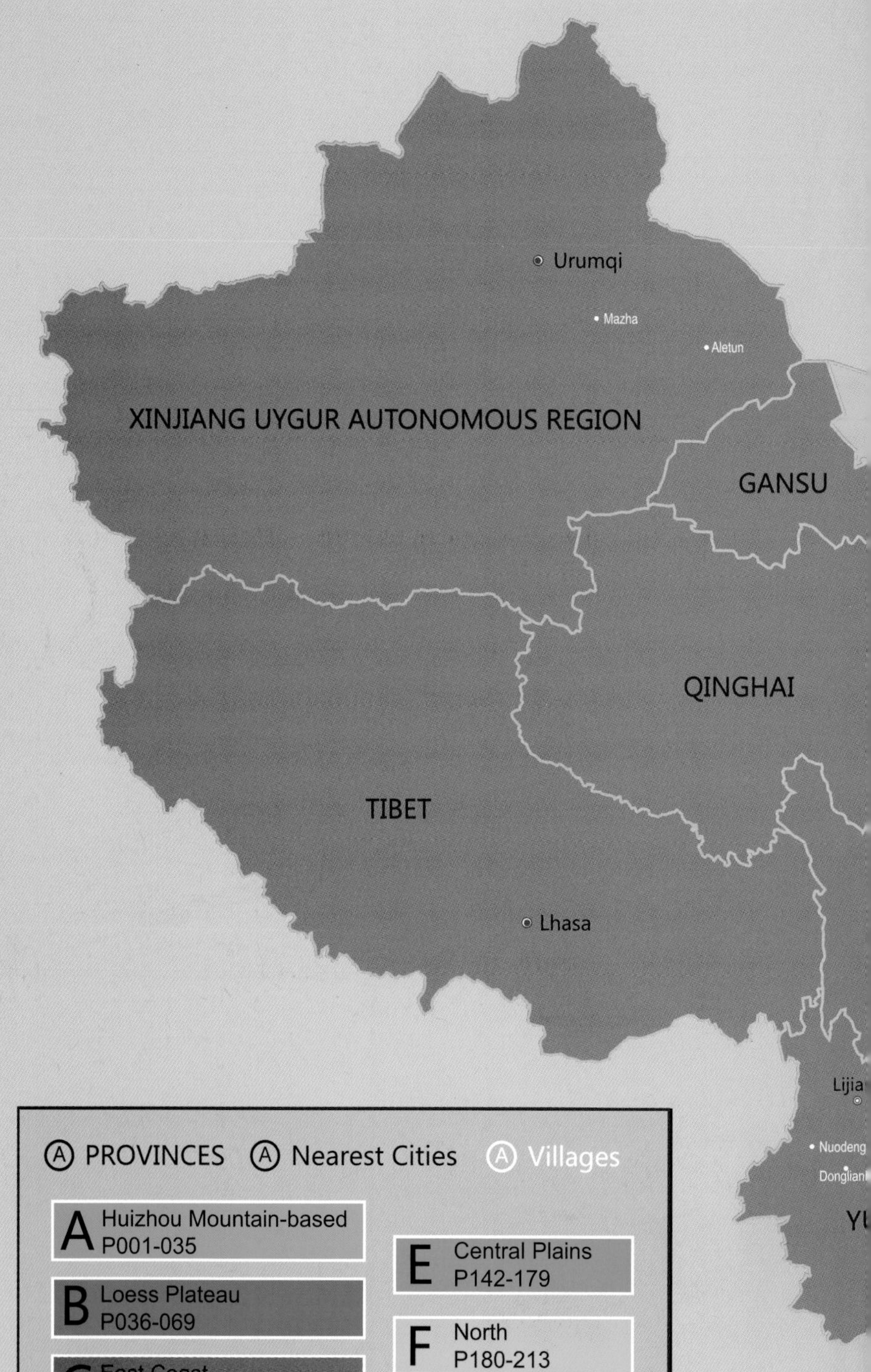

HEILONGJIANG
Harbin
Changchun
JILIN
Shenyang
LIAONING
INNER MONGOLIA
Hebei
Baotou
Holhot
Wudangzhao
Meidaizhao
Beijing
Tianjin
Tianjin
Guandixia
Beifangcheng
Ranzhuang
SHANXI
Yulin
Taiyuan
Yinchuan
Ningxia
Lanzhou
Nanchangtan
Yangjiagou
Xiwan
Xiaohe
Lijiashan
Liang
Zhangbi
Xiamen
Shijiagou
Shijiazhuang
Yingtan
Xingtai
Handan
Jinan
Zhujiayu
Weihai
Dongzhu Island
Xiongyasuo
Qingdao
SHANDONG
Piancheng
Douzhuang
Jincheng
Xiwenxing
Lianghu
Dangjia
Shangzhuang
Huangcheng
Guoyu
Luoyang
Zhengzhou
Xi´an
SHAANXI
HENAN
Linfeng
Zhangdian
JIANGSU
Nanjing
Hefei
Suzhou
Mingyuewan
Luxiang
Shanghai
ANHUI
HUBEI
Dayuwan
Hangzhou
Huangshan
Jinhua
Hong
Luobozhai
Moluo
Chengdu
Gunlongba
Enshizhou
Wuhan
Jingdezhen
CHONGQING
Chongqing
Lianghekou
Nanchang
Zhangguying
Luotian
Shangrao
ZHEJIANG
Tianbao
Jiajia
Xiamei
Bing'an
Changsha
Zunyi
Tongren
Huaihua
GUIZHOU
Loushang
JIANGXI
Cheng
Yanfang
Liukeng
Pixia
Meipi
Jixia
Lian
Matou
Baiwu
Guiyang
Qiaodongnan
Gaoyi
HUNAN
Nanping
Guifeng
Fuzhou
Yunshantun
Zengchong
Longli
Yongzhou
Sanming
Bailu
Laifang
Zhaoxingzhai
Ganyantou
Ganzhou
Peitian
FUJIAN
Longyan
Fuquan
Quanzhou
Xiamen
Shanggantang
Xiushui
Nangang
Gupai
Tianluokeng
TAIWAN
GUANGDONG
Daling
Tangwei
Qianmei
Guangzhou
Daqitou
Dongguan
Shantou
GUANGXI
Nanning
Bijiang
Nanshe
Gaoshan
Cuiheng
Shenzhen
Pengcheng
Zhuhai
Xima
Dalu
HONGKONG
MACAU
Zili
Haikou
HAINAN
Sanya
Chaji
Jiang
Pingshan
Hong
Nanping
Xidi
Yantai
Chengkan
Shen'ao
Tangyue
Yuliang
Tangmo
Likeng
Yan
Wangkou
Guodong
Houwu
Yuyuan
Sanmenyuan

# Ancient

In the last few years, the aggressive roll-out of a high-speed rail network has transformed travel in China. Ancient China: Villages is a guide to a formerly remote world of 108 Chinese villages that have remained largely unchanged for generations.

Many of the villages contain hundreds of stunning ancient residences, temples, bridges, theatre stages, memorial arches and shrines – from the Han (206 BCE-220) through to the Qing Dynasty (1644-1911). The villages also house numerous precious artworks, carvings and calligraphic inscriptions, which are regarded as national treasures.

## Clan Legacy

China's ancient villages were often dominated by families with a particular surname. For example, since the Southern Song Dynasty (1172-1279), almost all the residents of Bailu Village in southern Jianxi Province have shared the same family name – Zhong. Almost all the villages contain ancestral temples and halls, many of which were built by merchants and government officials who returned home after making their fortunes outside the village.

## Village Architecture

Given the vastness of China, there is unsurprisingly a commensurate variety of village architectures. Wealthy merchants of the Huizhou region developed the classic Anhui style famous for its white walls, black tiles and horse-head outer walls. Ancestral temples, studies and yards and lanes of the river villages of Jiangnan (south of the Yangtze River) exhibit a special architectural delicacy. Danba County in Sichuan Province, on the other hand, is renowned for its many unique stone Tibetan blockhouses. In the Dong villages of Guizhou Province, flower bridges and wooden drum tower were built as symbols of prosperity.

## Education and Culture

Since ancient times, the Chinese have placed a heavy emphasis on Confucian education and literature. As a result, the imperial examination system of feudal China, which lasted from the Sui Dynasty (589-618) through to its abolition in 1905, has had a huge influence on the culture of China's ancient villages. The achievments of those villagers who succeeded in the examinations have been memorialised in village buildings, monuments and inscriptions.

There were several classes of award scholars: Shengyuan, also called Xiucai, was a successful candidate in the annual county level exams; Juren was a graduate of the exams held at the provincial level every three years; and Jinshi was a graduate of the palace examination. Equally prestigious was membership in the Hanlin Academy, an elite group of court scholars. As you wander the village lanes you

will encounter many scholarly buildings such as Jinshi Mansions and Hanlin Memorial Archways.

**Religions**

The villages are also physical embodiments of China's religious system, which merged Buddhism, Daoism, Confucianism, and a pantheon of other ancient philosophies, religions and local gods. A typical ancient Chinese village may have shrines dedicated to Buddhist deities Maitreya and Guanyin, as well as the Town God, the God of War, and maybe others such as the Dragon King and the God of Wealth.

**Arts and Festivals**

The villages were also incubators of ancient Chinese arts such as martial arts and Chinese opera. There is a wide range of opera forms, from Peking Opera and Anhui Opera to Wu Opera and Shanxi Clapper Opera. In Jiangxi Province's Wuyuan Village, there are more than 50 varieties of masks for performing the art known as Nuo Dance.

Other villages like Jixia Village in Fujian Province or Xiema Village in Guangdong Province boast a long history of martial arts, and visitors will be able see practice facilities like stone locks, stone eggs, race grounds and practice halls in those villages.

Most villages also maintain ancient ceremonies held on traditional holidays like Chinese New Year, Tomb-Sweeping Day, Dragon Boat Festival and Mid-Autumn Festival. There is also a fascinating variety of local festivals such as the "Dream Interpretation" Festival of Yuyuan Village in Zhejiang Province and the "Wang Gong Welcoming" Festival of Guizhou Province's Yunshantun Village.

Make-Do Publishing

## Getting There

The development of high-speed rail has made it possible for tourists to explore a once mysterious world of ancient Chinese villages in a relatively short period of time. While many of the villages in this book are quite easy to find, visiting some the more remote or isolated locations may require a little extra effort. To make the villages easier to locate, each chapter provides directions (public transport where possible) to the village from its nearest major city. An introduction to these cities can be found on pages **viii-xi**. Develop your own travel plan with care – it will be well worth it.

# Getting there



## Anhui

**Huangshan City** is the jumping off point for visits to the famous Yellow Mountain (Huangshan) and the surrounding countryside contains some of the most beautiful ancient villages in China. Huangshan Tunxi Airport offers connections to major cities across China. Huangshan Railway Station on the Jianxi-Anhui line is linked to regional centres such as Nanjing and Hangzhou. *Hong Village (p2), Xidi Village (p3), Nanping Village (p8), Tangmo Village (p11), Pingshan Village (p14), Chengkan Village (p16), Yuliang Village (p18), Tangyue Village (p20), Jiang Village (p22), Chaji Village (p25).*

## Beijing

The big, bad and often bewildering capital of China. *Cuandixia Village (p181), .Lingshui Village (p184), Liuliqu Village (p190), Jimingyi Village (p198), Beifangcheng Village (p204).*

## Fujian

Fujian's capital **Fuzhou** is a heartland of the Mindong linguistic and cultural area. Fujian Changle International Airport offers routes to most major Chinese cities. Fuzhou's two railway stations – Fuzhou and the new Fuzhou South - mean that the city is well connected to other cities along China's eastern seaboard. *Guifeng Village (p78), Lian Village (p83), Jixia Village (p88).*

**Ganzhou**, the second biggest city of Jiangxi Province, revels in the moniker of "orange capital of the world".. Ganzhou Huangjin Airport has routes to China's major cities while Ganzhou with its several stations is also something of a regional railway hub. *Bailu Village (p157).*

**Longyan** City, located on the west shore of the Taiwan Strait, has a high concentration (about 75%) of Hakka people. Liancheng Airport has flight connections to Shanghai, Fuzhou and Shenzhen while there are frequent rail services between Longyan Train Station and Xiamen (4 hours). *Peitian Village (p74).*

**Nanping** is a picturesque city in northwestern Fujian, surrounded by high stone walls. Nanping's Wuyishan Airport has routes to and from Beijing, Xiamen,Shanghai and Shenzhen. Nanping Station is now just a 2 hour high-speed rail journey from Fuzhou South Station. *Xiamei Village (p80), Cheng Village (p86).*

**Quanzhou**, located in the southeast of Fujian, was once (during the Yuan and Song dynasties) one of China's largest seaports. Quanzhou Jinjiang Airport is linked to destinations elsewhere in Fujian and beyond. Quanzhou also has good high speed rail connections - the service to Xiamen takes under 45 minutes. *Fuquan Village (p90).*

**Sanming** is a green city in western Fujian, well-known for its diverse natural landforms. Sanming's Shaxian Airport has flights to major cities while Sanming Train Station is served by routes to and from Xiamen and Shanghai among other places. *Laifang Village (p76).*

**Xiamen**, also known as Amoy, is a major coastal city and the ancestral home of large communities of overseas Chinese. Xiamen Gaoqi International Airport has routes to and from cities across China. Xiamen is also connected to an expanding matrix of high-speed railway services. *Tianluokeng Village.*

## Guangdong

**Dongguan** is a factory town, located 50km from Guangzhou, and home to the world's largest shopping mall. High-speed trains connect Dongguan with Guangzhou, Shenzhen and Hong Kong. *Tangwei Village.*

## Guangxi

**Guangzhou**, located about 120km north of Hong Kong, is the capital of Guangdong Province and the third-largest city in China. In the eighteenth century the city emerged as one of the world's great trading ports. These days, Guangzhou Baiyun International Airport is the second busiest in China, and Guangzhou's four railways stations are connected with cities across China through an ever-expanding number of high-speed railway lines. *Daqitou Village (p114), Bijiang Village (p116), Daling Village (p118),Cuiheng Village (p124), Nangang Gupai Village (p134).*

**Shantou**, one of the original Special Economic Zones established in the 1980s, is situated on the eastern coast of Guangdong province. The city is about a 3.5 bus ride from Shenzhen. Meanwhile Jieyang Chaoshan Airport has flights to and from a variety of destinations. *Qianmei Village (p131).*

**Shenzhen**, located adjacent to Hong Kong, was a lowly fishing village before the 1980s when it was selected as another of China's Special Economic Zone. Shenzhen Baoan airport is one of China's busiest airports. Meanwhile Shenzhen is integrated into China's fast developing high speed rail network, providing easy access to Guangzhou and destinations further afield. *Pengcheng Village (p111), Nanshe Village (p120).*

**Zhuhai** borders on Macau to the south and is one of the top tourist destinations for Chinese domestic tourism. Zhuhai Sanzao Airport has routes to and from major cities in other provinces. *Zili Village (p126), Xiema Village (p128).*

## Guizhou

**Nanning**, the provincial capital, is situated 160km from China's border with Vietnam and its warm climate ensures an abundance of tropical foliage. Nanning Wuwei International Airport offers a large selection of domestic and some international routes. A high-speed rail link has cut travel time from Guangzhou to Nanning to 3 hours. *Dalu Village, Xiushui Village (p138), Gaoshan Village (p140).*

## Hebei

**Guiyang**, the provincial capital is populated by 23 different ethnic minorities, of which the Miao are the most numerous. Guiyang Longdongbao International Airport has routes to other major Chinese cities. Guiyang is also a railway hub, with high-speed connections to Chengdu, Chongqing, Guangzhou, Changsha, and Kunming due to be launched in 2012. *Matou Village (p224), Yunshantun Village (p227).*

**Tongren** is located in the Northeast of Guizhou Province. There are regular flights between Tongren Phoenix Airport and the provincial capital Guiyang. Alternatively, trains running between Huaihuai (in Hunan Province) and Tongren take about 1hour. *Loushang Village (p222).*

**Zunyi**, located in the north of Guizhou Province, is famous for its spicy hot local cuisine and for the rice liquor Maotai, which is brewed nearby. There are regular flights between Xinzhou Airport and Beijing, Shanghai and other destinations. Alternatively, there are regular rail connections with the provincial capital Guiyang as well as more distant destinations. *Bingan Village (p230).*

**Qiandongnan Miao & Dong Autonomous County** is served by Liping Airport, which offers services to Guiyang, the capital city of Guizhou, and Guangzhou. Kaili Station can be reached by train from Guiyang in about 2.5 hours. *Zengchong Village (p215), Zhaoxingzhai Village (p218), Longli Village (p220).*

**Shijiazhuang**, the capital city of Hebei Province is only a 2 hour train journey from Beijing West Station. Hebei Zhengding International Airport is served by a wide variety of domestic routes. *Yujia Village (p187), Ranzhuang Village (o192), Yingtan Village (p194), Piancheng Village (p196).*

## Henan

**Luoyang** is one of the ancient dynastic capitals of China – although the casual visitor may find it hard to detect any sense of that glorious history. Luoyang Airport has flights to cities across China while Luoyang Longmen Station offers routes to Beijing, Xian and Zhengzhou. *Zhangdian Village (p159).*

**Zhengzhou**, located on the southern banks of the Yellow River, is another of China's ancient capitals. The city is a major railway hub and Zhengzhou Xinzheng International Airport is also one of the country's gateway airports. *Linfeng Stockade (p160).*

## Hubei

**Enshizhou**, a county-level city in the Miao Autonomous Prefecture of southwest Hubei Province, is on the Yichang-Wanzhou (Chongqing) railway line, which after it was completed in 2010 was described as the most difficult ever built in China. Enshi Xujiaping Airport has services to Wuhan. *Gunlongba Village (p164), Lianghekou Village (p166).*

**Wuhan** is the provincial capital and an important economic centre located on the Yangtze River. Wuhan Tianhe International Airport is one of China's busiest airports. The new Wuhan Railway Station is used by Wuhan-Guangzhou high-speed trains, while the old Hangkou and Wuchang stations offer regular connections to destinations across China. *Dawuyuan Village (p162).*

## Hunan

**Changsha** is the capital city of Mao Zedong's home province, and the site of his conversion to communism. Changsha Huanghua International Airport is served by a large number of domestic routes. Changsha Railway Station has connections to cities across China – and a high-speed rail link now eats the distance between Changsha and Guangzhou in about 4 hours. *Zhangguying Village (p168).*

Huaihua is located in a mountainous area of southwest Hunan Province. Flights between Huaihua Zhijiang Airport and the provincial capital Changsha take 1 hour. Alternatively, the same journey takes about 6 hours by train. *Gaoyi Village (p171).*

Yongzhou is situated on the south side of the Xiang river. In recent years many industries have relocated here from more expensive coastal areas. Yongzhou Lingning Airport is served by flights to and from Changsha, Guangzhou, Shenzhen and Beijing. The city also has good rail connections with the provincial capital Changsha. *Ganyantou Village (p174), Shanggantang Village (p177).*

## Inner Mongolia

Baotou is the industrial hub of the Inner Mongolia autonomous region and also a major railway hub with two main train stations, Baotou East Station and Baotou Station. There are regular flights between Baotou Airport and Beijing, Shanghai and Taiyuan. *Wudangzhao Village (p206), Meidaizhao Village (p208).*

## Jiangsu

Suzhou in southeast Jiangsu is a major tourist draw on account of its canals, stone bridges and exquisite gardens. Downtown Suzhou is a 50 minute drive from Southern Jiangsu Shuofang International Airport. High-speed trains from Shanghai and Nanjing disembark at Suzhou Station or Suzhou South Station. *Luxiang Village (p92), Mingyuewan Village (p95).*

## Jiangxi

Jingdezhen in Jiangxi province is deservedly known as the "capital of Chinese porcelain". Jingdezhen Station on the Jianxi-Anhui railway line is connected to key centres such as Nanjing and Shanghai. There are also direct flights between Shanghai and Jingdezhen Airport (1 hour). *Yantai Village (p34).*

Shangrao is a medium-sized city in the north-east of Jiangxi. Shangrao Sanqingshan Airport offers services to a selection of major Chinese cities while Shangrao Train Station on the Jianxi-Anhui line is linked with larger regional centres such as Shanghai. *Wangkou Village (p28), Yan Village (p30), Likeng Village (p32).*

Nanchang, the capital of Jiangxi, is famous for both its history and its scenery. There are regular flights between Nanchang Changbei Airport and Beijing, Shanghai, Guangzhou, Shenzhen and Haikou. Nanchang is also linked to Hangzhou, Changsha and Shanghai by high-speed rail. *Luotian Village (P143), Liukeng Village (p145), Tianbao Village (p148), Jiajia Village (p150), Meipi Village (p152), Pixia Village (p154), Yanfang Village (p156).*

## Ningxia

Yinchuan, the capital city of Ningxia Hui Autonomous Region, boasts attractions such as the Western Xia Tombs. The city is served by Yinchuan Hedong Airport while Yinchuan Station is connected to China's national rail network. *Nanchangtan Village (p250).*

## Qinghai

Xining, the provincial capital, is the biggest city on the Qinghai-Tibet Plateau. There are regular flights between Xining Caojiabao Airport and Beijing, Shanghai, Chengdu, Hong Kong and other cities. Xining is also connected by rail to Lanzhou in Gansu province. *Guomari Village (p252).*

## Shaanxi

Yulin is an isolated coal mining city which has preserved a fair amount of classical architecture, including parts of the old city walls. Yulin Yuyang Airport has a selection of routes to and from major cities while there are also rail connections with Beijing and other destinations. *Yangjiagou Village (p68).*

Xian, the provincial capital, was once the site of "Chang'an" one of the four great ancient capitals of China. Xian Xianyang International Airport is the largest airport in the northwest of China. Xian Railway Station offers more than 100 services daily. *Dangjia Village (p66).*

## Shandong

Jinan, the provincial capital, is known for its large number of natural artesian springs. Jinan Yaoqiang International Airport offers services to many other Chinese cities. Jinan is a major railway hub and the new high-speed Beijing-Shanghai route connects Jinan with Beijing West Station in an amazing 1.5 hours. *Zhujiayu Village (p201).*

Weihai is a major seaport which was the base for the Beiyang Fleet of China during the Qing Dynasty. Weihai Dashuipo International Airport has connections with Beijing, Shanghai and Guangzhou – as well as Seoul and Pusan. There are regular routes between Weihai Station and provincial capital Jinan as well as Beijing and Hankou, Wuhan. *Dongchudao Village (p212)*

Qingdao, located in Shandong Province on the shores of the Yellow Sea, is known as "City of Sails". The city is also the home of the Qingdao brewery. Qingdao Liuting International Airport offers a wide selection of routes, including some international ones. Qingdao has several rail stations and connections to major cities of other provinces. *Xiongyasuo Village (p210).*

## Shanxi

Jincheng is a prefecture-level city located in an important coal producing region of China. A train to Jincheng from the provincial capital Taiyuan takes about 6hours. *Lianghu Village, Douzhuang Village, Xiwenxing Village, Huangcheng Village, Guoyu Village, Shangzhuang Village.*

Taiyuan, the provincial capital, was founded in 497BC and was an ancient capital of the Zhao Kingdom. Taiyuan Wusu International Airport has good connections with major cities. A high-speed train from Beijing can now reach Taiyuan Station in less than 3hours. *Xiwan Village, Lijiashan Village, Liang Village, Zhangbi Village, Xiamen Village, Shijiagou Village, Xiaohe Village.*

## Sichuan

Chengdu, is the cultural heart of West China, and during its 2000 year history, has been capital to at least six breakaway regimes. Chengdu Shuangliu International Airport is the busiest airport in Western China. The city is also a major rail terminus with four railway stations. *Moluo Village (p233), Luobozhai Village (p238).*

Panzhihua is located on the confluence of the Jinsha and Yalong rivers in the far south of Sichuan. There are direct flights between Panzhihua and Chengdu, Beijing and Chongqing, while Panzhihua is also linked by rail to regional centres Chengdu and Kunming. *Yishala Village (p236).*

## Xijiang

Urumchi (Xinjiang Uygur Autonomous Region), located at the north of the Tianshan Mountains, is the most remote city from any sea in the world. Urumchi Diwobao International Airport is one of China's top airports while Urumchi is Xinjiang's major rail hub. *Mazha Village (p254), Aletun Village (p256).*

## Yunnan

Kunming, the provincial capital, is a gateway to the delights of China's exotic and culturally diverse south-west. There are direct flights between Kunming Wujiaba International Airport and other leading Chinese cities, while a new airport Kunming Changshui, was due to become operational during 2012. Kunming is the main rail hub of Yunnan province. *Baiwu Village (p240), Zhengying Village (p246).*

Picture-esque Lijiang has a history of almost a thousand years and is a hot tourist destination for Chinese and foreign visitors alike. Lijiang Qihe Airport offers a wide selection of connections. Lijiang Station is an 8-hour train ride from the provincial capital Kunming. *Nuodeng Village (p243), Donglianhua Village (p248).*

## Zhejiang

Jinhua, which borders Hangzhou in central Zhejiang, is best-known for its dry-cured Jinhua ham. Jinhua Yiwu International Airport has routes to a limited number of key Chinese cities. The city is also an intersection point for three railways. *Guodong Village (p98), Yuyuan Village (p104), Sanmenyuan Village (p106).*

Hangzhou has been celebrated throughout history for the scenic beauty of its West Lake. Hangzhou Xiaoshan Internataional Airport offers a wide selection of routes. Direct trains link Hangzhou to more than 20 cities and a high-speed service covers the 200km from Shanghai in about 1.15 hours. *Houwu Village (p101), Shen'ao Village (p108).*

# Formation of Ancient Villages

Ancient villages in China usually began as clan settlements, providing individuals with a community for living, trading and economic development. By contrast, Chinese cities were developed more for political and military functions.

The many unique ancient villages contained in this book are distinguished by distinctive features, including: villages designed according to feng shui principles; villages built within ancient city walls; villages associated with China's twentieth century revolutions; ethnic culture villages; post station villages; religious villages.

However the layouts of China's ancient villages can be grouped into four main types:

## Water Villages

This type of village is situated beside a river and typically features water, bridges and elegant residences (Xidi Village is an outstanding example). River Villages integrate natural landscapes with cultural traditions, and contain a strong sense of feng shui and an agricultural education system where students split their time between study and farming. Such villages are very particular about their distribution of memorial arches, colleges, temples and ancestral halls. The distinctive stilted dwelling, known as Diaojiaolou ("hanging-foot" house), is both artistic and practical – some stand alone, while others are built in groups — all are extraordinary buildings; warm in winter and cool in summer, neither dry nor damp, and in perfect harmony with nature.

## Mountain Villages

This type of village typically features mountain slopes, towering old trees and crystal clear streams (Lijia Village is a great example). Commonly featured architecture include Siheyuan (courrtyard residences with rooms on 4 sides) Diaojiaolou and cave dwellings. These villages are filled with interesting laneways, white walls with black tiles, tall and magnificent horse-head walls and delicate carvings.

## Fortress–style Villages

Built to withstand invasion, this type of village typically contain castles and fortresses (the best known is probably Zhangbi Village). Strategically located on steep mountains, these villages are easy to protect and hard to attack. Tall city gates, grand city walls and neat and tidy streets are the common features of fortress-style villages.

## Scenic Villages

This kind of village usually grew prosperous because of the exceptional advantages it enjoyed from being built near picturesque scenic spots (the perfect example is Jimingyi Village). Often situated nearby to famous temples, well-known mountains, or residences of celebrities, these villages were eulogised in poetry and song and gradually developed into unique places with profound cultural associations.

# Architectural Styles

Ancient Chinese villages typically have an organic culture that blends traditional feng shui philosophies, local folk traditions, and aspects of national culture in a blend which is on display in every corner.

Most ancient villages are typically situated near mountains and rivers. In addition to ditches and ponds, trees and flowers, village architecture mainly include residences, temples, colleges, wells, bridges, stages, memorial arches, towers, shrines and tombs. Of these, the temples and the residences of wealthy families are the most extravagant. Characteristic features include:

祠堂 Larger and more intricately constructed than most residences, temples (including ancestral halls, branch temples and family temples) were built to worship ancestors, deliberate on family issues, hold ceremonies, as well as educating future generations. The building of temples began to flourish during the Ming Dynasty. As temples symbolise wealth and family honour, the richer the family the more likely the temple will feature grand halls, delicate carvings and precious ornamentations.

旗杆石The mast stone is generally set at the front of a temple to mark the clan members' scholarly honour or official rank.

匾额 Hung above the door, plaques (decorative boards inscribed with writings) are an integral element of ancient Chinese architecture. Typically bearing a building's name and features, it is an art form which reflects one's doctrines and emotions. The size and the number of plaques in a temple symbolises the honor and pride of a clan

堂号 The "Tang Hao" (symbol of a clan) is written by a skilled family member or calligrapher, then made into a gold plaque and hung atop the inside of the main hall. Beside it, you may find plaques detailing the origin of the family's name, clan honour, female chastity and so on.

正堂 The main hall is the most important part of a temple, in which there are altars, ancestor memorial tablets and portraits, family trees, and tables for religious offerings.

牌坊 A memorial arch is primarily for conferring honour on the virtuous and the worthy, and is usually located at the front or middle of a village as an iconic structure of feudal etiquette.

戏台 For operas and ceremonies, most villages also have a simple yet elegant theatre stage, which will be bustling with excited crowds during major festivals.

山 Many ancient villages are located near mountains or at least with a mountain as the backdrop. An ideal village site is one surrounded by mountains like city walls and with flowing streams.

水口 Water outlets are commonly seen at the entrance of villages and form a cultural landscape with landmarks such as towers and bridges.

塔 Towers often stand at the entrance of a village to adjust the FengShui or to decorate the scenery.

府第 The mansions of wealthy families with big, complex courtyards and rich decorations are generally situated at the best locations of a village. These mansions pay particular attention to building and carving techniques, and some even have their own gardens. A luxurious mansion symbolises family honour.

池塘 Ponds are an indispensable element in ancient villages, used for fishing, washing clothes and fetching water, as well as accumulating feng shui. The artistic beauty of a mountain reflected perfectly in the water has always been a much sought after sight since ancient times.

# Cultural Significance

China's ancient villages reflect the country's many different regions, cultures, ethnicities and architectural preferences:

**Historical** Each ancient village embodies centuries of history, and many contain old wharves, ports and streets that have remained largely unchanged for generations. Plenty of beautiful and ingeniously pragmatic ancient buildings and dwellings still have their original features, from Ming and Qing Dynasty residences to ancient post stations, theatre stages, gatehouses and bridges.

**Feng shui philosophy** Feng shui philosophy regards human beings as part of nature. China's ancient villages represent the goal of "unity of heaven and humanity", which has been a goal of the Chinese for thousands of years. Almost all villages place significant emphasis on FengShui when it comes to site selection, planning and layout. Hong Village, shaped like a crouched ox, is beautiful and tranquil; Tai Chi Horoscope Village is filled with mysteries; Nuodeng Village offers the marvellous natural spectacle of the Tai Chi map.

**Clan System** Most of China's ancient villages are characterised by clans, giving them a sense of orderliness and hierarchy as well as traditional family and cultural values, which are typically passed down through the bloodlines. The ubiquitous memorial archways and ancestral temples are the symbols of this phenomenon.

**Architectural Culture** The tiny Diaojiaolou ("hanging-foot" houses) near hills and rivers; the simple and dignified Siheyuan (four-sided courtyards); the nine halls and eighteen wells of Peitian Village – all of these are proud

representations of ancient village architecture. Yujia Village is a world of stone; the seaweed houses of Dongzhu Island Village are unique. Watchtowers, drum towers, earth buildings and castles – each structure has its own unique style and features. Whether it is dwellings, pavilions or pagodas, stone bridges, sculptures, plaques or couplets, architecture in China's ancient villages often symbolises the ancient villagers' pursuit of beauty.

**Gengdu (Farming and Education) Culture** The traditional concepts of "returning to one's roots" and "farming while studying" are engrained in China's ancient villages. The ancients took education very seriously, and their longing for culture is reflected everywhere in the overall architectural structure of the villages. The "four treasures" in the study room of Daqitou Village is a classic representation of the "Gengdu" (farming and education) philosophy.

**Culture and Festivals** Each ancient village has its own unique cultural traditions, anging from Nuo Opera to dragon dancses and the Welcoming Wang Gong Festival of Yunshantun Village

# CONTENTS

A
Huizhou Mountain-based Villages
P1—35

B
Loess Plateau Villages
P36—69

# D South of the Five Ridges

P110—141

## Central Plains Villages

## North

CONTENTS

# 徽州山区古村

# Huizhou Mountains

## Rivers, Courtyards and Lanes

# Hong Village

## The Village from a Chinese Painting

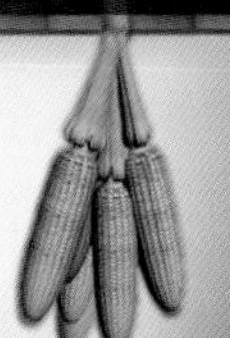

Hong Village, located in northwest Yu Country at the foot of Huangshan (the Yellow Mountain), is a stunning ancient village with a history that goes back to the Northern Song Dynasty.

### Getting there

Hong Village, Yi County, Anhui Province.
Nearest City: Huangshan.
安徽省黄山市黟县宏村镇宏村
Take a long distance bus (2 hours) from Huangshan's Tunxi Coach Station (屯溪汽车站) to Yi County (黟县). Tourist buses from Yi County Bus Station (黟县汽车站) to Hong Village depart every 20 minutes (RMB2). Alternatively, shuttle buses departing from Huangshan Scenic Area (黄山风景区) at 7:40 and 13:40 will pass Hong Village on their way to Yi County.

Flanked by the Yellow Mountain, on sunny days, Hong Village offers sublime views that unveil like a slow-spreading landscape scroll, in which the surrounding mountains, white walls and black tiles are reflected on the lake.

Hong Village's cinematic qualities were recognised by director Ang Lee when he chose the village as a location in his martial arts epic "Crouching Tiger, Hidden Dragon". The Song dynasty village was originally a settlement of the Wang (汪) clan but was later renamed Hong (宏) Village during the reign of Emperor Qianlong (1711-1799) in the Qing Dynasty.

From the hills, Hong Village is said to look like a buffalo lying leisurely among the scenic landscape. A star village attraction are the more than 140 well-preserved ancient folk houses dating back to the Ming and Qing Dynasties. Of these, Chengzhi Hall (承志堂) is a stand-out, regarded as one of the best ancient folk houses in all of southern Anhui province.

Chengzhi Hall was built in the sixth year of the Xianfeng Period during the Qing Dynasty (1855) and originally belonged to local salt tycoon Wang Dinggui. Located in the middle of the Hong Village's watercourse, the hall is a magnificent half-timbered building with exquisite woodcarvings in the beams, brackets, doors and traceries of window lattices. These ornate carvings, featuring an

The Song Dynasty Chinese Ink Painting

Village houses reflected in the lake

assortment of people with many different faces and expressions, are considered classic representations of one of Anhui's "Three Carving Arts" (being wood, stone and tile).

At Chengzhi Hall, the murmuring sound of water from the fish pond helps to create an impression of timelessness. The impressive mansion boasts inner and outer courtyards, a front room and back room, and east and west wing rooms, as well as a study room, fish pond, kitchen and stable. The Wang family's leisure was amply provided for: the Paishan Pavilion (排山阁) was built to play mahjong while the Tunyun Pavilion (吞云轩) was for smoking opium.

The front room has an unusual woodcarving joist featuring a pair of lions standing on their heads while playing with a ball. The doors of the wing rooms display four celestial symbols (福禄寿喜) which represent "blessing, fortune, longevity and happiness", as well as the famous "Eight Immortals" (八仙) from Chinese mythology. Elsewhere, woodcarvings on the beams show Emperor Suzong dining with officials during the Tang Dynasty.

The man-made South Lake's poetic beauty is another highlight as the lake curls around the southernmost part of Hong Village in the shape of an archer's bow. The surface of the water is as smooth as a piece of glass, reflecting green hills and blue skies; white walls and black tiles, flowers and trees.

South Lake was designed in accordance with the principles of "rhythmic vitality" in Chinese landscape paintings, and each season offers a different artistic imagery: in Spring, green and blooming flowers in Summer, the sweet fragrance of white lilies; Autumn offers the unique spectacle of the dual full moons — one hanging in sky, the other reflected in the tranquil waters below; and in Winter, the lake turns into a "silver bow lying in the snowy earth," resembling a "jade plate".

For a panoramic view of the South Lake and the green hills in the distance, hike up to the "Lake Watching Pavilion" of the South Lake College (南湖书院) (a former family private school). Beneath the Lake-Watching Pavilion lies Zhi Garden (抵园), formerly a living quarter for tutors. In Chinese, "Zhi" (抵) means good luck and also underlies the value of education and being respectful towards teachers. At a corner of the garden, a marble tablet rests snugly in the shade. While it looks natural, the marble is actually artificial; locals call it the "Scholars' Stone".

In the shape of a half-moon, Moon Pond, (月沼) the "stomach of the buffalo", was originally built during the Yongle period (1400-1424) of the Ming Dynasty. The pond is encircled by paved

### TEMPLE

Zilu Temple is located at the foot of Ziling Mountain, three kilometers southwest of Hong Village. Originally built in the third year of the Huichang reign during the Tang Dynasty (843), Zilu Temple continues to be a popular international meditation centre for visitors and Buddhist pilgrims.

blue stones and bordered by houses with white walls and black-tiled roofs. On bright days, clouds and houses appear as perfect reflections on the clear surface of the pond. Moon Pond has become a shared public place for villagers, a stage for opening folk customs and a venue for festivals.

North of the Moon Pond lies Lexutang ancestral hall (乐叙堂), also known as "All Happiness Hall". It was built during the Yongle period in the 15th century and originally served as the general ancestral hall of the village founding Wang family. The archway is essentially unchanged since ancient times, and the Ming Dynasty crescent beams, shaped braces, decorated brackets and short transverse timbers all feature exquisite sculptures. Together with the Moon Pond, Lexutang ancestral hall has the cute moniker of "Breeze-Ruffled Lotus on the Moon Pond" (月沼风荷).

The architecture in Hong Village is heavily influenced by the celebrated Suzhou Gardens (in Jiangsu province), which are famous for their exhibits of miniature mountains and lakes. These influences can be seen in the man-made ponds, the pavilions on the water and the trees and flowers cultivated by taking advantage of the village's irrigation system.

The 300 years from the late period of the Ming Dynasty to late period of the Qing Dynasty was a time of great prosperity for the descendants of the Wang family. This was also a time when Huizhou merchants were making major strides and the numbers of high officials and erudite scholars were on the rise. It was customary for those who had earned great achievements or made considerable fortunes abroad to return home to raise family honor by setting up ancestral halls, building mansions, digging ponds and drainages and paving roads.

Nearly every ancient folk house in Hong Village boasts a picturesque garden. "Longevity Hall" (松鹤堂) has a pavilion named "Crane-attraction" (in Chinese culture, the crane represents longevity), where occasionally waterfowls come to rest. "Genxin Pond" (根心塘) is shaped like the letter "U" and offers unique views.

The planning and design of the artificial water system inside and outside Hong Village is downright ingenious. Hundreds of years ago, the residents of the village dug a one-meter-deep canal to divert water from the river in the west of village into town. The canal still zigzags through the village, offering water for every household, as well as the added benefit of regulating temperatures.

The "Green Garden" (碧园) is situated at the source of the canal, where the water meanders through the garden's fishpond. The water in the pond is as described in Zhu Xi's poem (Zhu Xi (1130-1200) a Song Dynasty philosopher), The Book:

"There lies a glassy oblong pool, where light and shade pursue their course. How could it be so clear and cool? For fresh water comes from the source".

By the pond, you'll find a pavilion with three rest chairs. Originally built for fishing and to enjoy the evening breeze, the pavilion has become a place where locals come to admire the full moon and recite poems during the Mid-Autumn Festival. There is a ventilation wall to the north of the fishpond and a stone transparent window engraved in it, the designs of window constitute four Chinese characters "祥云瑞气" (means luck and blessing). It is a pleasant spot to kick back for a while and soak up the unique ambience of Hong Village.

Ang Lee used Hong Village as a location for "Crouching Tiger, Hidden Dragon"

# Xidi Village

## The Land of Peach Blossoms

Located on the south side of Huangshan, Xidi Village boasts hundreds of well-preserved residences from the Ming and Qing Dynasties and roads paved with marble. Be warned that is alarmingly easy to become lost in its labyrinth of its 99 high-walled lanes.

### Getting there

Xidi Village, Yi County, Anhui Province.
Nearest City: Huangshan.
安徽省黄山市黟县西递镇西递村
Take a long distance bus from Huangshan's Tunxi Coach Station(屯溪汽车站) to Yi County (黟县) (2 hours). There are buses from Yi County Bus Station (黟县汽车站) to Xidi Village (西递村) every 20 minutes. The distance is 8km and the ride costs RMB2 per person. Alternatively, buses departing from Huangshan Scenic Area at 09:40 and 15:40 will pass Xidi on their way to Yi County.

Xidi Village, with its cute moniker of "The Land of Peach Blossoms", is located only 40 km from the Huangshan Scenic Area. Originally named Xichuan (literally "West River"), Xidi Village was established during the Yuan Feng period of the Northern Song dynasty, over 900 years ago. The village is surrounded by mountains and two streams flow through it. There used to be a "dipu" (递铺, the ancient Chinese version of a post office) in the village, so it was eventually renamed Xidi. According to historical records, the village was founded when Li Hua, son of Emperor Tang Zhao Zong, fled to the area to avoid civil unrest. During Xidi's most prosperous period, believed to be at the beginning of the Qing Dynasty, there were said to be almost 600 residences in the village. Xidi Village was listed as a UNESCO World Heritage site in 2000.

The layout of Xidi Village has been likened to a ship: the continuous rows of houses are the cabins; the tall arbors and thirteen decorated archways are the mast and sails;

Residences of Xidi

The floral window of Xidi's East Garden

the surrounding mountains are the waves of the sea; and the Moon Lake and clusters of fields outside the village are the calm harbour in which the ship rests.

Xidi Village contains 124 wonderfully preserved residences dating back to the Ming and Qing Dynasties. With high firewalls and bluish tiles, the delicacy and refinement of the structures and decorations are regarded as extremely rare, prompting Chinese scholars to bestow Xidi Village with flowery nomenaclatures such as "Treasure Vault of Ancient Residences".

Inside most residences there is a tianjing (天井, inner courtyard), a feature of Anhui-style architecture where the rooms are specifically structured around the yard so that light and air can pass through smoothly. In ancient times the merchants protected their wealth with high walls and they rarely opened windows, so tianjings became a way to let "nature" into the buildings. A more allegorical notion was that tianjings would help merchants collect wealth and prevent it from leaving their house – just like the rain when it has rolled off their roofs and accumulated inside the courtyard.

The first thing you will see upon entering Xidi is Lingyun Tower (凌云阁), also called Zoumalou (走马楼), built during the Daoguang period of the Qing Dynasty. It is said to have been built by the village's wealthiest person, Hu Guansan, to welcome his father-in-law, the then prime minister. The present Zoumalou has been rebuilt and is now a single attraction together with Qizhe Temple (七哲祠). Zoumalou has two floors, and stands above a stone arch bridge called Wugeng Bridge (赓古桥). The best views are on offer after sunset: standing on Zoumalou watching the stream flowing past you under the bridge, with the bright round moon glowing in the evening sky has been deemed one of the "Eight Sights of Xidi."

East of Lingyun Tower stands the Hu Wenguang Memorial Archway (胡文光刺史坊), founded in 1578. With five floors and four pillars, it is a grand statement of respect, and a reflection of the position the Hu family held in the area. Overlooking the ship-shaped Xidi Village from afar, the archway stands tall and firm, like a mast.

Situated at the centre of the village, Taoli Garden (桃李园) was built during the Xianfeng period of the Qing dynasty (1850-1861) by two brothers, a scholar and a merchant. The garden has three domains – the first was built as shared space, the second was for the merchant and the third for the scholar. Above the door leading to the scholar's domain, a stone carving reads "The Land of Peach Blossoms." Inside the room is a wood carving called "The Roadside Hut of the Drunkard" by Huang Yuanzhi, a famous calligrapher from the Kangxi period of the Qing dynasty (1661-1722).

Taoli Garden leads into the West Garden (西园), which was built during the Daoguang period of the Qing dynasty (1820-1850) and is a fine model of Anhui-style structure.

Jingai Hall is the largest ancestral hall of Xidi Village, famous for its 24 filial piety figures carved on 12 wooden doors

Xidi was once the location of an ancient post station

Inside the garden there are stone-carved windows featuring the patterns of pines, stones, bamboos and plum blossoms. Divided into eight layers, this brilliant art utilises all the techniques of ancient Chinese stone carving. On the long narrow table in the middle of the garden' s main structure lies a bottle ("ping"), a mirror ("jing") and an ancient chime clock ("zhong"), which together symbolise "lifelong serenity" (as "pingjing" means serenity and "zhong" represents time.) The decorated floral window in East Garden (东园) is also quite special, as it symbolises the old Chinese saying "fallen leaves return to their roots" (落叶归根).

Built in 1691, Dafu House (大夫第) is a pavilion and former residence of senior government official Hu Wenzhao. At the front there is a small and delicate gazebo named Guanjinglou (观景楼), which means "a place to enjoy the scenery". It was built smaller than originally designed because the master wanted to make it easier for people to walk by, and written on the lintel of the door is the phrase "Step Back and Rethink" (热抛绣球).

East of Dafu House are two houses called Jingai Hall (敬爱堂) and Lvfu Hall (履福堂). Jingai Hall used to be the residence of village notable Shi Chegong, and was built during the Wanli period of the Ming Dynasty (1572-1620) but was ruined in a fire. Following reconstruction during the Qianlong period of the Qing Dynasty (1735-1796). it became the largest ancestral temple in Xidi Village, with an area over 1800 square metres. Apart from being an ancestral temple, it is also a place for villagers to discuss business, hold marriages and instruct children. Lvfu Hall was built during the reign of Kangxi and was the residence of famous collector Hu Jitang. Carved on the 12 wooden back doors are 24 representations of filial peity.

West of Dafu Hall, past Ruiyu Courtyard, you will find Zhuimu Hall (追慕堂) and Diji Hall (迪吉堂). Zhuimu Hall was built by Hu Guansan during the Kangxi reign to commemorate the noble morality and philanthropy of his grandfather and father. Diji Hall was used to welcome lords and high ranking officials and has a suitably refined atmosphere.

If you are starting to feel like you may have overdosed on ancient buildings, then it could be time to relax and admire a few more of the "Eight Sights of Xidi", which include: "Hidden Leopard on the Mountain Peak", "Fallen Rainbow in the Courtyard", "Flowing Spring from a Stone Lion", "Resting Bridge Stretching in the Valley", "Shade of Pagoda Trees Along the Lanes" and "Shade of Willow Trees Along the Lakeside".

## LONGEVITY TEA

Huangshan is a tea-growing area and the local Shimo tea (石墨茶) is believed to ward off senility and promote long life. Xidi village also offers hearty local cuisine including dried beef, roast sweet potatoes, roast pheasant and Laba tofu (腊八豆腐).

# Nanping Village

## China's Ancient Architecture Museum

Nanping Village may strike you as a lonely place despite its thousand-year-old history. It has always been a quiet little village, claiming few famous residents and untouched by war. Or, as poet Tao Yuanming described it, Nanping Village is a "heavenly place undisturbed by the outside world".



**Getting there**

Nanping Village, Yi County, Anhui Province.
Nearest City: Huangshan..
安徽省黄山市黟县碧阳镇南屏村
Take a long distance bus (2 hours) from Huangshan's Tunxi Coach Station (屯溪汽车站) to Yi County (黟县).Yi County Bus Station (黟县汽车站) has direct buses to Xiwu County (西武乡)which will pass by Nanping Village (南屏村) (15mins).

Just 4 km west of Yi County, Nanping Village has a population of only 1000 people but a history of more than 1100 years. The village contains 300 well-preserved and amazingly constructed residences from the Ming and Qing Dynasties.

Surprisingly, the way into the village is actually through one of the family residences occupied. The yard has vines twisted around the stone wall and chairs in the corner for chatting and sipping tea.

There are 72 lanes in Nanping Village, which has earned it the nickname of "Labyrinth of Lanes". The longest lane is Bubugaosheng (步步高升, meaning "rise with every step"), at the end of which there are 23 steps, each one higher than the one before it. There is also an interesting well in the village, where the shape of the rope eerily resembles eyelashes.

Nanping Village is associated with three major family names: Ye (叶), Cheng (程) and Li (李), and each family has their own ancestral hall, thus forming an impressive cluster of ancestral halls along the village' s main road, especially the eight major

Nanping's Ye Family Ancestral Hall (Xu

halls on either side. With so many large, grand ancestral halls and smaller, more elegant family temples, it is no wonder that Nanping Village fancies itself as "China's Ancient Architecture Museum".

The Ye Family Ancestral Hall (叶氏宗祠) is located in in the centre of Nanping Village. Built during the Chenghua period of the Ming Dynasty (1464-1487), it is 2000 square metres in size and more than 300 years old. Eighty giant ginko trees support the hall, which is split into three sections. In 1989, superstar director Zhang Yimou made his film Ju Dou here, and the Ye Family Ancestral Hall was transformed into the noble Yang family's dyehouse; even now there are posters on the walls of Chinese cinema's leading lady Gong Li.

The Cheng Family Ancestral Hall (程氏宗祠), built during the Qianlong period of the Qing Dynasty (1735-1796), is famous for its delicate stone carvings. Beside the gate of the hall stand characteristic Yi County stone carvings – of "three dragons in the clouds" on the right and "five phoenixes flying towards the sun" on the left – which are supposed to symbolise prosperity. There are also carvings of eight steeds and ten deers, which are so intricate that even the individual strands of fur can be seen, a testimony to the amazing skill of Huizhou's stone carving artists.

The four-storey Xiaosilou (孝思楼) is also called "Little Villa" because of its bold Roman architectural style. On the fourth floor there is a pavilion from which you can see the entire village.

Bingling Pavilion (冰凌阁), built in the middle of the Qing Dynasty, is split into three parts: the main hall, the side hall and the winding corridor. On the doors of the side hall is a map of

## EGG TEA

Nanping Village boasts a range of local delicacies such as "xige egg tea" (锡格蛋茶), black-boned chicken (乌骨鸡), "three yellow" chicken (三黄鸡), red taro, little red rice, buckwheat noodle, snow-white lotus root, roast duck, beans, bacon, wild carp, smoked mutton, ice-roast taro, and fruit pie.

The Yang family's dyehouse from Zhang Yimou's movie Ju Dou

the inevitable "10 sights of West Lake".

The constructions at the old water gate in Nanping Village are amazing too. There is a 40-meter bridge lover the Wuling River, the Wansong Bridge (万松桥), and over the bridge stand a magnificent array of halls and pavilions such as Leizudian (雷祖殿), Wenchangge (文昌阁), Guanyinlou (观音楼) and Wansongting (万松亭). Further back is Wansong forest, which contains hundreds of ancient trees. In the old days there used to be a couplet on the front doors of Leizudian which said "Work for the People and Be Just" (有功德于民则祀，能正直而一者神) - a timely admonition which governments everywhere would do well to heed.

Nanping Village's Dunmu Hall

# Tangmo Village

## Water Street

According to the ancients, Tangmo Village has "purple clouds in the west, waterfalls in the east, gold in the north, and mountains all around." Tangan River runs through the Tang Dynasty village, and the mountains and rivers do provide amazing sceneries.

### Getting there

Tangmo Village, Huizhou District, Anhui Province.
Nearest City: Huangshan.
安徽省黄山市徽州区潜口镇唐模村
Take a bus from Huangshan's Tunxi Coach Station(屯溪汽车站) to Qiankou (潜口) (50 mins), then walk 2 km or take a direct bus to Tangmo Village (唐模村). Alternatively, you can also go to She County (歙县) first, then take a taxi to Tangmo Village (about RMB30 & 15mins)

Located on the south side of Huangshan. Tangmo Village was built during the Tang Dynasty by the great-grandfather of Yue ruler Wanghua, who designed the village according to the style and mode of the Tang Dynasty (hence the name.)

Through the village flows the twisting Tangan River, which is over 1000 metres long and has 13 distinctive stone bridges built across it. The most famous bridge is called Gaoyang Bridge (高阳桥), built during the Yongzheng period of the Qing Dynasty (1722-1735). Nowadays, there is a teahouse on the bridge. Having a cup of Maofeng tea while enjoying a performance of the local Huangmei Opera is a not to be missed delight of visiting the village.

At the heart of Tangmo village is Shui (Water) Street (水街), which runs along both sides of the river. Tangan River made Shui Street prosperous and holds reflections of its long open corridors with green walls and white tiles. Along the banks there are long rest chairs, known as "Beauty Chairs" (in ancient times women were not often allowed

Rest chairs on Shui (Water) Street

Tangan Garden

outside and could only view the world from such chairs in the courtyards of their homes). Hundreds of years later, Shui Street still retains a prosperous feel, with red lanterns hung high on either side, emanating a sense of peace and serenity.

Shangyi Hall (尚义堂), one of the ancestral halls of the Xu family, was built during the reign of Emperor Zhengtong (1435-1449) in the Ming Dynasty and is located on the most important part of Shui Street. There are three parts to the hall, with two yards and five rooms, in front of which stands a wooden archway. The horse-mounting (上马石) and horse dis-mounting (下马石) stones on either side of the archway enhance the sense of grandeur.

The name Mingde Hall (铭德堂) can be translated as "inscribe virtue hall". Built in the traditional Anhui style, the hall features a wide tiangjing (inner courtyard) in the front, and is built with materials made out of precious woods, bricks and stones.

Tangan Garden (檀干园) is the biggest private garden in the south of Anhui Province. Built at the beginning of the Qing Dynasty and repaired during the reign of Emperor Qianlong (1735-1796), it is famous for the large amounts of wingceltis and Chinese redbud trees on the bank outside the gate. Like other places in Huizhou, Tangmo bred many rich merchants and high government officials. At the beginning of the Qing Dynasty, in order to fulfill his ill mother's wish to see Hangzhou's West Lake, a wealthy merchant by the name of Xu spent a small fortune so that he could duplicate West Lake's scenery within the village, hence giving Tangan Garden the nickname of "Little West Lake." In a little pavilion in the garden, there are 18 stone tablets with various masterpieces carved by famous calligraphers from different eras, a rare collection of artistic treasures.

Shui Street retains a prosperous feel

The mountains and rivers surrounding Tangmo Village provide impressive sights

The garden has a timeless feel, with flowing water, waving willows and blossoming lotuses.

Beside Tangan Garden there is a 400-year-old pagoda tree. The underpart of the tree is hollow, with a resemblance to an old man's open mouth. After it was once featured in a local television drama, a red ribbon was tied around the tree to wish a pair of fictional star-crossed lovers an everlasting love. Apart from the giant pagoda tree, Tangmo Village is also renowned for its ginkgo trees, which can be seen throughout the village. A particularly famous one was planted by the ancestors of the Wang family. At more than 1400 years old, it is still green and healthy, and requires 10 people just to wrap their arms around it. The people of Tangmo Village consider that the outstretched branches of the ancient gingko tree are protecting them, and to this day they continue to pray to it for health and longevity.

Built during the Kangxi period of the Qing Dynasty (1661-1722), Shadi Pavilion (沙堤亭), also called Bagua Pavilion, is situated not far away an old camphor tree. It has two storeys – the upper level is hollow in the middle, with empty cabinet on four sides and horse-like bells on the eight-cornered eaves of the roof.

Past Shadi Pavilion lies the Tongbao Hanlin Memorial Archway (同胞翰林石坊). There is a saying that "There are one and half memorial archways in Huizhou." The "one" refers to the tallest archway, Xixian Xuguo Memorial Archway, and the "half" refers to Tongbao Hanlin. In the 15th and 24th years of Emperor Kangxi's reign, two brothers, Xu Chengxuan and Xu Chengjia, were honoured as members of the Hanlin Imperial Academy by the Emperor himself, and Tongbao Hanlin Memorial Archway was built for them as a symbol of that honour. Sixteen metres high and 9.6 metres wide, it has three storeys, three rooms and four pillars, and features delicate carvings of plum blossoms, cranes, clouds, jumping fish and other auspicious symbols.

## CHICKEN vs. CULTURE

One ancient saying was "one would willingly starve to death to see Tangmo". These days, rather than starve, you might try the "old chicken" soup (老母鸡汤) – the broth is light and clear. For those with more of an appetite for culture, in the front hall of Shangyi Hall there are stone-carved calligraphy books for sale while in the back hall there are free Huizhou folk opera performances.

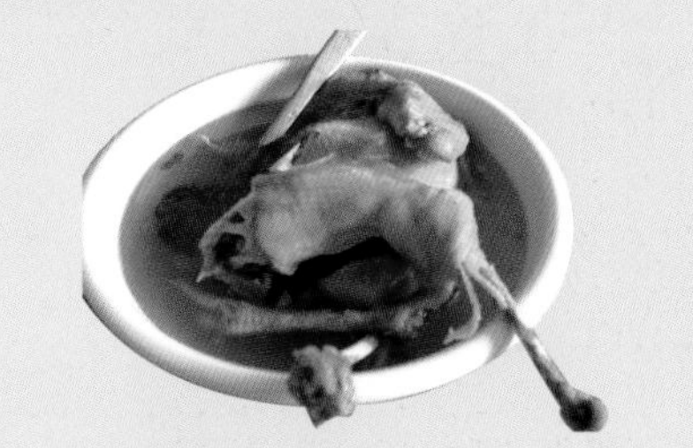

# Pingshan Village

## Village of Three Thousand Stoves

Pingshan Village stands at the foot of Pingfeng Mountain. Although it is located between the world-famous Xidi and Hong Villages, tourists have often made the mistake of ignoring this stunning village. On the other hand, for this reason, Pingshan Village has been able to maintain a rare tranquility that only small villages can offer.

### Getting there

Pingshan Village, Yi County, Anhui Province.
Nearest City: Huangshan.
安徽省黄山市黟县宏村镇屏山村
Takea long distance bus from Huangshan's Tunxi Coach Station (屯溪汽车站) to Yi County (黟县) (2 hours), then take a regular taxi ( RMB15) from Yi County to Pingshan Village (屏山村) (about 10mins).Tourist entry tickets to the village are RMB32 during peak season and RMB20 in the off-peak season.

Pingshan was originally called Changningli during the Tang and Song Dynasties and was renamed because of the screen-shaped Pingfeng Mountain north of the village. ("Ping" is the Chinese character for a screen. ) Shu (舒) is a common surname here because the Shu family, ninth generation descendants of the legendary Fuxi (the first of the Three Sovereigns of ancient China), moved over from Lujiang River during the last years of Tang Dynasty, more than 1100 years ago.

Pingshan Village is also known as a "Feng Shui Village" for its overall arrangement was made according to the principles of feng shui, yin and yang and bagua (the eight diagrams of Taoist cosmology.)

Backed by the green Ruping Mountain, Pingshan Village lies at a corner of the basin in Yi County that combines the scenery of the mountain areas and the water villages of South China. While many experts regard it as a mountain village, a

Ancient dwellings in the South Anhui style

little river passes through Pingshan Village and divides it into two parts, which are connected by dozens of single-arch stone bridges. Pingshan Village can therefore also be considered a water village, albeit one surrounded by mountains. The debate may seem academic but the village's scenery of small bridges, flowing water and old-style houses is undeniably charming.

Since ancient times, Pingshan Village has been known for its "Three Thousand Stoves and Five-Li Street." To this day, there are still more than 200 ancient buildings from the Ming and Qing Dynasties, including Changning Eight Old Bridges (长宁八古桥), Chengdao Hall (成道堂), Sangu Temple (三姑庙), Red Temple (红庙), Changning Lake (长宁湖), Yulan Hall (玉兰厅), Calabash Well (葫芦井) and the Small Embroided Tower (小绣楼). In particular, Shikejiadi Ancestral Hall Gatehouse (世科甲第祠堂) is regarded as the best gatehouse in Huizhou for its incomparable architectural style, tile and stone carvings and layout.

Shu Xiuwen (舒秀文) was known as "the people's artist." Her former residence, Shugu Hall (黍谷堂), is located in the centre of Pingshan Village. Built during the late Qing Dynasty and the early years of the Chinese Republic, the hall comprises two houses and several gardens and small courtyards. The architectural style here is very different from that of the traditional style of South Anhui, for it abandons the traditional courtyard and compensates for the insufficient lighting with six connected lotus doors. Both sides of the study hall are decorated with carved doors, which is rarely seen in Huizhou.

Established during the Wanli period of the Ming Dynasty (1572-1620), Shuqingyu Hall (舒庆余堂) is the largest ancestral temple in South Anhui, with an area of 480 square metres. The front gate is a 10-metre high memorial archway with two columns. The inside is divided into two houses and the main framework was made of gingkgo wood.

Shu Xiuwen's former residence

Guangyu Hall (光裕堂)was established during the Wanli period of the Ming Dynasty and is located west of Pingshan Village . The branch roads cutting through the village pass this ancestral temple and form four main roadways to the village in front of the Ancestral Temple Square, making the location of Guangyu Hall very important. With 300 exquisitely painted bodhisattva tile carvings and arhat sculptures in the temple, it is known colloquially as Bodhisattva Hall.

Since ancient times, Pingshan Village has placed heavy emphasis on Confucian education and literature. The village has given birth to a large number of well-respected people, and the tradition continues in the present day with the likes of philosopher Shu Weiguang and the wealthy Anhui merchant Shu Xiangeng.

## LEADING LADY

Locally-born actress and film star Shu Xiuwen (舒绣文) remains one of the most revered stars in the history of Chinese cinema. The Spring River Flows East (一江春水向东流) (1947) is regarded as among her most memorable masterpieces.

# Chengkan Village

## The Feng Shui Village

Once called "The first village of South China" by Confucian philosopher Zhu Xi, Chengkan Village is located in the north of Huizhou District and just a short ride from Huangshan City.

Chengkan Village, Huizhou District, Anhui Province.
Nearest City: Huangshan.
安徽省黄山市徽州区呈坎镇呈坎村
Take a taxi (RMB40) or pedicab taxi (RMB10) from Huangshan's Tunxi Coach Station (屯溪汽车站) directly to Chengkan Village, (1/2hour).

Chengkan was called Longxi (龙溪) in ancient times, but was renamed during the latter part of the Tang Dynasty more than 1000 years ago. It remains one of the best-preserved ancient villages in China.

The whole of Chengkan Village is structured around the principles of bagua (八卦, the eight diagrams of Taoist philosophy) and feng shui in accordance with The Book of Changes (otherwise known as I Ching) (易经)). The old Longxi River passes through the village from north to south in the shape of an "S", like the boundary line of the yin and yang diagram, while the two temples in the north and south of the village form the dots on either side of the line. The eight mountains outside the village form the eight positions of bagua while te three streets and ninety-nine lanes of the village are connected like a chessboard labyrinth. One gets the feeling that Chengkan Villagge is one of the more intriguing miracles of Chinese ancient village architecture.

Backed by mountains and close to water, the east-facing Chengkan Village is in perfect accordance with the ancient feng shui principle of "resting on mountain, surrounded by water and facing the screen." Two ditches introduce numerous streams through the streets of the village to provide fire control, flood discharge and irrigation. As a result, Chengkan Village has many bridges, among which the

Chengkan features diverse styles of pagodas, pavilions and temples

The entrance to Chengkan Village

most famous are the graceful Huanxiu Bridge (环秀桥) built during the Yuan Dynasty and the stone-arched Longxing Bridge (隆兴桥), whose single span is the largest built during the Ming Dynasty in South China.

Anhui merchants emerged in Chengkan Village during the Song Dynasty. Their respect for the morality of Confucianism guided their businesses and their wealth supported a flourishing of culture, education and architecture.

Chengkan village features different styles of pavilions, terraces, towers, bridges, wells, ancestral temples, community houses and residences. At present, there are more than a hundred buildings from the Ming and Qing (1644-1911) Dynasties, among which there are three state and provincial protected historic sites – Baolun Pavilion (宝纶阁), Changchun House (长春社) and Luo Runkun Residence (罗润坤宅). The exquisite and delicate stone, brick and wood carvings and colorful decorations of these buildings are reflective of the history, size, beauty and elegance of Huizhou's ancient architecture.

Established in 1542, the grand Baolun Pavilion was originally named Zhenjing Luo Dongshu Ancestral Temple and was expanded 70 years later after several floors collapsed. This ancestral temple consists of three bays – the courtyard and the building are seperated by the Yi County blue flagstone, which is regarded as having high artistic value due to its flower, grass and geometric pattern embossments as well as the colourful decorations on the beams. Despite a history of 400 years, they remain dazzlingly beautiful and lively. The 30th floor of Baolun Pavilion is the pinnacle of Chengkan Village, with a view of the clouds hovering around Huangshan's Tiandu Peak and Lotus Peak.

Ancient plaques (decorative boards inscribed with writings) are symbols of the Chengkan family's generational glory. There are many plaques left from the Song to Qing Dynasties, though only 30 of these are well-preserved. The oldest is the Dasicheng (大司成) plaque, which has a history of more than 700 years. Written by the famous calligrapher Dong Qichang (董其昌) during the Ming Dynasty, the Chinese characters on it say "Common Sense and Unmodifiable Sequence" (彝伦攸叙)_. With dimensions of 6.5 by 2.5 metres and giant strokes up to 2 metres long, it is justly known as the "King of Plaques."

Nearby Changchun House (长春社) is commonly called Community House. With a history of 1500 years, it was the only public building in Huizhou used for offering sacrifices to the village god inn ancient times.

## BAMBOO FOREST

Peaceful Lingshan Village (灵山村), southeast of Chengkan Village, is worth a visit. Attractions include the one-and-a-half-kilometre-long ancient street paved with blue flagstones (古水街), 36 ancient stone bridges and historic buildings such as the Hanyuan Memorial Archway (翰苑牌坊). Uniquely, the village is surrounded by a seemingly boundless bamboo forest .

# Yuliang Village

## An Ancient Port

With few modern buildings to be seen, the ancient flavour of Yuliang village feels more real and natural, giving visitors the sense that the people of the village have been unable to let go of tradition.

**Getting there**

Yuliang Village, She County, Anhui Province.
Nearest City:Huangshan..
安徽省黄山市歙县徽城镇渔梁村
Take a bus from Huangshan's Tunxi Coach Station(屯溪汽车站) to She County(歙县) (40mins). Since Yuliang Village is only 1 km away from She County (歙县), you may continue there by pedicab, taxi or motorcycle taxi.

Established during the Tang Dynasty, Yuliang Village is located 1.5 km southeast of She County. In the second year of Emperor Qianyuan's reign (759), the Yao family moved to Yuliang and founded a village. Shaped like a fish and nestling under a mountain and near a river, Yuliang Village is famous for its primitive simplicity. It is also commonly known as Liangxia and lies at the drainage outlet of Lianjiang River, which was once the busy and prosperous port of She County.

Yuliang Village can attract large crowds, so it is best to avoid visiting during public holiday. if you arrive during the rainy summer months, be alert for possible flooding around Yuliang Dam. Mornings and evenings are best for a stroll followed by sampling the specialty dish of Yuliang Village, delicious fresh fish from the Lianjiang River.

The rugged Yuliang Street (渔梁商业街), otherwise known as "Fish Scale Street", has essentially retained the style of the ancient port. The prosperous street itself is lined on both sides with buildings erected during the Ming and Qing Dynasties. The tall horse-head wall, black Chinese-style tiles, lofty eaves and natural-coloured boarded doors are seeped in deep Anhui flavour, known for its harmonious and natural feel.

At No.77 Yuliang Street stands the former residence of the School of She's Yinren Ba Weizu (巴慰祖故居). Built in the early years of the Qing Dynasty, it is the largest existing

Yuliang Street faces the south of Xinan River and the famous Yuliang Dam.

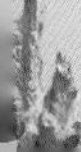

The present appearance of the port.

ancient dwelling in Yuliang Village. This former residence is divided into three houses, each of which borders a side of a courtyard. Additionally, there is also an eastern hall, western hall and back garden. The middle house is supported by a shuttle-shaped column, whose base is like a distintive over-turned bowl. Following repairs throughout the generations, the former residence has been changed into the Ba Weizu Memorial Hall (巴慰祖纪念馆), where there are many cultural relics such as a plaque inscribed with Chinese characters which are translated to mean "House of Sun Lovers" (爱日居).

Yuliang Street faces the south of Xinan River and the old shipyard still remains close to the river. At the bottom of the stairs is the famous Yuliang Dam, after which Yuliang Village is named. It is the distribution centre and port for Anhui merchants to deliver goods to South China. The dam is said to flow directly into Qingyi River and then the Yangtze River. Anhui merchants, who ruled in business circles during the Ming and Qing Dynasties for 300 years, began their earliest businesses here. Yuliang Dam was built by Wang Hua, an official from the Sui Dynasty, before being repaired in the latter years of the Ming Dynasty. The dam is 138 metres long, with a bottom width of 27 metres and a top width of 4 metres. Built entirely with whole-colored solid stones, the dam is divided into three water gates. The left gate is used to flow water, while the middle and right gates are used to prevent waterlogging and drought. As the oldest and largest barrage on Xinan River, Yuliang Dam is also known as the "Triumphal Arch of China."

The surface of the dam is calm and peaceful. Fish swim deep in the water and boats create ripples on top. Ziyang Mountain standing firmly at the western bank is full of verdant green woods. Ziyang Bridge (紫阳桥), built during the Ming Dynasty, is like a rainbow spanning over the river. Of the three ancient bridges in She County, it is the highest and widest.

Starting from the south gate of She County, the Old Xinan Path (新安古道) zigzags for several miles, passing through Yuliang Village before reaching the port under Yuliang Dam. The path cleaves to the mountain and the river. Along the river, stone hand rails evoke a local legend (see below). The name of the local wine shop "Taibailou" (太白楼) is another allusion to this story.

Beside Taibailou stands Xinan Stele Garden, (新安碑园) which was rebuilt from an official's residence from the Ming Dynasty. Its structure is typical of the private landscape style architecture in Huizhou. Leaning against Piyun Peak, taking advantage of Lianjiang River and facing Taiping Bridge (太平桥), Xinan Stele Garden is famous for two sets of famous calligraphy carvings of Yuqing Room (余清斋) and Qingjian Hall (清鉴堂). The garden includes scenic spots such as the Zhenshang Pavilion Courtyard, She Pool, Xiaotiandu Courtyard and Piyun Villa Courtyard, which form an organic whole through the winding corridor.

## A POET CALLS

It is said that the great Tang Dynasty poet Li Bai once tried to visit hermit Xu Xuanping, who lived in the area. Li took a boat on the Xinan River and inquired about Xu's residence from the old boatman, who said, "The house with a bamboo pole before it belongs to Xu", a subtle hint that he was in fact Xu himself. Sadly, Li Bai did not realise this, so he simply drowned his sorrows alone.

# Tangyue Village

## Huangshan's Memorial Archways

The cluster of memorial archways in Tangyue Village is unique, as they do not adopt the conventional usage of a wooden structure, instead opting for black stones without the use of nails. These ingeniously designed stone structures are regarded as profound cultural treasures.



### Getting there

Tangyue Village, She County, Anhui Province.
Nearest City: HuangShan.
安徽省黄山市歙县郑村镇棠樾村
Take a bus from Huangshan's Tunxi Coach Station (屯溪汽车站) to Shexian Bus Station(歙县汽车站) (about 40mins) and get off at Zhengcun Town(郑村镇) Station, then take the No. 4 bus to Tangyue Village (5mins).

Tangyue Village is 5 km west of She County. "Tang" symbolises a kind of tree called "Tangli" (Chinese Bush Cherry) and "Yue" means "under the shades of two trees." Literally, "Tangyue" suggests that there are so many Tangli trees planted in the village that their collective shade can block out all sunlight.

Tangyue Village was originally a settlement of the Bao (鲍) family from Qingzhou in Shandong Province. The Baos were a family of officials during the Ming Dynasty that commenced a family business during the Qing Dynasty. The family, best known for their wealth, enjoyed prosperity that lasted for 18 generations, spanning approximately 400 years.

The memorial archways cluster, the most famous in all of Huizhou, is located at the eastern edge of the village. Together with ancestral halls and folk residences, memorial archways are regarded as one of the "Three Greatest Ancient Architectures" of Huizhou.

There are seven memorial archways which honour the qualities of loyalty, filial piety, moral integrity and justice. Three were built during the Ming Dynasty and four during the Qing dynasty. The oldest one is the second archway, Cixiaoli (filial piety), built in the 18th year of the Yongle period during the Ming Dynasty (1520). The newest one is the fourth archway, Leshanhaoshi (philanthropy), constructed 300 years later in the 19th year of the Jiaqing period during the Qing dynasty (1814).

Tangyue's Memorial Archway

The ancient archways are surrounded with ancient ancestral halls, folk residences and pavilions, making it a perfect film location. Over 30 films and TV series, including a famous adapation of Chinese

The Bao Family Garden fish viewing corridor

classic The Dream of the Red Chamber (红楼梦) have been shot here.

The Bao family's ancestral hall, Dunben Hall, is colloquially known as "Temple for Men" (男祠). Built at the end of the Jiajing period of the Ming dynasty (1561) and reconstructed in the sixth year of the Jiaqing period during the Qing Dynasty (1801), it is considered the quintessential Huizhou ancestral hall from the Qing dynasty. Inside, there are 17 inscribed tablets depicting the glory of the Bao family, such as the Shangyu Tablet (上谕碑) bestowed by Emperor Jiaqing.

There is also a unique "Temple for Women" called Qingyi Hall (清懿堂). The hall' s name represents chastity and morality, the highest praise for women in feudal society. It was built during the Jiaqing period of the Qing Dynasty, (1796-1820) when Bao Qiyun commanded his son Youlai to build a temple for women, breaking the tradition of keeping women out of ancestral halls.

The Bao Family Garden (鲍家花园) is 350 metres south of Tangyue Village and after several reconstructions, it has now become the biggest private gardenin the country. The Bao Family Garden was originally the backyard of Bao Qiyun, a Qing Dynasty businessman. The garden has everything from mountains, water, stones, and trees to paths, corridors, pavilions and bonsais. There are nealy 10,000 bonsais in the garden, all mixed in with the charm of Huizhou culture.

**CANDY**

Huizhou tofu (徽州豆腐), Yuliang dried tofu (渔梁豆腐干) and Jinhua candy (金花糖) are all very popular among visitors to Tangyue Village.

The Bao Family Garden has views of mountains, water, stones, trees, long corridors and pavilions

# Jiang Village

## Feng Shui Treasure Land

Jiang Village is an historic village in the mountains with ancient temples, tall archways, folk residences and stone pathways. Like other ancient villages, it has been formed by culture, time and individual lives.

### Getting there

Jiang Village, Jingde County, Anhui Province.
Nearest City: Huangshan.
安徽省宣城市旌德县白地镇江村
Take a train from Huangshan Station(黄山站) to Jixi Station(绩溪站) (about 1hour & RMB3.5). After arrival at Jixi Train Station, take a long-distance bus from the nearby Jixi Bus Station(绩溪汽车站) to Caijiaqiao Town(蔡家桥镇) (1hour). At Caijiaqiao Town, transfer to a service to Baidi Town(白地镇),which will pass Jiang Village (1hour).

Built in late the Sui and early Tang Dynasties, Jiang Village is also known as "Little Hangzhou" for its resemblance to the Zhejiang capital. The shape of the village has been liked to an old armchair, surrounded by mountains in the east, south and north, while the west side is wide open. The village sits in the middle, with two rivers passing by and Juxiu Lake in the front. Shi Mountain and Xiang Mountain are supposedly like the two arms of the chair.

Jiang Village not only offers stunning natural views but also cultural heritage attractions such as the Jiang Village Temple (江村总祠), Pugong Temple (溥公祠), Xiaozi Temple (孝子祠), and Jinshi Temple (进士坊). With old dwellings, streets and archways, Jiang Village shares some similarities with other ancient villages of southern Anhui, but at the same time it manages to convey its own uniqueness.

Jiang Village was designed with deep allegorical considerations: Juxiu Lake is supposedly like an ink-stone, the archway is the ink, the Wenchang Tower (文昌塔) a writing brush and the earth a huge paper – a reflection of the villagers' wish for cultural prosperity. Long River and Feng River run parallel and come together to form Juxiu Lake at the entrance to the village.

Jiang Village once had 18 archways but only two have survived – the "father and son" pair of Jinshi Archways honouring Jiang Han and Jiang Wenmin, the 48th and 49th generations of the Jinao Jiang family (金鳌江) who had both become "Jinshi" (third-degree scholars) and imperial officials during the Ming Dynasty. The "father" Jinshi archway has numerous engravings, each with a certain meaning; at the front there is a lion (stateliness), the mythical beast qiling (auspice) and phoenix (prosperity), and at the back there are two phoenixes representing Jiang Han and his cousin

Jiang Putang and their academic achievements. The "son" archway has a carp on the right side suggesting an old saying "carp jumping over the dragon gate" (鲤鱼跳龙门), which symbolised success in civil service exams. These two archways are said to be the only remaining non-governmental white marble archways in all of China.

The former residences belonging to Jiang Village celebrities include Jinxiu Hall (进修堂), which has delicate wood carvings, Maocheng Hall (茂承堂), which was the ancestral home of the acting premier of the Republic of China, Jiang Chaozong, as well as Duxiu Hall (笃修堂) and Anran Villa (黯然别墅).

Duxiu Hall was built during the Ming Dynasty and is the oldest remaining folk residence in Jiang Village. "Du" means honesty and "xiu" means self-cultivation. It is the former residence of the high-achieving Jiang family, whose numbers in Qing dynasty times included doctors, medical scientists and members of the Imperial Academy. Only one fifth of the hall remains. The two thin stones on both sides of the hall are a symbol of status because only high ranking officials were allowed to have them. The magnificent front gate is in the style of an archway. The threshold is high with several steps in the front because the height of the threshold symbolizes the height of the status. Upon entering the room, there is a door which can only be used to welcome officials above the seventh rank. Women could only enter for marriages and funerals. The rules of Duxiu Hall illustrate how strict the caste system was in ancient China.

**GREEN GARDENS**

The forests of Jiang Village boast flax gardens, bamboos gardens, tea gardens and fruit gardens. This natural environment is a focus of Anhui Province's innovative "Two Mountains and One Lake" green tourism project which emphasises visitors' ability to "live in the houses, eat local food and enjoy the sights of an ancient village".

The grey-stoned Old Street (石老街) of Jiang Village is 350 metres long, starting from Yuangong Temple (溥公祠) and ending at the Jiang Family Temple. (江氏宗祠). There are several stores along the high-walled, grey-tiled road, most of which have a storefront and a workshop in the back. The north and south ends of the street each has three bends to guard against wind, fire and the cold.

Pugong Hall is also called Liufen Hall. The original owner, Jiang Bo, was a 48th generation jinshi of the Ming Dynasty. The temple is also the ancestral hall of former Chinese President Jiang Zemin. This magnificent yet delicate landmark has a three-hall structure. The first entrance is the gate tower. The second is Xiang Hall (享堂), where family meetings take place. The third is Qin Hall (寝堂) for honouring ancestors. There are 36 wooden columns in the temple and 22 granite square columns around the courtyard.

Juxiu Lake

Wenchang Tower

Carved turtles can be found on the ridge of the roof, a symbol which represents "coming in first place." In the middle there is a gourd-shaped roof with an upside down prong and a tiangou (天狗, celestial dog) to ward off bad luck. Under the ridge there is a 500-year mural which reflects hope for better life. The three gods of longevity, "Fu" (福), "Lu" (禄) and "Shou" (寿), are in the middle of the picture, blessing the Jiang family. The picture's colours remain clear and unfaded.

Xiaozi Temple, located in the middle of Old Street., is a three-hall building with two yards and is said to be the only temple built in honour of filial piety in the country. Above the door are eight Chinese characters explaining that the temple was built for a filial son from the Ming Dynasty. The couplets on the wooden pillars all contain the word "xiao" (孝), which means filial piety.

The Jiang Family Ancestral Hall (江氏宗祠) is the main temple of the Jiang family and Jiang Village. It has four halls, two wings, two pools and three yards. The first hall was burned down though you can still see the remains. The two pools on either side of the gate are for fire prevention with three arch bridges leading to the second gate. On the walls of the hall you can still see slogans from the Cultural Revolution. There are also vase-shaped wood carvings of the 24 solar terms on the screens left from the Republic of China period, though only 21 remain now. Up above is a structure called Zhonggulou (钟鼓楼), used for storing clocks, drums and genealogy records.

Shishan Temple (狮山古庙) is located at the southern shore of Juxiu Lake and is alternatively known as Haishen Temple and Tianhou Niangniang Temple. It was built in the fifth year of the Chongning period during the Song dynasty (1106) and is the only Mazu temple in southern Anhui Province.

Great feng shui and the cultural tradition of attaching particular importance to education apparently aided the success of many talented locals. According to records, although there were only nine schools in the village, 126 people from Jiang Village succeeded in the civil service examinations during the Ming and Qing Dynasties.

One of Jiang Village's many archways

# Chaji Village

## A Classic Anhui Village

Chaji Village is an ancient village located among the Huangshan mountains. Its scale ranks as the largest in Anhui Province and it is home to the biggest cluster of ancient folk residences in China.

### Getting there

Chaji Village, Jing County, Anhui Province.
Nearest City: Huangshan.
安徽省宣城市泾县桃花潭镇查济村
Take a train from Huangshan Station to Xuancheng Station(宣城站) (3 hours). There are direct buses from Xuancheng Coach Station(宣城汽车站) to Jing County (泾县) (about 1.5 hours), where you can transfer to a local bus to Houan Village (厚岸村). Then take a "tiaotiao" ("jump-jump") car from Houan Village to Chaji village (RMB3-10).

With a 1380-year history, Chaji Village was established in the early years of the Sui Dynasty, developed during the Song and Yuan Dynasties and reached its greatest prosperity in the Ming and Qing Dynasties, before experiencing decline in the final years of the Qing Dynasty and modern times. Most villagers have the surname Zha (查), a large family with many famous descendants such as calligraphers and painters Zha Bingjun and Zha Chunru and martial arts novelist Jin Yong (Zha Liangyong).

The residences of Chaji are all in the classic Anhui style with white walls, black tiles and horse-head outer walls. Most residences have a wooden structure with several halls and yards surrounded by wing rooms. The woodcarvings are very vivid, making an even greater pity that many were ruined during the Cultural Revolution. Propaganda graffiti left from the Cultural Revolution can be found everywhere. In some halls there are still portraits of Chairman Mao, which seem to have become a part of the village. The villagers never lock their doors and tourists are generally welcomed.

The peaceful scenery at the entrance of Chaji Village

There are three types of architectural engravings in Chaji

Village: wood, tile and stone. They are usually seen in residences, temples, archways, bridges and coffin chambers, exhibiting a wide range of shapes and styles and relecting the ancient villager's delicate tastes, professional dedication and perpetual pursuit of beauty.

Erjia Hall (二甲祠) is the biggest hall in the village. Built in the Ming Dynasty, it has high eaves and engravings of drama pictures. The white stone panelling is carved with flowers and the dooryard is thin and long. Upon entering the second hall, you can see exquisite wood and stone carvings, especially the lively "Magpie and Plum" (喜鹊登梅). There are also magnificent carvings in the third hall.

Built in the Hongxi period of the Ming Dynasty, the 600-year-old Baogong Temple (宝公祠) has two grand embossments of a lion playing a silk ball on the crossbeam. The dozens of wooden pillars inside the main hall are said to rival even those in the Imperial Palace.

Built during the brief Tianqi period of the Ming Dynasty (1620), Airi Hall (爱日堂) is filled with exquisite decorations from the gates to the columns, dougong (system of brackets inserted between the top of a column and a crossbeam,) and window lattices.

Chaji Village's Zoumalou (走马楼) is a quality piece of Ming Dynasty architecture, with a living room right in the middle, an engraved and gold-plated bed in the bedroom and a bright red and green silk quilt – a stunning example of the extravagance and warmth enjoyed by wealthy families in ancient times.

Chaji Village's only remaining Yuan

**Surrounded by green trees, Chaji Village is elegant and enchanting**

Dynasty architecture, Degong House (德公厅屋), has a gate, Zhuanmen Lou (幢门楼) which can be seen as an independent archway. The gate has four pillars and three levels and the dougong roofing looks classical and dignified . In the back of Zhuanmen Lou, there are skilled carvings of double dragons, a soaring phoenix and a lion playing with a silk ball. Inside, the building is held up by 16 columns made of precious wood, implying the importance of this house to the Zha family.

It is said that there were originally 108 bridges in Chaji Village, but now only a relative handful remain, including Honglou, Tianzhong and Lingzhi. Built during the Ming Dynasty, Honglou Bridge (红楼桥) is most famous, as there used to be a teahouse on the bridge where scholars would often come to drink wine and sample teas. The teahouse is sadly no more but you may want to check out the GuangYuan Lou hotel. The roof of the hotel is the only place that offers panoramic views of Chaji village. Meanwhile there are plenty of places around the village where you can try local edibles like chestnuts, dazhang bamboo shoots (大障笋), Jixi plums (绩溪李), Fuling cakes (伏岭饼), Choujue fish (臭鳜鱼) and stone chicken (石鸡).

Degong House

## ALLEGORICAL FANCIES

Some locals say that Chaji village is like a modest old man with a big heart, guarding his homeland. Others say Chaji is a young and energetic maiden: "the mountains are her clothes, the clouds are her sleeves, the springs are her blood and the villagers' kindness is her pure heart..." Old man or maiden - readers, you decide!

# Wangkou Village

## Land of a Thousand Mists

Wangkou Village, encircled by mountains and rivers, was on the land route from the ancient city of Huizhou to the city of Raozhou in Jiangxi Province. During the Ming and Qing Dynasties, Wangkou was a prosperous village full of shops and swarming with merchants. Many historic relics from that era still remain.



### Getting there

Wangkou Village, Wuyuan County, Jiangxi Province.
Nearest city: Shangrao.
江西省上饶市婺源县江湾镇汪口村
Take a long distance bus from Shangrao Bus Station (上饶汽车站) to Wuyuan North Coach Station (婺源县汽车北站) (2hours). From Wuyuan there are plenty of buses heading towards Qiukou Town(秋口镇) and Jiangwan Town (江湾镇) which will pass Wangkou Village (about RMB60 & 1/2hour).

With Jingde Town to the west, Sanqing Mountain to the south and Huangshan to the east, the 1100-year-old Wangkou Village is conveniently located only 30 km from the centre of Wuyuan Country. The name "Wangkou" (literally means a pool) comes from a green pool in the village. As a well-resourced village in Huizhou, Wangkou has nurtured a number of renowned talents and enjoyed the reputation of being a "Scholars Village" since the Song and Qing Dynasties.

Colloquially called "The Land of a Thousand Mists" (千烟之地), Wangkou Village has managed to maintain most of its Ming and Qing Dynasty features. Leaning against mountains and facing a river, the village is lower at the front and higher behind, extending east to west along the water. Inside the village, a central street and 18 roads that lead directly to Xihu Dock (溪埠码头) are crisscrossed by numerous alleys, forming the shape of a large net. There are also more than 60 lanes and two stone bridges (Juxing Bridge and Caogong Bridage) as well as many ancient mansions like Yuyunxing Mansion (俞运行宅), Dahudi Mansion (大夫第), Xudu Hall (述德堂), Shenzhi Hall (慎知堂), Shengxun Hall (生训堂), Shouxun Hall (守训堂), Jishan Hall (积善堂) and Cunyu Academy (存與斋书院).

The ancient street along the river is officially known as Main Street (正街). It was paved during the Daguan period of the Song Dynasty and flourished at the beginning of the Qing Dynasty. The 600-metre street is covered with flagstones and is shaped like a crescent. Of the 340 residences in the village, more than 150 are built on the street. These ancient half-timbered houses, with white walls and black tiles, contain no courtyards but only storefronts, living rooms and kitchens. Take a walk along this tranquil and serene ancient street and you can easily imagine its former prosperity.

Overlooking Wangkou Village

At the east end of the village is Yushi Ancestral Hall (俞

Thousand year old village streets

氏宗祠). Built in 1744, it has three courtyards and a three-storey main hall. The hall is known for its meticulous wood carvings, including shallow and deep carving, openwork carving and full relief , all of which are of fine workmanship.

Maode Hall (懋德堂), built in 1795, is the house of the once famous "First Family of the East Gate" of Wuyuan County. "Maode", literally meaning "encouraging people in kindness and virtue", aims to remind younger generations to be kind and to help others. There are three courtyards and five rooms in the hall. A chamber with exquisite craftwork in the north of the hall is the ladies' living room. Animals and other designs carved on the eaves, doors, brick and stones of the main hall are vivid and lifelike.

Yijing Hall (一经堂), built during the era of Emperor Qianlong (1735-1796), is located in the middle of Lijia Alley (李家巷). It was named "Yijing" (a volume of books) because the owner of the house was greatly influenced by the ancient proverb: "While others leave wealth to their offspring, I leave mine with a volume of books" (人遗子，金满，吾教子，唯一经). He preferred to educate his children to become learned scholars rather than leaving them material wealth. This residence comprises three chambers and two side-rooms. Wood carvings on the beams, doors and thresholds inside the house are detailed and delicate , and the court is installed with meticulous drainage, all of which are well-preserved.

Yangyuan Academy (源书屋), built in 1879, is situated at the top of the stone steps in Tongmu Alley (桐木岭巷). Covering an area of 120 square metres, it has a frontcourt with an old osmanthus tree, classroom, tutor's office and kitchen. Pingdu Weir (平渡堰), lying inside the village river, is similar to a zigzag ruler in shape, and was designed and built by Jiang Yong, an economist and phonologist, between 1723 and 1735. Though without a water gate, Pingdu Weir serves the functions of water storage, navigation and flood prevention. At 120 metres long and 15 metres wide, it is unsuprisingly considered a masterpiece in the history of water conservation construction in China.

The dialect spoken in Wangkou Village still amazing contains a lot of words and intonations from that used in ancient Huizhou. Grand recreational activities are held on all the traditional holidays like Chinese New Year (春节), Tomb-Sweeping Day (清明), Dragon-Boat Festival (端午) and Mid-Autumn Festival (中秋). Venues like Gongwen Pavilion (拱文亭) and Wenchang Pavilion (文昌阁) were specially built by the villagers for poets and scholars to perform literature pieces.

## CHILLED-OUT VILLAGE

Other ceremonies and recreational activities participated in by the villagers include an ancestsor-worshipping ceremony, a local god-worshipping ceremony, lantern-lighting and opera – events which occupy an enviable 36 days of the year.!

Many historic relics are still perfectly preserved in Wangkou

# Yan Village

## A Village of Confucian Businessmen

The varying heights of the white-walled, black-tiled folk residences in Yan Village create a beautifully ragged skyline. No steps can be found in the village, and the flatness of the landscape was reputed to reflect the open heart and frankness of the villagers and to promote smoothness in business ventures.

### Getting there

Yan Village, Wuyuan County, Jiangxi Province.
Nearest city: Shangrao.
江西省上饶市婺源县思口镇延村
Take a long distance bus from Shangrao Bus Station (上饶汽车站)to Wuyuan North Coach Station (婺源县汽车北站) (3 hours), then take one of the many buses bound for Sikou Town (思口镇) (RMB4 & 45 mins).Get off at the entrance to Yan Village (延村) and the village is about a 10-minute walk from there.

Established during the Yuanfeng period of the Northern Song Dynasty (1078-1085), Yan Village, also called Yanchuan Village, was originally built around a well, which in China symbolises wealth. Two roads meet at the well in an inverted "V' shape, which resembles either the Chinese character "人" (Mandarin pronunciation "ren"), meaning human, or "八", the character for "eight" which also symbolises wealth. Designed around such concepts, the entire village is a incarnation of society and culture at that time. All the houses are linked to each other, creating a cluster of mansions. There are 56 ancient residences remaining in the village, most of which were built during the Qianglong and Jiaqing periods of the Qing Dynasty.

From afar, the village looks like a large cluster of blank white walls. Several small windows in the walls highlight the contrast between the whole and the part, and embodies the spirit of Taoist natural humanism. With gables, black-tiled roofs and stone-ringed doors made of grey bricks, the houses usually consist of a front hall, back room, kitchen and so forth. On the cross beams, decorated brackets, doors and windows of the houses are carvings of dragons,

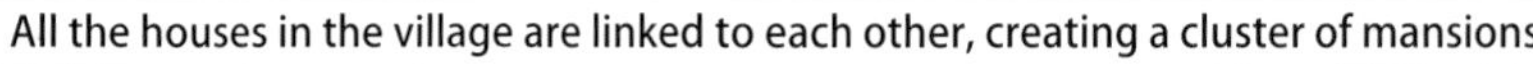

All the houses in the village are linked to each other, creating a cluster of mansions

phoenixes, unicorns, pine trees, cranes, deer, waterside pavilions and folklore characters. The designs are vivid and breathtaking, demonstrating not only the excellent craftsmanship but also the rich culture of the time. Most interestingly, a carving of a mouse was a must for every house as it symbolised the wish be as good at producing offspring and hoarding grains as mice!

Yuqing Hall (余庆堂) was built by a businessman named Jin Shiqiu during Emperor Qianlong' s reign in the Qing Dynasty (1735-1796). The wood carvings on the door planks of the wing rooms located at both sides of the courtyard are exquisite. Several animals are carved on the plank of the left wing-room: there is the "qilin" (麒麟), a mythical creature that can bring sons to the family according to Chinese culture; crane and deer, the symbols of longevity and happiness. In the back courtyard there is a vat called "Vat of Peace" (太平缸), made out of a natural piece of jute stone. The water contained in the vat is rainwater, which symbolises bliss fallen from heaven. It is said that the rainwater in the vat can forecast the weather: it becomes turbid before raining and turns clean when it is sunny...

Congting Hall (聪听堂), the house of a prestigious family in Yan Village, was built during the Kangxi period of the Qing Dynasty. The inscription on a plaque in the house was written by Yaonai, a renowned Confucian master. The wood carvings on cross beams in the front court and wing rooms depict four scenes from the poem Song of Pipa by Bai Juyi, a famous poet from the Tang Dynasty. The four scenes are: "seeing a friend off at Xunyang River", "maple leaves and Anaphalis wavering in autumn winds", "only after our repeated calls did the singer appear" amd "her face is still half hidden behind a pipa lute". All are considered wood carving masterpieces.

On the gates of every house hangs an inscription of the word "business" (商). As rainwater is said to symbolise wealth, most houses have hidden pipes at either side of the gate to allow rainwater to flow through into the yard. The architects of ancient times also used turtles to dig underground waterways to prevent clogging and to keep courtyards clean. In South China there was a shortage of coal, so villagers burned wood to cook. However, instead of erecting chimneys, villagers dug a hole on the wall of kitchen, and the smoke would float through the white wall, creating a very unique sight around dinner time.

Dujing Hall (笃经堂) was built at the beginning of the Qing Dynasty. The owner of the hall had three sons, and the sons' rooms, connected by a passage, were laid out in order of seniority: the room of the youngest son is at the entrance, followed by the room of the second son, and the room of the oldest son lies deep inside the house. Further, the room inside is higher than the one in the middle, and middle one higher than the one at the entrance. If a visitor wanted to meet the oldest son, he would have to wait on the narrow bench in the passage while his request was relayed through the three rooms. It is said that from this sprung the Chinese idiom: "To sit on a cold bench" (坐冷板凳).

### TEA CRAZY

Yan Village is famous for its tea. Every family performs elaborate tea ceremonies, and free tea is served before dinner at local restaurants.

# Likeng Village

## A Remote Mountain Village

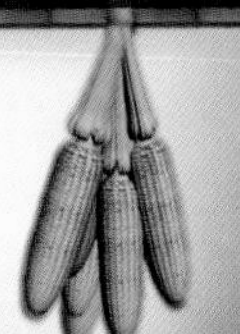

White walls and black tiles, broad and misty bricks, a red-rail bridge across the clear stream... beside an old camphor tree lies Likeng Village, an ancient village with a history of more than a thousand years.

### Getting there

Likeng Village, Wuyuan County, Jiangxi Province.
Nearest city: Shangrao.
江西省上饶市婺源县沱川乡理坑村
Take a long distance bus from Shangrao Bus Station (上饶汽车站)to Wuyuan North Coach Station (婺源县汽车北站) (3 hours). Take the bus from there to Tuochuan County (坨川县) (RMB7) and then continue to Likeng Village by foot (5 mins).

Likeng Village, initially called Liyuan, was built at the end of the Northern Song Dynasty. The "keng" in "Linkeng" means "pit", while "li" comes from the village's original name "Liyuan", which literally means "tthe cradle of Neo-Confucianism".

Likeng Village is a village of scholars which according to local sources has nurtured 36 government officials, 16 third-degree scholars and 92 famous intellectuals. These people have apparently written 582 volumes of 330 works, of which 78 volumes of 5 works were included into the imperial collection.

Well-preserved ancient buildings in the village include: the mansion owned by Yu Maoxue (余懋学), vice-minister of the Ministry of Revenue and an official of the Ministry of Works during the Wanli period of the Ming Dynasty (1572-1620); Yiyu Hall (诒裕堂), owned by Yu Xianhui, a tea businessman from the Daoguang period of the Qing Dynasty (1820-1850); a garden-style cottage, a garden-style lounge, the legendary Jinjia Well (金家井) and so on. These ancient architectures, with white walls, black tiles, curved rooftops,

Bird's-eye view of Likeng

A harmonious balance of water, bridge and residences

meticulous carvings, decorations and ingenious layouts, are ecologically-friendly,warm in winter and cool in summer.

There are more than 120 Ming and Qing Dynasty official residences in Likeng Village, most of which are perfectly-preserved. These ancient mansions are equipped with stairs, which were exclusively for the use of government officials and reflective of their rank. Usually the walls at both sides of the gate slope down, forming a shape of the auspicious number eight ( "八" ) in Chinese. The outer wall corners are made of stone columns embedded in bricks, and the end of the columns are sliced off. This sliced part forms a triangular prism with the wall' s corner lines, which are said to be reminders of modesty.

Guanting (官厅), also called Jiamu Hall and later renamed Yousong Hall, is a mansion built at imperial command. Originally owned by Yu Ziyi, governor of Guangzhou during the Chongzhen period of the Ming Dynasty (1627-1644), this magnificient mansion has two courtyards, five rooms in the center and winding corridors in three directions. All the pillars in the central hall are square, symbolising the uprightness and integrity of the owner.

Tianguan Shangqing (天官上卿), literally "Senior Minister", is the mansion of Yu Maoheng, a senior minister of the Tianqi period during the Ming Dynasty. (1620-1627). With front, middle and back halls, the mansion is grand as well as solemn. Interestingly, the outer wall is crooked and shapeless, but the interior of the mansion is very straight and balanced. Legend has it, such a design represents the owner' s philosophy: appearance doesn' t matter as long as one is upright and honest.

Sima Mansion (司马第) is the residence of Yu Weishu, the head of the Ministry of Military Affairs at the beginning of the Qing Dynasty. Facing east, this three-storey mansion has grey-brick doors and four-brick arches. The beams of the rooms before the front courtyard are decorated with carvings of plants and characters from Chinese dramas. The rooms behind the back courtyard are decorated with painted pillars and carved beams.

The stream beside Likeng Village flows from northeast to southwest and is clean but it flowed too fast and so the path of the stream was too straight. To slow it down, locals built a bridge over the stream at the entrance of the village (a "water gate" in feng shui theory) and put logs and rocks in the riverbed between the water gate and the village to slow the current, creating lovely swirls in the flowing stream.

The water in Jinjia Well drains from mountain walls. Free from bacteria, it is reportedly mellow and sweet and never dries up. Pouch Red Carp (荷包红鲤鱼), a famous specialty of Wuyuan often selected as an ingredient for state banquets, comes from this well. Green dumplings made from Artemisia (小饺子) can be seem almost everywhere in the streets. Some are sweet and some are savoury, and you can take your pick of four for 1 RMB. Home-made berry and mead are sold at RMB10-20 per bottle.

## MASKS

Nuo Dance (傩舞) is an artistic form combining classical dance with painted wood carvings. In Wuyuan Village there are more than 50 varieties of masks for performing Nuo Dance including pretty and ugly faces and loyal and treacherous faces. Meticulously carved, these masks are very vivid and lifelike.

Green trees and lofty horse-head walls

# Yantai Village

## The Hometown of Tea

Viewed from afar, Yantai Village presents a "timeless" scene of morning sunlight, thin mist, mountains, farmlands, winding paths, barking dogs, crowing cocks and singing birds. Inside the village, a winding flagstone path leads to Anhui courtyard residences and ancestral halls.

### Getting there

Yantai Village, Fuliang County, Jiangxi Province/
Nearest city: Jingdezhen.
江西省景德镇市浮梁县江村乡严台村
Take a taxi from Jingdezhen train station (景德镇火车站) to Fuliang County coach station (浮梁汽车站) (40 mins). There are direct buses from Fuliang coach station to Jiangcun County (江村乡) (40 mins), where you can change to another bus bound for Yantai Village (严台村) (10 mins). An alternative is to take a train from Fuliang (浮梁) to Zhitan Town (峙滩镇) (about 1hour), and then continue by taxi to Yantai Village (50 mins).

Yantai Village, called Yanxi in ancient times, was initially built during the Guangwu period of the Eastern Han Dynasty more than 1100 years ago. Seventy-four kilometres from Fuliang County, this ancient village is situated in a valley stretching eastward at the north end of Jiang Village. The crystal-clear Yan Stream flows across the head of the village, and changes its course when it hits the valley. The ancient theatre in the village was made of grey flagstones and has a history of more than 1000 years. There are also more than 140 well-preserved Anhui-style residences.

The village gate is the only way into Yantai Village. There are two ways to the village gate: you can take the ancient flagstone path built along the stream after crossing Fuchun Bridge (富春桥), built in 1502. The other way is through the concrete bridge across the stream. Though small, the village

Yantai Village scenery

is equipped with road signs.

The doors of typical Anhui-style residences are usually decorated with tile carvings and overhanging eaves. The door framemade of big flagstones is decorated with intricate carvings. The gold-plated windows of the wing rooms at both sides of the front hall reflect the former glory of the residence. Baskets with preserved pork, salted fish and delicacies from the mountains such as mushrooms and dried bamboo shoots hang from the ceiling. The walls of most buildings are decorated with horse-head walls, beneath which are many fine paintings.

The courtyard of every Anhui-style residence is a must-see. The gate of the residence is at the left of a gable wall with painted murals. Above the gable wall there is an attic. At each side there are wing rooms separated from the hall by wood carving windows. Behind the gable wall stands a screen wall on which the images of ancestors or landscape paintings are usually hung. Before the screen wall is a table with incense burners and offerings for ancestor-worshipping. At each side of the screen wall is a side door linked to the back hall and leads to the kitchen and store house. Near the gable wall there is a vast vat for breeding fish. The water in the vat is known as "heavenly water" (无根水) and is kept to ward off fire.

Among the many ancestral halls in Yantai Village, Fish Ancestral Hall (鱼祠堂) is particularly famous. Its main building has been replaced by two classrooms, which were then abandoned due to the increasing number of students. There are two stone drums at each side of the gate of the hall, decorated with cloud-shaped carvings and relief scriptures, but unfortunately they are now mostly covered with graffiti.

## PERFECT BREW

Situated amongst high mountains and thick forests, Yantai Village is the perfect place for cultivating tea. There used to be more than 4000 acres of quality tea fields in Yantai Village during the Daoguang period of the Qing Dynasty (1820-1850). The local Tianxiang Tea Shop (天祥茶号) is definitely worth a visit .

Yantai Village ancient residences

Valley setting

# 黴州山区古村
# Loess Plateau
## Castles, Cave Houses and Comrades

# Xiwan Village

## The Village is a Yard and a Yard is a Village

The main part of Xiwan Village lies on a slope between two mountains. With layer upon layer of houses, the layout of the village is harmonious and natural. The peaceful Qiushui River winds through the village, bearing witness to its tumultuous history.

### Getting there

Xiwan Village, Qikou Town, Lin County, Luliang City, Shanxi Province.
Nearest City: Taiyuan.
山西省吕梁市临县碛口镇西湾村。
From Taiyuan, there is a high-speed rail line link to Lvliang City ((吕梁)(2 hours). Lishi West bus station(离石西客运站) ( a 1/2 hour taxi-ride from the train station) has several bus routes heading to Qikou Town(碛口镇) (1 hour). From Qikou Town, take a taxi to Xiwan Village (about 1km).

Xiwan Village is situated in Lin County, east of Huang He (Yellow River) in mid-west Shanxi Province. The village's Ming and Qing Dynasty-style ancient architectures are well-preserved. Sitting northwest, facing southeast and surrounded by mountains and rivers. Xiwan Village enjoys enviable feng shui because its buildings are sheltered from the wind while facing the sun. As descendants of the village's founder, Chen Shifan (a wealthy businessman), most villagers also have Chen (陈) as their surname. After hundreds of years of expansion, the village has evolved into a fort-like complex with dozens of courtyards.

The village was established on a 30-degree slanting slope, rising up from the front to the back, from the south to the north. The courtyards are about 250 metres long and 120 metres wide. Five stone roads, each representing one of

Xiwan Village Courtyard

A stone roller inside a residence

the traditional Chinese "five elements" – metal, wood, water, fire and earth – connect the 30 or so courtyards together. A 2-metre wall surrounds all the courtyards (the gate and most of the village walls are ruined), creating a huge enclosed area. The only entrances are the three gates facing the south, representing heaven, earth and man under Taoist philosophy. If these main gates are closed, no one can get inside. However, inner doors link each courtyard, so once you are in one courtyard, you can go to all the others.

The streets of Xiwan Village demonstrate the idea of building archways in and towers above the walls for stability and convenience of transportation. Interestingly, the house of village founder Chen Shifan is hidden in an unobtrusive alley but is regarded as the best residence in the village due to its site selection, appearance, design and interior decoration. Inside an unflashy wooden gate on the outer wall is a delicate gate with lively carvings known as the second gate. There are two lions on the both sides of the gate and even the rings on the gate have beautiful engravings. The first gate is relatively shabby because the Chen family ancestors believed that it was prudent to be inconspicuous with their wealth.

The folk residences in Xiwan Village are typical quadrangle dwellings of the west Shanxi province Luliang style (吕梁风格), featuring columns, wide eaves and high fences. The courtyard is divided into front and back by a half-metre stone wall and each one contains a complete set of facilities such as a main room, wing room, pavilion, bathroom, stable, fuel-house, mill and grinding mill. The main room is a stone cave-house sitting on a stone platform with exquisite beams and wooden columns supporting the wide eaves. The wing rooms are built with bricks and wood, most of which are structured like lofts. The alleys are filled with beautiful tablets and brick, wood and stone carvings. The refined door

Lady's chamber

Hidden small door

carvings and decorations have high artistic value and are regarded as a perfect combination of art and utility.

Above the doors of many of the residences of Xiwan Village, there are wooden or stone tablets with Chinese characters which say "Sui Jinshi" (岁进士), "En Jinshi" (恩进士), or "Mingjing Di" (明经第). Jinshi was a title given to scholars who performed well in civil service examinations, but sui jinshi and mingjing jinshi were not considered official jinshi (third-degree scholars) – they were just titles to comfort old scholars who never made it through the exams. The Chen family was a family of businessmen and they didn't produce as many successful scholars as the more intellectual families of Nanyan and Qinshui in eastern Shanxi Province.

Simply from the luxuriousness of the structures, it is clear that the residences in Xiwan Village were not owned by common businessmen, but by the wealthy and powerful. There are two ancestral temples in the village. Sixiao Ancestral Hall (思孝堂) in the southwest is a stone cave house and the Chen Family Ancestral Temple (陈氏宗祠) in the southeast is built with bricks and wood. In winter, the fields outside the Chen Family Ancestral Hall are usually covered with snow. - making this a picturesque, if cold, time to visit the village.

### IDEAL HOMES EXHIBITION

A Chinese saying is, "If you want to see royal architecture, go to the Imperial Palace. If you want to see folk houses, go to Shanxi province".

Layer upon layer of ancient residences

# Lijiashan Village

## The Cave Houses of Phoenix Mountain

Famous painter Wu Guanzhong once said: "From the outside, Lijiashan Village looks like a Han Dynasty Tomb, but on the inside, it's Shangri-La".

### Getting there

Li Family Village, Qikou Town, Lin County, Luliang City, Shanxi Province.
Nearest City : Taiyuan City.
山西省吕梁市临县碛口镇李家山村。
From Taiyuan, there is a high-speed rail line link to Lvliang City ((吕梁)(2 hours). Lishi West bus station(离石西客运站) (a 1/2hour taxi-ride from the train station) has several bus routes heading to Qikou Town(碛口镇) (1 hour). From Qikou, get a taxi to Li Family Village (1/2hour).

5 kilometers south of Qikou Town, Lijiashan Village (literally "Li Family Mountain Village") was built on two slopes with a valley in the middle. Because it looks like the two wings of a phoenix, Lijiashan Village is also called "Phoenix Mountain". Most of the residents of have Li (李) as their surname. The village features hundreds of courtyards and more than 400 cave houses. The residences on the west side of the village were built during the Qing Dynasty, and although they have seen better days they remain intact. An unusual feature of the village is that the villagers keep camels for commercial transportation.

Most residences in Lijiashan Village are cave houses which cover the mountain from bottom to the top, forming a mountain village. Both the interiors and the outer walls boast delicate brick and wood carvings. Landslides and mudslides occur regularly, which is why the village has stone gutters as deep as 30-40 metres.

The front gate of the cave houses is usually on the left and the entrance may be perpendicular, vertical or at a 45-degree angle. There are cellars to store potatoes, radishes and sweet potatoes. The main room is the living quarters and the wing rooms are used to store food while the rooms beside the gate facing the main room are used as the livestock shed and fuel house. The main and wing rooms only have a 1-metre eave to shelter the house and wall, and as such, the hearth can only be placed in the open space between the main and wing rooms. With a roof on top, it becomes a "summer kitchen". The kangs (heated sleeping platforms) are usually set beside the windows, and the hearth underneath can be used for heating and cooking. If the cave house has a second floor, the roofs of the main and wing rooms become the courtyard of the second floor.

Ancient residences of Lijiashan Village

There are more than eight types of residences in the Lijiashan Village ranging from the luxurious Qing Dynasty houses to the earth cave houses.

The Xinyao Courtyard (新窑院) was built in the 5th year of the Republic of China (1916). The courtyard is wide open, the architectural quality is high and it is well-preserved. The building is layered with grey bricks and was crafted with fine workmanship. The cellar cascades down like stairs, different from the the traditional style which is dug vertically. The east wall of the room facing the main room has stone hoops to tie the horses.

The East Caizhu Courtyard (东财主院) was built by wealthy local Li Dengxiang during the late Qing dynasty. It has two storeys and the front gate is widely regarded as the best in the village. Houdi Courtyard (后地院), on the west hillside of Big Village (大村), was built by the affluent Li Daifen, and is bigger than East Caizhu Courtyard. As Li Daifen is also known as Xiangting, the courtyard is also known as Xiangtinglou.

Old Village (旧村), also known as Small Village , is located in the left gully of Phoenix Mountain. Before the Li family moved there, locals called it Chenjiawan (literally "Chen Family Bay"). Small Village has a completely different architectural style to Big Village – some villagers are still livng in one room earth cave houses, and stone and brick dwellings are rare.

The 200-acre Qilin River Beach (麒麟滩) is situated at the foot of Lijiashan Village. This narrow plain is prolific in the production of wild pepper, chili pepper and red jujube. Lots of giant and strangely-shaped Yellow River stones can also be found there..

## STAYING THE NIGHT

It is possible to overnight in a few of the cave residences - usually it is preferable to fix this up after arrival. Villagers Li Jiangxing (tel: 13753388943) and Li Yinlan (tel: 0358-4451308) can each arrange lodging in stone cave houses for up to 20 people.





Cave houses on the mountain

# Liang Village

## One Village and Five Castles

Liang Village forms the shape of a phoenix and is regarded as an outstanding example of ancient Chinese architecture. Standing on the 1060-metre long Guyuan Street is Beizhenwu Temple, the head of the phoenix. Donghe Castle and Xining Castle on the east and west sides are like wings. Nanqian Castle and Changtai Castle are tucked inside the belly while Tianshun Castle in the south is supposedly like a rising tail.

### Getting there

Liang Village, Yuebi Town, Pingyao County, Jizhong City, Shanxi Province.
Nearest City: Taiyuan.
山西省晋中市平遥县岳壁乡梁村。
From Taiyuan, take a train to Jinzhong City (晋中市) (1/2 hour). After arrival at Jinzhon's, Yuci Train Station(榆次站) take a local train to Pingyao Train Station(平遥站)(1hour). From the nearby Pingyao bus station (平遥汽车站) there are many buses to Liang Village (20 mins).

Liang Village is situated on hilly ground 6 km southeast of Pingyao Ancient City . The main draw for visitors is the village's five ancient castles - Donghe Castle (东和堡), Xining Castle (西宁堡), Changtai Castle (昌泰堡), Nanqian Castle (南乾堡) and Tianshun Castle (天顺堡) - but the village boasts many other attractions including tombs - Zhao King's Tomb (赵王墓) and the Northern Song Dynasty Ji's Tomb (冀氏古墓); five temples – Zhufu Temple (祝福寺), Zhenwu Temple, (真武庙) Guanyin Temple (观音堂), Laoye Temple (老爷庙), and Yuan Temple (源祠); Yuangong Pagoda (渊公宝塔); a theatre stage (古戏台) and two ancient streets – Guyuan Street (古源街) and Xi (West) Street (西街).

Liang Village's five castles all have different styles which can be dated back to the Xia Dynasty, Shang Dynasty and the period of the Five Dynasties and Ten Kingdoms. Donghe Castle was designed according to the shape of the Big Dipper; the designs of the Nanqian, Changtai and Tianshun castles were based on the Chinese characters "Yu" (玉, Jade), "Tu" (土, Earth), and "Wang" (王, King), and the cultural belief that "Yu is from Tu" (土生玉). In the castles, the streets are narrow, the walls high and the courtyards connected.

The five castles contain most of the residences in Liang Village. Tianshun Castle and Nanqian Castle are considered the most complete ones; Donghe Castle is the oldest and steepest; Xining Castle is surrounded by water and offers the best views and Changtai Castle, although somewhat dilapidated, has lots of quadrangle dwellings. All walls are built with earth - Nanqian Castle still has some extant walls which are about 1-metre wide, The more than 20 cave houses in the village are relics of ancient cave dwellers.

The ancient temples in Liang Village are very famous.

Liang Village Gatehouse

The big temples are clustered in the village while the small temples are spread more diffusely around the castles. The largest group of temples, which also includes the Jifu (积福寺) and Guangsheng (广胜寺) temples, is located in the northern part of the village. Guangsheng Temple has become the location where most Buddhist activities take place.

## TEMPLE FAIRS AND WEDDINGS

Liang Village's colourful folk culture encompasses traditional wedding festivities, temple fairs, festivals, embroidery, and paper cutting - making the village a valuable site for the study of Han ethnic culture in North China.

Liang Village is situated at the corner of Huiji River (which is a branch of Fen River) with the tall Mengshanin the south and the Yinhui Reservoir in the north. The physical layout is said to be like two dragons drinking water from the river with their heads close together.. There are more than 2000 acres of marshlands and a lakeshore of more than 3000 metres.

Liang Village's good feng shui is attributed by locals to the achivements of such local success stories as Mao Honghan, manager of the famous bank "Wei Tai Hou" (蔚泰厚), and businessmen Ji Gui and Deng Wanqing, second-degree scholars of the Qing Dynasty. During the Ming and Qing Dynasties, hundreds of the villagers ran or managed banks and stores.

Liang Village has a diverse architectural legacy

# Zhangbi Village

## An Impregnable Fortress Village

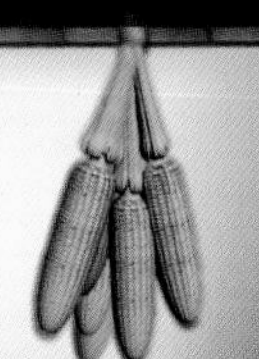

Zhangbi Village is a small village which is rich in features of military, social, religious, industrial and cultural interest. This architectural treasure trove featuring an assortment of tunnels, temples, alleys, gates and coloured glazes.

### Getting there

Zhangbi Village, Longfeng Town, Jiexiu County, Jinzhong City, Shanxi Province.
Nearest City : Taiyuan .
山西省晋中市介休市龙凤镇张壁村。
From Taiyuan Airport take a taxi to Jiexiu City (介休市) (about 1 hour). There is a special tourist shuttle bus line from Jiexiu City to Zhangbi Ancient Castle (张壁古堡) ( RMB 40, 1.5hours).

Zhangbi Village, also known as Zhangbi Ancient Castle, is situated in the southeast of Jiexiu Basin, 10 km from the downtown area of Jiexiu City. Despite its small size, Zhangbi Village is rich with cultural heritage interest, with attractions such as ruins from the Xia and Shang Dynasties, tunnels from the Sui and Tang Dynasties, tombs from the Jin Dynasty, theater stages from the Yuan Dynasty and cultural relics and historic sites from the Ming and Qing Dynasties. Some of these features are unique to Zhangbi Village - including the Sui and Tang Dynasty tunnels (隋唐地道), Liuwuzhou Temple (刘武周庙) and a long tradition of glazed tablet production.

Built during the late Sui and early Tang Dynasties, Zhangbi Village is supposedly shaped like a dragon, with a stone dragon head on the south gate and nine red stone paths as the dragon's beard. On either side of the road, quaint stores, simple houses and luxurious temples along with old trees add more charm to the village.

At present, most of the well-preserved residences in the castle are concentrated in Hujia Garden (户家园) and Jiahui Hall (嘉会堂) in Jiangjia Alley (贾家巷). In Zhangbi, village, "lifangs" (里坊, residential areas) from the Sui and Tang Dynasties, which have disappeared from most ancient cities in China, can still be found. When its gate is closed, the lifang becomes a castle within a castle.

The defense system of Zhangbi Village makes it easy to defend and difficult to attack. There are three steep gullies at the northern part of the village and three direct exits at the south. The 30-metre deep Yaowan Gulley is in the west. In the east, the castle occupies a commanding position, making it virtually impregnable.

In order to fully utilise the castle's advantages, villagers built forts and stationed troops on the ground, and constructed a 3000-metre, three-storey tunnel underground for both attack and defense. The wider sections of the tunnel allow two people to walk side-by-side but most parts of the tunnel are less than 1.8 metres high. There are also traps, communication channels, observation holes, ambush channels, retreat channels and drain gates, as well as tiny breathing holes connected to the surface.

In Xichang Alley (西场巷) there lies an exquisite residence with a tunnel entrance in the second room east of the main room. The entrance is hidden in a black closet. There are 10 wells in Zhangbi Village and at least eight of these are connected through underground tunnels. The inner walls of the wells have manholes on either side, allowing people to travel between them simply by using a board to bridge the gap. Removing the board after crossing to the other side prevents enemies from following. Remarkably, this massive underground network was kept so secret that it left no historical record.

Apart from the large-scale fortress, temples are also considered a highlight of Zhangbi Village. There are 16 temples remaining – among the best ones are Zhenwu Temple (真武殿), Kongwang Temple (空王殿), Sandashi Temple (三大士殿), Erlang Temple (二郎庙), Kehanwang Temple (可汗王祠), and Guandi Temple (关帝庙). However, the Ming Dynasty Kongwang Buddha Palace (空王佛行宫) is most famous. Inside the palace, there are three big halls with the statue of Kongwang Buddha and a mural detailing his life story. There are two coloured glaze tablets in front of the palace: the one in the east tells how Kongwang Buddha became a Buddha, while the one in the west side explains how the palace was built.

According to records, the coloured glaze industry existed in thei Jiexiu area as far back as the Tang and Song Dynasties, and reached its peak during the Ming Dynasty. Before the Tang Dynasty there were already three types of kilns – coal pit, stall and bowl. During the late Tang and early Song Dynasties, the ceramic and vinegar industries commenced large-scale productions, and Jiexiu became famous for its white porcelain. Zhangbi Village's Chenghuang Temple (城隍庙), Guangwenji Temple in north Shitun and Zishou Temple in Lingshi are all regarded as masterpieces of Jiexiu craftsmenship.

### MATURE VINEGAR

One Zhangbi Village specialty is mature vinegar. Many visitors like to bring home a bottle of vinegar as gifts or souvenirs, but to avoid disappointment, note that vinegar must usually be placed in check-in luggage on planes!



Zhangbi Village's outstanding cultural heritage includes 16 extant temples

# Xiamen Village

## Mysterious Ancient Castles

Xiamen Village is a symbol of historic splendour. The residences are a fascinating blend of northern and southern styles, and the famous castle complex is considered a pinnacle of northern Han architecture.

### Getting there

Xiamen Village, Xiamen Town, Lingshi County, Jinzhong City, Shanxi Province. Nearest City: Taiyuan.
山西省晋中市灵石县夏门镇夏门村。

From Taiyuan long-distance bus station(太原长途客运站) (located next to Taiyuan Rail Station) take a long-distance bus to Lingshi County(灵石县) (about 2hours). From Lingshi County, there are direct bus routes to Xiamen Village (1/2 hour).

According to legend, Xiamen Village lies at "Lingshikou" (灵石口), the point where the legendary founder of the Xia Dynasty, Yu the Great (夏禹) allegedly cut into the mountain to create flood-controlling irrigation channels. In order to demonstrate their gratitude towards Yu, locals named the village after him. Located 9 km from Xingshi County, Xiamen Village is famous for its unique physical features, great feng shui and beautiful scenery.

Xiamen Village was built on Qinwang Mountain's Longtou Hill. The cliffs in the front provide natural defenses while mountains in the back provide support, with Fen River below acting as a moat. The village's complex of castles is considered to embody both the magnificence of northern residences and the delicacy of southern gardens.

Xiamen Village still has nine well-preserved traditional streets. There are three streets which lie from east to west (East Street, Middle Street and West Street), one road (Houbao Road) and five alleys (Dafu Alley, Xushi Alley, Baojiu Alley, Liangjia Alley and Tianjiu Alley). One of the unique features of the village is that every house is linked by the streets, roads and alleys, and there are secret tunnels for transportation, hiding and drainage.

The complex of ancient castles in Xiamen Village was originally the residence of the Liang (梁) Family – one of the four leading families in Lingshi County. Construction began during the Wanli period of the Ming Dynasty (1572-1620) and finished in the Guangxu period of the Qing Dynasty (1875-1908), taking more than 300 years. Now there are six

sets of well-preserved courtyards, around 60 buildings and over a thousand cave houses and traditional folk residences. The main buildings are Dafu House (大夫第), Yushi House (御史府), Zhifu Courtyard (知府院), Shenxiu House (深秀宅), and the courtyards outside Hou Castle (后堡), and Daotai Courtyard (道台院). Additionally, there are a large number of other interesting buildings from the Ming and Qing periods including ancestral halls and temples, schools, and a post house.

Built in the 24th year of the Daoguang period in the Qing Dynasty (1843), The God of War Temple (关帝庙) is a two-storey building covering 750 square km situated at the entrance of the architectural complex. The first floor has a brick arch structure and the second floor is half-timbered.

Baichilou (百尺楼) was built by the seventh generation of the Liang family, Liang Shu, during the Qianlong period of the Qing Dynasty (1735-1796). The building ("lou") is called "Baichi" ("bai" means 100 and "chi" is a traditional Chinese measure of size equivalent to around a third of one metre) because it is 40 metres high. With cliffs ahead and mountains behind and Fen River below acting as a moat, Baichilou is divided into four floors. The first and second floors have three rooms and the third floor has four. The fourth floor is known as Yun HallIn spring; go to the top of the building and you will see a magnificent view of mountains, rivers, fields and trees.

As a family of officials, the Liang Family made significant contributions to the prosperity of Xiamen Village. During the Ming and Qing Dynasties, the Liang Family produced 185 government officials, among which 66 were above the fifth rank and 18 were above the third rank, making the Liang Family a local aristocracy. The family is also known for a legendarily incorruptible figure – Liang Zhongjing, whose great efforts to vindicate the innocent during the infamous "Zhao Ergu" (赵二姑案) case from the Daoguang period of the Qing Dynasty (1820-1850) cemented his reputation across the country.

Toubao Gate

Ancient residence of Xiamen Village

### FEEDING THE DRAGON

On the second day of the lunar calendar (late January or early February), every local family cooks a millet pancake called "tan tan" (摊摊) in order to tame the dragon king and make him promise them a great year.

# Shijiagou Village

## Manor in the Mountain

Situated on the Loess Plateau, Shijjiagou Village is a place that attracts travellers with her antiquity and sense of mystery - it is possible to spend the night here.



### Getting there

Shijia gou village, Sengnian town, Fenxi xian, Linfen city, Shanxi province.
Nearest City: Taiyuann.
山西省临汾市汾西县僧念镇师家沟村。
From Taiyuan Station there is a high-speed service to Houzhou railway station(霍州火车站) (about 3 hours). From Houzhou station, take a bus to Fenxi County(汾西县)(1/2hour), and then get off at Shijiagou village - the ride costs RMB6.

Surrounded by mountains, Shijiagou Village is 5 km southeast of Fenxi Town in northwest Huozhou City. Inside the village a cluster of Qing Dynasty architecture known as "Shijia Compound" (师家大院) is regarded as the essence of ancient Shanxi architecture. The buildings are large and unique and filled with carvings on brick, wood and stone, providing invaluable information about China' s ancient residences.

The layout of the Shijia compound has been

A two-story residence in Shijiagou

The layout of Shijiagou village is like a ladder, with three sides resting against the mountains

moulded by the landform here. Shijiaguo Village is supposedly shaped like a phoenix, with the Shijia Compound as the phoenix's heart. The buildings are surrounded by mountains from three sides, with a river on the fourth.

Built in the 34th year of Emperor Qianlong's reign during the Qing Dynasty (1769), Shijia Compound is located in the north of Shijiagou Village. It was allegedly built by the four brothers of the Shi (师) family, and the construction spanned 70 years and the reigns of four emperors. It is divided into two parts. The major part consists of five compounds, and the auxiliary part consists of 31 yards. Most of the cave dwellings are 4 metres high and deep, warm in winter and cool in summer, making it quite a cozy place to live.

The architecture in each courtyard has its own style. Every courtyard has a living room, a corridor, a principal room, a side room, a study, a working room and a resting room for the workers. Doors with different names link the rooms, creating layouts where there are buildings within buildings, yards within yards and rooms within rooms.

The gates of the courtyards are connected by laneways divided by traditional moon gates (月洞门) essentially connecting every house to each other. Under the 1500-metre-long pavement are drainage ditches connected to every house, so there is hardly any water on the road, giving rise to the local saying "No wet shoes after half a month of rain" (下雨半月不湿鞋). On the outer circle of Shijia Compound there are spirit shops, vinegar shops, oil shops and chemists. This demonstrates that Shijiaguo Village can exist quite comfortably without having to deal with the outside world, but at the same time it highlights the economic and cultural limitations of a closed-off society.

Shijia Compound boasts 10 sets of wood and stone carvings of flowers and plants, people and arts related subjects, as well as wooden engravings in 163 places and brick engravings in 47 places. Many of the engravings are considered masterworks. Worth special mention is the floral window based around the word "longevity" (寿) in Chinese, which features 108 different patterns. Some say the patterns represent the 108 types of businesses of the Shi family, while others say they represent the 108 towns of Shanxi.

Due to the uniqueness of its architecture, elegance and prosperity, Shijiaguo Village enjoyed the reputation of "The No. 1 Village in the World" during the Qing Dynasty - it is still a special place.

## SHIJIAGOU SLEEPOVERS

Visitors to Shijiagou Village can ask to stay in the ancient residences - bear in mind though that the winters here are very cold. Popular village foods worth a try include "Six flavour pork" (六味斋酱肉) and Jishan jujube (稷山板).

# Lianghu Village

## A Living Fossil of Ancient Villages

Lianghu village has many well-preserved residences and is known for its detailed carvings, especially the patterns of animals and flowers on the stone window sills and door frames.

### Getting there

Lianghu village, Yuancun town, Gaoping city, Jincheng city, Shanxi province.
Nearest City : Jincheng.
山西省晋城市高平市原村乡良户村。
Take a bus from Jincheng bus station(晋城汽车站), (a ten-minute walk from the train station) to Gaoping City(高平市) (1hour). From Gaoping, your best option is to take a taxi to Lianghu Village (1/2hour).

Lianghu Village is blessed with a fabulous setting, its three sides pressed up against mountains and the fourth facing a river. The village is located in the west of Gaoping City, with Fengchishan (Phoenix Wing Mountain) to the north and Shuanglong (Two Dragon) ridge to the south. Linaghu Village has a long and illustrious history. It was founded in the middle of the Tang Dynasty, when the Guo (郭) and Tian (田) families decided to stay and form a village. Hence it was named "两户" ("Lianghu" - similar pronounciation), which means "Two Families", before later being changed to "良户", which means "Good Family". The village was the home of Tian Fengji, one of the esteemed "Three Ministers" of the Qing Dynasty.

The old village streets are long and the residences are well-preserved.The main streets in Lianghu Village are Hou (back) Street, West Street, East Street and Taiping Street, most of which are paved by sand and stones to dry up excess water. The village's handicraft industry is quite developed, with numerous blacksmiths, coppersmiths, silversmiths shops, mills, dyehouses and oil mills. There is also an abundance of natural resources like coal, wood and stone, giving villagers easy access to materials like bricks and stones to build.

Panlongzhai (蟠龙寨, coiled dragon stockade) is a large complex of castle-like Qing Dynasty architecture. The interior resembles a palace, combining the grandeur of the northern architectural st as well as the graceful beauty of the south. The Office for Assistant Ministers" (侍郎府) lies right in front of Panlongzhai, and as the former residence of Tian Fengji, it is also known as Tian Fu (Tian's residence.)

The grand Office for Assistant Ministers has a huge brick wall, on which there are carvings of the mythical beast qilin, waves, flowers, phoenixes, fireballs and various other designs. The Office for Assistant Ministers features four courtyards.

The front yard is long, providing a contrast to the spacious main courtyard. The three other halls are grand and graceful, containing wood carvings of phoenixes and oxen. The doors and windows of the side rooms are also quite delicate. While the courtyards may look somewhat delapidated, the majestic grandiosity of their past still shines through.

The building emphasises the orderly use of space. In a straight line from the south to north lie the door room, hall and inside room , exhibiting the philosophy of finding the right balance between heaven and earth and reflecting the fundamental principles of feng shui.

For safety reasons, the front hall is not connected with the inner rooms, requiring visitors to pass a long, narrow lane along the back in order to enter. Behind the back room is a garden called "Juzhenji" (居贞吉), which used to be a place for the girls of the Tian family to play in. The narrow lane to this garden faces the east, reflecting the belief that children should live a happy childhood and listen to their elders in order to develop into upstanding adults.

There are also many ancient temples in Lianghu Village, predominately concentrated in the village's southeast. It is an area seemingly designated for religious activities, with the King's Temple (皇王宫) for legendary king Shangtang, the "God of War" Temple (关帝庙) for the god Guanyu, the "White Lord" Temple (白爷宫) for local gods, the "Goddess of Mercy" Temple (玉虚观) for the Buddhist deity Guanyin and many other sacred buildings.

Among these temples, the oldest and grandest is the Jade Void Temple (玉虚观), built

A temple

Office for Assistant Ministers

in the fifth year of the Mingchang era of the Jin Dynasty (1194). The temple exhibits a stone tablet with writings by Li Junmin, a "zhuangyuan" (scholar who came in first place in the civil service exams) from the Jin Dynasty. The main hall is 10 metres high, and the "spout" shapes of the doors and windows are like those of Mongolian yurts. The style of the temple resembles the Ji family residences of Gaoping in Shanxi which are regarded as the earliest ancient residences in China.

Lianghu Village has enjoyed much prosperity throughout history. From the inscriptions on the plaques in the village it is apparent how much attention locals paid to education and culture. The village produced its fair share of "jinshi", "juren" and "xiucai", all of which were titles bestowed on those that enjoyed success in the all important imperial examinations.

## MAKING SACRIFICES

On the 17th of the first lunar month of each year, (usually mid-February), Lianghu residents offer sacrifices to their gods and ancestors, and in the evenings there are traditional rituals such as Sanludeng (散路灯), lighting lanterns to help the ghosts of those killed in accidents find their way to the next world, and Datiehua (打铁花), Taoist-inspired fireworks).

# Douzhuang Village

## A Masterpiece of Castle Villages

Douzhuang Village is a typical Shanxi village with defensive castle-like architecture. The village's design, layout and carvings were created over a period of 700 years during the Yuan, Ming and Qing Dynasties.

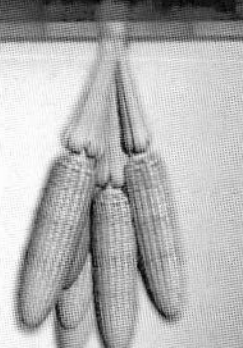

### Getting there

Douzhuang village, Jiafeng town, Qinshui xian, Jincheng city, Shanxi province..
Nearest City : Jincheng .
山西省晋城市沁水县嘉峰镇窦庄村。
Take a bus from Jincheng bus station(晋城汽车站), (a ten-minute walk from the train station) to Qinshui county(沁水县) (1hour). From Qinshui county, take a bus to Jiafeng town(嘉峰镇), and then get off at Douzhuang Villlage (1hour).

Douzhuang Village is situated on the bank of the Qin River, southeast of Qinshui Town and 50 km from Qinshui County. The village, which provides a pleasing environment and rich culture, is best known for its huge complex of castle-style structures, which has been famous in Shanxi since the latter years of the Ming Dynasty. Apart from folk residences, the village also has many temples, pavilions, ancestral halls, studies, drill grounds, courts, jails, walls, memorial archways, shops and stone carvings.

Douzhuang Village is regarded as a pioneer of castle-style architecture and is often the subject of studies into local lifestyle, economic development and folk customs.

Douzhuang Castle is 2000 metres long, 12 metres high and 15 metres wide. Built in the shape of a "卍" (a traditional buddhist symbol before it was mis-appropriated in mirror-image form by the Nazis), it is divided in four streets and four lanes. Because the layout is similar to that of the Forbidden City, locals like to call it "Little Beijing". Only four of the nine grand gates remain. In the front,a moat runs around the castle. Above the north gate is an iron gate called the Neicheng (Inner City) gate, connected to the lanes inside, while the Waicheng (Outer City) gates are connected to the streets .

The famous grand gardens of Douzhuang Village feature orderly and well-preserved buildings with skilful carvings on the rails, window sills and pillars.

Fo Hall

The garden of the Chang Family Mansion (常氏宅院) is particularly large and splendid, and was once used as dowry for the daughter of a government officer during the Qing Dynasty.

The Zhang Family Mansion garden (张氏宅院) was built for a tomb keeper. The Zhangs have been a prosperous family since the Ming Dynasty. The top of the 9-metre tall, east-facing gate is decorated with a brick carving of three Chinese characters" "尚书府" ("Minister's Residence"). The garden is divided in two parts: the upper part has the Five Phoenix Building (五凤楼), the River Gazing Building (望河楼), and Heaven Bridge (天桥). . The lower part consists of three yards located off Chenbao Xi Street (城堡西街) . On the corner of the street there is a grand gate with carvings in bricks, stones and wood.

The gracefully extravagant Jia Family Mansion (贾氏宅院) has three connecting yards and a classic brick-carved gate. The boards of the gate are inscribed with the Chinese characters "怡善" (Virtue), "忠 (Loyalty), and "孝 (filial piety). The roof of the Jia family's "treasure room" (藏宝房) is particularly unique. The location and design is careful and delicate – it is not connected with any other buildings; the outside wall is smooth to avoid climbing thieves, and the entrance has the same colour and pattern as the floors to make it hard to find. Built with huge stones, bricks and lime, the walls of the treasure room are almost five foot thick and made with fire-proof materials.

Gugong Hall (古公堂) in the north consists of a tribunal building (公堂) and a dungeon (地牢). The passages are wide, held up by stone pillars, and the rooms on the left and right are higher up than the main hall. In the front, the doors are small and the windows are large. In the middle of the main hall is the inquisition hall, while on the sides are the discussion halls. In an area 20 metres away and 5 metres underground, there are eight brick caves for the construction of prisons . Inside each cave there is a stone grill and iron chains on the walls. At the end of the passage is a brick watchtower to guard the prisoners. The jail is an extreme rare piece of ancient architecture.

Duozhuang Village, which has the nickname of "Little Beijing", once had 13 ancient temples in total. The remaining ones include Fo Temple (佛庙), Caishen Temple (财神庙), Huoxing Temple (观音堂) and Guanyin Temple (观音堂). Fo Temple was built in 1346 and comprises three main halls, Er Hall (耳殿), east and west halls and the grand gate (大门楼) . The main halls faces south, with 3 rooms.

## "LADY CASTLE"

During the upheavals of the Ming Dynasty, the female members of the Zhang family were said to have thrice fought off the attacks of bandits, thus also giving the village the nickname "Lady Castle" ("夫人堡").

Chilling out in downtown Douzhuang Village

# Xiwexing Village

## The Ancient Site of the Liu Family Settlement

Xiwenxing Village has been famous for its ancient residences since the Yongle period of the Ming Dynasty (1360-1424). The residences, surrounded by green slopes and trees, were built high in the west and low in the east..

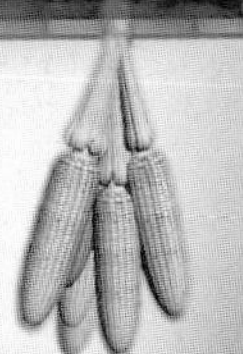

### Getting there

Xiwenxing village, Qinshui County, Gaoping City, Jingcheng, Shanxi province.
Nearest City : Jincheng.
山西省晋城市高平市沁水县土沃乡西文兴村。
Take a bus from Jincheng bus station(晋城汽车站), (a ten-minute walk from the train station) to Qinshui county(沁水县) (1hour). From Qinshui county, take a bus to Xiwenxing village (about 20mins).

At the foot of Li Mountain, Xiwenxing Village is enclosed by the Taihang, Taiyue and Zhongtiao mountains, 25 km southwest of Qinshui Town, 378 km away from Taiyuan City and 228 km from Zhengzhou City. Ninety percent of the villagers have the surname Liu (柳), and it is one of the only ancient villages in northern China dominated by people from the same bloodline.

With a layout supposedly resembling a flying phoenix, this archetypal castle village is more than 30 acres in size. The core of the village is a passage encircling several large courtyards. One of the widest streets in the village's south, Paifang Street (牌坊街), has two stone archways on either side. The stones have eroded over time, and even the features of the stone lions beneath the arches have become indistinct, though on the whole they remain well-preserved.

The Liu family residences combined the essence of Ming

God of War Temple

Liu Residence Gate

and Qing constructral art with styles from north and south, and are decorated with calligraphy in the style of various famous masters. They comprise a typical "huanshanju" (环山居), which means a "residence surrounded by mountains".

The layout of the Liu family residence is shaped like a "卍", an ancient buddhist symbol which is supposed to represent good fortune. The complex is divided in three sections. In the south is the outer section, which includes the Liu Family Ancestral Hall (柳氏祠堂), The God of War Temple (关帝庙), Temple of Literature (文庙) and other buildings and pavilions. The middle section comprises several small alleys and the Literature Pavilion (文昌阁), a school ground and two grand stone buildings. The enclosed inner section has barbed wires, alarm bells, underground passages and firewalls, and on its four corners there are a small theatre (小戏台), the River Watching Pavilion (观河亭), Admiring the View Pavilion (赏景楼) and a Gatehouse (府门楼). Together, the three sections measure 1.5 km and traverse 18 ancient streets.

The Liu family residence is decorated with traditional patterns that are pronounced like auspicious sayings. For example, lotus and cassia twigs represent having "successive sons" (连生贵子); and five bats flying around the character "寿" "Shou" - meaning "longevity") represents "a long life with five blessings". There are 30 such patterns inside the residence, which also features a large number of ancient artistic creations by past masters such as Southern Song dynasty philosopher Zhu Xi (朱熹), Ming dynasty philosopher Wang Yangming (王阳明); Ming dynasty painter and calligrapher Wen Zhengming (文征明), and famous Tang dynasty painter Wu Daozi (吴道子).

Seated at the entrance of the village, the Kuixinglou building (魁星楼, named for the four

Memorial archway

## SWEET CEMETERY

The Liu family cemetery is in the northern mountains 2km from the Lui family residence. It is a sweet spot, with swimming turtles, green pines, abundant sunshine and sweet spings. You can also sample the fresh spring water and the fresh fruits growing on the trees.

Sculpture of village founder Liu Zongyuan

stars in the bowl of the Big Dipper) was built during the Jiaqing period of the Qing Dynasty (1760-1820). What is seen today is actually a reconstruction of the original. The building's pavilion, the highest point of the village, offers magnificent views of the nearby mountains.

Next to Kuixinglou there is the God of War Temple (关帝庙), which was rebuilt in 1559 and is the main temple of Xiwenxing Village. The middle of the temple contains a courtyard enclosed by building on all four sides. On the north base of the courtyard is the main hall, opposite of which is a theatre stage (戏台) for religious offerings and performances, making it the most important public activity centre in the village.

The Zhongxiandi gate (中宪第) is located in the middle part of Xiwenxing Village. The decoration of the two-storey gate is quite outstanding, with the high middle roof and wooden carvings underneath, plus a magnificent and graceful stone lion guarding the front entrance.

Simadi (司马第) is a large residence comprising two "siheyuan" (四合院, courtyards surrounded by buildings on four sides). Above the southwest-facing gate is a four-storey board with the name of the building inscribed on the lowest part. In front of the gate there is a horse-mounting block and on either side of the gate sit two stone lions. Facing the gate is an elegant screen wall with carvings made out of brick, stone and wood. Beside the doors are more stone lions.

The rich culture of Xiwenxing Village is apparent from its location, structure, residences, detailed decorations and folk customs. It is a living fossil of the Liu family's ancestral culture and a fine architectural museum.

Kuixinglou

# Huangcheng Village

## The Prime Minister's Village

Stand in the deep courtyards of Huangcheng Village ("Imperial Palace Village') and admire timeless architecture while you listen to melodious music played by ancient bell chimes and savour the aroma of fresh tea.

### Getting there

Huangcheng Village, Beiliu Town, Yangcheng County, Jincheng City, Shanxi.
Nearest City:: Jincheng..
山西省晋城市阳城县北留镇皇城村。
Take a bus from Jincheng bus station(晋城汽车站), (a ten-minute walk from the train station) directly to Huangcheng Tourist District (皇城相府景区)( RMB10 & 1.5 hours).

Originally named Zhongdao Village, Huangcheng Village is conveniently located 20 km west of Jincheng City. Nestled at the foot of a mountain and resting alongside the river, the village is home to 234 families. With its proud collection of historical relics, Huangcheng Village has claimed the reputation of "The First Village of Shanxi". The village's unique architectural complex of official mansions and residences is regarded by some as an epitome of Chinese civilisation.

Huangcheng Village's Prime Minister's Mansion (皇城相府), with its multiple structures and numerous courtyards, was built by Qing government official Chen Yanjing for his mother. It is said that when Chen Yanjing took up an official position in the capital, his mother wanted to pay him a visit but was too old and weak to make the journey. To fulfill his mother's wish, Chen specially built this Imperial Palace-like mansion in his hometown. Chen was Emperor Kangxi's tutor as well as Prime Minister of the country. He was also chief editor of both the Kangxi Dictionary (康熙字典) and The Standard Phrase Dictionary (佩文韵府), two huge landmarks in the history of Chinese letters. Because Chen was also known as "Wuting", the mansion is also called "Wuting Cottage."

The Prime Minister's Mansion was built during the Xuande period of the Ming Dynasty, 570 years ago, but

Old Commercial Street of the Ming and Qing Dynasties

did not begin to develop into what we see today until Emperor Kangxi's reign in the Qing Dynasty (1644-1911). Covering an area of 60 thousand square metres, the mansion is divided into two parts: inner city and outer city. All together, the mansion has 9 gates, 1700 metres of walls and 19 large courts. The Prime Minister's Mansion is effectively an architectural cluster of Ming and Qing Dynasty-style official mansions and residences of intellectuals and civilians. Some highlights include the splendid Yushu Pavilion (御书), the majestic River and Mountain Pavillion (河山楼, the lofty Zhongdao Hall (中道庄巍峨壮观), the intriguing "Army-hiding Cave" (藏兵洞), the winding South Study, (南书院), the elegant West Garden (西花园) and the Purple Cloud Pavilion, (紫芸) which contains a forest of imperial stone tablets (碑林).

The Prime Minister's Mansion was previously known as Zhongdao Hall (中道庄). Nowadays, this usually refers to the outer portion of the mansion, which includes the outer wall, Zhongzai House (冢宰第), Dianhan Hall (点翰堂), Ladies' Chamber (小姐院), Hanlin Academy (翰林院), and the Virtue Memorial Archway (书院).

Yushu Pavilion stands at the front gate of Zhongdao Hall. With carved beams, painted brackets and red pillars, the pavilion was initially built in the 50th year of Emperor Kangxi's reign (1710 ). The words "Wuting Cottage" (冢宰总宪), written with bold strokes by Emperor Kangxi himself, are inscribed in a plaque hanging over the door.

"Virtue Memorial Archway" is the most eye-catching archway in the mansion, being three storeys high and with four pillars made of stone. Its foundations are decorated with the carvings of auspicious animals and the brackets with spectacular dragons and phoenixes. Inside the mansion, there are more small memorial archways which record all the official positions of Chen Jingting's ancestors.

Prime Minister's Hall (相府大院) also called "Academian Hall" (大学士第) was the former residence of Chen Jingting. It is a courthouse and the main building of the outer portion of Huangcheng Village. Behind the gate there is a screen wall and a board with the Chinese characters for "Academician Hall" written on it. The North Hall (北大堂) is the main building of Prime Minister's Hall, and it is a symbol of many generations of imperial favour. A board inscribed with more calligraphy by Emperor Kangxi hangs atop the gate. This two-storey building, with overhanging rooftops, meticulously-carved brackets, doors, windows, rails and screen walls represents a prefect combination of feudal Chinese palace culture and local traditional workmanship.

The inner portion of the mansion, also called "Douzhu Hall" (斗筑居) is a castle-like building built by the Chen family during the Ming Dynasty. These living quarters comprise eight independent yet connected courtyards enclosed by rooms on all four sides. The "army-hiding caves", RongShan Mansion (荣山公府), General's Mansion (御史府), the Chen Family Ancestral Hall, Shide Hall (世德院), Shude House (树德居) and Qilin Court (麒麟院) are located here. The stone lions

The "Prime Minister's Mansion" of Huangcheng Village is an elaborate structure

on both sides of each court, the bearing stones, the decorated brackets and the screen walls are all well-preserved. Rooms with carved beams and decorated pillars can be seen everywhere, and the patterns carved on doors and windows are vivid and lifelike

The walls of the inner part of Huangcheng Village were built at the end of Ming Dynasty. Army-hiding caves (in use at the end of the Ming Dynasty) are ubiquitous, and crenels (cut out portions of castle walls) line the walls of the entrance. The Literature Pavilion (文昌阁) and the God of War Temple (关帝阁) sit at the southeast and northeast corners, respectively. The wooden stairs lead to the top of the walls, from where visitors can enjoy a sweeping view of the picturesque world outside the village.

Built in 1632, The River and Mountain Pavilion is actually a defensive structure built by the Chen family to protect themselves from invasion. Made of bricks and stones, the pavilion has seven storeys and can accommodate more than 1000 people at a time. The passages inside are linked to each other and there are no windows until the third floor. The stone gate of the pavilion hangs high on the second floor, and the gate is connected to the ground with a suspension bridge. To make it easier to observe and react to the enemy, crenels and forts were built atop of the pavilion and secret tunnels were dug below. The River and Mountain Pavilion is also equipped with living facilities such as a well, stone roller, millstone, as well as room for stocking food in the event of a long-term besiegement.

The North Study was built in 1642. Situated in the south of the mansion inside Zhiyuan Garden (止园花园), this study provided a place for young men in the Chen family to study and develop their talents. Chen Jingting and most of the Chen family received their primary education here before entering into an official career. During the Ming and Qing Dynasties, the Chen family produced a large number of scholars and academics. Chen Jingting in particular was praised by Emperor Kangxi as being "as elegant as Minister Fang and Minister Yao from the Tang Dynasty; as gifted in poetry as famous poets Li Bai and Du Fu". Emperor Qianlong also wrote couplets to show his appreciation of Chen Jingting and the Chen family.

West Mountain Court (西山院) derived its name from its location – it is located near the mountain at the west bank of Fan River. The plaque at the entrance was originally written by Chen Changyan, a general who had served two successive emperors. It is a venue for meetings of the "Jinding Society" (金顶会), a Taoist organisation founded by the ancestors of the Chen family. On the third day of the third month in the lunar calendar (late April or early May), villagers gather here to discuss donations, building temples and paying tribute to mountain gods.

These days, the Prime Minister's Mansion has become a filming hotspot: in recent years, it has been a location for several large-scale Chinese TV serials and cultural documentaries.

Purple Cloud Pavilion, the burial site of Chen Jingting, is located at Jingping pass (静坪山坳), 500 metres north of Huangcheng Village. Main buildings include a stone memorial archway, stone tablets with an imperial elegy, 10 large tombstones, four pairs of stone statues and Chen Jingting's tomb (陈廷敬墓).

## "GREETING THE EMPEROR"

Huangcheng Village stages regular entertainments for tourists: "Greeting The Emperor" at 09:30 (10:00 in winter) at Yingbin Square (迎宾广场); "Eight-Sound Concert" from 10:30-11:30 at Army-hiding Cave; and Bell Chime Dancing from 10:30-16:00 at Qilin Hall.

# Guoyu Village

## A Shanxi Castle Village

Built at the start of the Tang Dynasty (618-907), Guoyu Village is a castle-like village situated at the foot of Taihang Mountain. The village features tall walls, solemn ancient temples, magnificent officals' mansions, and a great number of battlements on the gate tower.

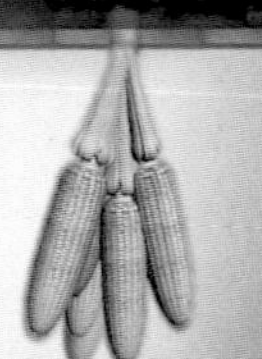

### Getting there

GuoYu Village, BeiLiu Town, YangCheng County, JinCheng City, Shanxi Province.
Nearest City: Jincheng.
山西省晋城市阳城县北留镇郭峪村。
Take a bus from Jincheng bus station(晋城汽车站), (a ten-minute walk from the train station) to BeiLiu Town(北留镇)( RMB10 & 40 mins). Then transfer to a minibus to Guoyu Village （郭峪村(15mins).

Guoyu Village is located in the middle of Han River Valley, 8 km north of Beiliu Town and only about a hundred metres from Huangcheng Village. The present-day village comprises three sectors, namely Guoyu Valley, Shilang Fortress and Heisha Slope. The village still has 40 well-preserved residences dating back to the Ming Dynasty, with a total of more than 1100 rooms spread across buildings such as Old Lion Hall (老狮院), Small Lion Hall (小狮院), the 12 houses of the Chen Clan (陈氏十二宅) and the 13 courtyards of the Wang family (王家十三院).

For both residential and defensive purposes, the villagers of Guoyu Village built Guoyu Fort (郭峪城) during the Chongzhen period of the Ming Dynasty (1627-1644). A cave house was added to the ramparts (defensive wall) so villagers could live inside while maintaining defenses.

Inside Small Lion Hall

As the cave house has three storeys and 628 openings, it was given the nickname "Honeycomb Fort". The fort has 10 watch towers and 18 shacks and wood pavilions, as well as three gates, one of which is the front entrance to the village. Once upon a time it was apparently possible to circle the entire city by horse by riding on the ramparts. Though only a section of the ramparts remain, it still remains an imposing part of the fort.

At the southwest corner of the village stands a flood-controlling water gate called West Water Gate (西水门). The east-to-west streets of the village, intersected by north-to-south streets, form an intriguing network. There are ancient residences from the Ming Dynasty on either side of the streets, most of which are two-storeys high and built with grey bricks. Guoyu Village has been economically prosperous since ancient times as the commercial centre of Fan River Valley.

Guoyu Walls

Old Lion Hall, built during the Ming Dynasty, is the ancestral home of former Chinese prime minister Chen Jingting. Before building a new mansion in nearby Zhongdao Village, the ancestors of Chen family lived here.

Yulou (豫楼), built in 1640, is a military building situated in the middle of Guoyu Village which serves the functions of bandit prevention and self-defense ("Yu" is pronounced the same as "precaution" in Chinese.) Yulou is seven-storeys and 30 metres high, with four vertical corners, four flat walls and a 2-metre bottom wall. Inside the first storey there is a stone roller, a stone mill, a well and a hidden hole which is linked to two tunnels, both of which lead to the outside of the fort. The ceilings of the third storey are made of ebony board and a battlement wall was set up above the seventh storey. There are impressive views from the very top of the building.

The Temple of Emperor Tang (汤帝庙), built during the Yuan Dynasty, is situated inside the village's west gate. The temple is divided into the upper and lower halls, which are are connected by stone stairs. In both the east and the west of the lower hall there is a two-storey house, with each storey containing 10 rooms. Watch rooms are situated on the upper floor, and living rooms and guest rooms are on the ground floor. A theatre can be found to the north of the upper hall. In ancient times, key decisions concerning the village were discussed at this temple.

From the Tang to Qing Dynasty, more than 80 people from the village gained official rankings through civil service examinations at all levels. In the Ming and Qing Dynasties alone, Guoyu Village produced 15 second-degree scholars and 18 third-degree scholars.

### FRIED BEAN JELLY

Pingyao Theatre (平遥大戏台) puts on shows for tourists. While watching a show, you might wnat to try a spicy local snack called fried bean jelly - it has been made in the area for more than 100 years.

# Shangzhuang Village

## Peaceful Home of A Ming Minister

Encircled by mountains and penetrated by clear streams, with its ancient architecture and beautiful location, Shangzhuang Village was the hometown of Wang Guoguang, a well-renowned statesman, economist and writer from the Ming Dynasty (1368-1644).

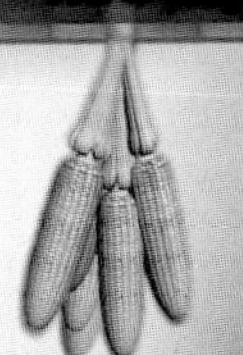

### Getting there

ShangZhuang Village, RunCheng Town, YangCheng County, JinCheng City, Shanxi Province.
Nearest City: Jincheng.
山西省晋城市阳城县润城镇上庄村。
Take a bus from Jincheng bus station(晋城汽车站), (a ten-minute walk from the train station) to Yangcheng Bus Station (阳城汽车站) (1.5 hours).You can then take a bus from Yangcheng to Runcheng Town(润村镇) (about 1/2hour), and then a pedicab to Shangzhuang Village(上庄村) (10mins).

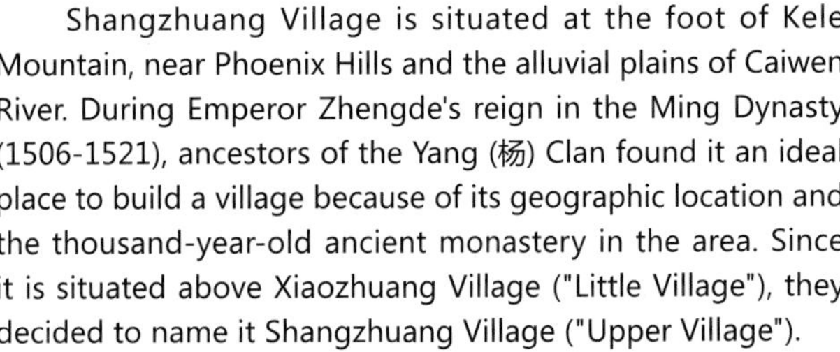

Shangzhuang Village is situated at the foot of Kele Mountain, near Phoenix Hills and the alluvial plains of Caiwen River. During Emperor Zhengde's reign in the Ming Dynasty (1506-1521), ancestors of the Yang (杨) Clan found it an ideal place to build a village because of its geographic location and the thousand-year-old ancient monastery in the area. Since it is situated above Xiaozhuang Village ("Little Village"), they decided to name it Shangzhuang Village ("Upper Village").

Yongding Gatehouse (永宁闸), built at the beginning of the Tang Dynasty, sits at the former entrance of the village. With a name that means "perpetual peace and stability", it is a large-span arch gatehouse made of stones and bricks. With old pines, red walls, golden tiles and clear streams rippling underneath, it is one of the symbols of Shangzhuang Village. An inscrption of four golden Chinese characters written on a black background ("水远云从", or "Far Waters Followed By Clouds") is hung high on the first arch gate.

Walking eastward along the pebble path you will reach the famous He Jie (河街, River Street) of the Ming and Qing Dynasties. Two dams made of sandrocks were built on the north and south sides of the river, and many tall blockhouses and ancient residences with grey tiles and bricks stand alongside the street. With the river as a central axis, the ancient architectural complex is laid out with order and balance: in the southern bank there is Minister's Hall (尚书第), Jinshi Hall (进士第) and Lufeng Nunnery (炉峰庵); in the northern bank there is Canzheng Hall (参政府), Sinong Hall (司农第) and Wangyue Pavilion (望月楼).

Atop the stairs of the southern bank of River Street lies Minister's Hall, the former residence of Wang Guoguang. Built between 1573-1575, it consists of the east hall and the west hall. The extant west hall comprises Dazun Hall (达尊

Decorated Archway in Shangzhuang Village

堂) and Tingchuan Pavilion (听泉居), which also acts as the backyard. The internal court is a typical courthouse and is elegantly decorated by painted beams and carved poles. Tingchuan Pavilion exemplifies Wang Guoguang's garden-building philosophies with their emphasis on the harmony between man and nature. Unlike traditional buildings with a higher main building and lower side buildings, Minister's Hall features a lower main hall and higher side houses.

Canzheng Hall, built at the end of the Ming Dynasty by Wang Guoguang's grandson Wang Zhengjun, is made up of five parts – Tingfang Hall (厅房院), Wuben Hall (务本堂), Yangshan Pavilion (仰山居), Wang Ancestral Hall (王氏祠堂) and Study H ll (书房院). It is equipped with all kinds of livin facilities such as a well, a roller and a mill. As a defensive mechanism, it is connected to the outside of the village by a tunnel. Wuben Hall is located west of Tingyuan Hall. At either side of the gate stands a brick screen wall facing the inside of the hall, featuring auspicious inscriptions such as "red phoenix greets the morning sun" (丹凤朝阳) and "pine and crane promise longevity" (松鹤延年).

Sinong Hall (龙章院) is made up of two courtyard residences, Longzhang Hall and Old Menli (老门里). The former is the residence of Wang Guoguang's ancestors. Above the gate is an ancient board dating back to the Ming Dynasty exhibiting its Chinese name. The extant east court and west court are linked by a door in the middle. Most buildings in the east court have been demolished, and only a house facing north at the bank of the river remains.

Old Menli, built by Wang Dao, Wang Guoguang's cousin, lies behind Longzhang Hall. In front of both the east and west gates are finely-carved stone lions and stone drums. The stairs inside the gate lead to the main hall, which is as large as five rooms and boasts an outside porch. Inside, there are two layers of wooded partitions and wing-rooms. Stone sculptures like "lions playing with an embroidered ball" can be found beneath the platform before the hall. These date back to the Ming Dynasty and are of high artistic value. An ancient wintersweet tree planted during the Ming Dynasty continues to stand inside the hall.

Full Moon Pavilion (望月楼), completed in the third year of Emperor Tianqi's reign during the Ming Dynasty (1622 ), comprises a front court and back court, linked by a passage. The main entrance is set at the southeast corner, and the lintel of the entrance is inscribed with Chinese characters for "honesty, prudence, diligence" ("诚"、"慎"、"勤"). Local visitors are encouraged to admire the moon from the balcony while listening to the sound of the wind rushing through the pines opposite Lufeng Nunnery.

Lufeng Nunnery is surrounded by ancient lacebark pines. In the upper part of the nunnery stands a God of War Temple (关帝殿), while the lower part is a theatre. Most of the buildings here date back to the Ming Dynasty and are divided into two areas. In the back area there is Gaomei Hall (高媒殿), Wenchang Hall (文昌阁), Fuzi Hall (夫子殿), and in the front there is the Three Churches (三教堂), Eighteen Arhats Hall (十八罗汉殿) and a Bell and Drum Tower (钟鼓楼).

### TEA CUP OF THE GODS

An ancient well at the southern bank of the village contains an inscription written by local luminary Wang Guoguang himself. The well is only as deep as a bucket but is regarded as a "heavenly spring", which according to legend was a "cup of tea" bestowed upon Wang by the gods. The water of the well is believed by villagers to expel illness and promote longevity.

# Xiaohe Village

## A World of its Own

Xiaohe Village is built on a slope, with a river lined with luxuriant trees flowing quietly through its streets. The village's Shi Family Garden features a unique design described as "yards within yards, yards above yards and yards beside yards." Combining tranquility and primitive simplicity, it is regarded as a treasure of Qing Dynasty architecture.

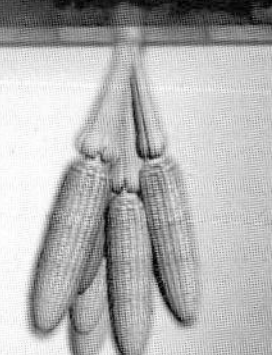



### Getting there

XiaoHe Village, YiJing Town, suburb of YangQuan City, Shanxi Province.
Nearest City : Taiyuan.
山西省阳泉市郊区义井镇小河村。
From Taiyuan Station take a high-speed train to Yangquan North Station(阳泉北站) (about 1/2hour). From Yangquan North Station take a minibus or taxi to Xiaohe Village (about 1 hour).

Xiaohe Village is situated in a belt between downtown and suburban areas, 4 km east of downtown Quayang City. According to the genealogy of the Shi (石) Clan, their ancestors settled here at the beginning of Ming Dynasty and named it Xiaohe Village (literally "River Village") after the river in front of the village. However the village has a history of more than 1,600 years.

Remaining buildings from the Ming and Qing Dynasties and the Republic of China period include 178 traditional residences which cover 30 thousand square metres. There are also traditional streets and lanes and commercial buildings such as pawn shops, stores and vinegar workshops; mansions such as the Shi Family Mansion (石家老院) and Li Family Mansion (李家大院); ancestral halls like the Shi (石家祠堂), Li (李家祠堂) and Dou (窦家祠堂) Family Ancestral Halls, and temples for the God of War (关帝庙) and Goddess of Mercy (观音庵).

Statue of Shi Pingmei

The Shi Family Garden (石家花园), built during the Yongzheng period of the Qing Dynasty (1722-1735), is located on the slope at the south entrance of Xiaohe Village. The main building, with nine gates front and back, 65 cave-dwellings and 112 pitched-roof rooms, covers an area of more than 10 thousand square metres. In the courtyard lies the small garden after which the whole building is named. The house faces east, and with a mountain at the back and a river in the front, it can keep out the northwest wind while taking in abundant sunshine. From the gate of the building, you can see range upon range of ancient residences with grey bricks and black tiles. Inside the house, there are more than 450 delicate wood carvings, 300 brick carvings and 300 stone carvings.

The main building of Shi Family Garden is a large court consisting of 21 smaller courts, such as Hanqing Hall (含清堂院落), Sanyuan Hall (三元堂院落) and Mingyuan Hall (远堂院落). These courtsyard buildings, laid out in a terrace pattern, are linked to one another by 72 doors. The study (书房), Ladies' Chamber (绣楼) and Yinian Hall (颐年堂) together with a small bridge over the flowing stream, fish pond, arbor and corridors, provide an exclusive place for members of the Shi family, especially young men, to study. The twelve animals from the Chinese horoscope are inscribed on the railing of the bridge leading to the garden.

Xiaohe Village is the hometown of Shi Pingmei, a famous Communist writer. Shi Pingmei Memorial Hall (石评梅纪念馆) can be found inside the Shi Family Garden, and features exhibits of how Shi Pingmei struggled against imperialism and feudalism while also fighting for the liberation of women! The memorial hall displays her literary works and details her tragic love affair with Gao Junyu, a revolutionary pioneer.

The Li Family Mansion covers a large area and contains many similar courts, exemplifying the characteristics of a conventional residence. Meanwhile the God of War Temple is intriguingly located on the hill beside Xiaohe Village, while the Buddhist Goddess of Mercy Temple stands halfway up Huyan Mountain (虎岩山) at the north entrance of the village.

### PIPE UP

The reed pipe (芦笙) music troupe of Xiaohe Village has participated in performances at the provincial level. Xiaohe Village also hosts intriguing local activities like cow goading (赶老牛), marble competitions 弹球) and coin piercing (砭钱).

A stone carving with the Chinese words for "A World of Its Own" is embedded into the lintel of the entrance of the Shi Family Garden

# Dangjia Village

## A Treasury of Chinese Residences

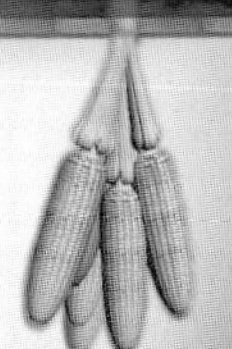

Dangjia Village is situated on the downstream side of Longmen. This elegant, dignified village attracts thousands of visitors every year, and is known as "The Treasury of Chinese Residences" because of its rare and well-preserved folk dwellings.

### Getting there

Dangjia Village, Xizhuang Town, Hancheng City, Weinan City, Shaanxi Province.. Nearest City :Xian.
陕西省渭南市韩城市西庄镇党家村。
Take a high-speed train from Xi' an North Station(西安北站) to Weinan North Station(渭南北站)(about 30mins) then take a bus from Hancheng Bus Station(韩城客运总站) heading to Xiayukou(下峪口) (RMB30, about 1hour), and get off at the entrance of Dangjia Village. From here it is a half hour walk to the main village.

Overlooking Dangjia Village

The ancient residences of Dangjia Village are located 9 km northeast of downtown Hancheng, just 3km from the Yellow River. The most common village family names are Dang (党) and Jia (贾). As the Dang family has a longer history, the village was named Dangjia Village (literally "Dang Family Village"). Developed from the second year of Emperor Yuanshun's reign in the Yuan Dynasty (1331), Dangjia Village is sheltered from the wind and exposed to ample sunshine. Sitting beside a long and narrow river channel, the village is boasts 100 siheyuans (四合, courtyards surrounded by rooms on all four sides) and temples.

From a distance, Dangjia village offers the impressive view of a mammoth complex of connected courtyards, a sea of green bricks and grey tiles. There is a tall gate tower in each siheyuan (四合院), and the lintels are inscribed with auspicious Chinese characters asking for happiness and success in civil service examinations. Most of the larger rooms have two or more doors and windows.

The hundred-plus lanes connecting the village's siheyuans are covered by bluestone or grey bricks. The tall gate towers and walls on both sides make the narrow lanes feel even longer and deeper. The zig-zagging lanes eventually converge, like streams flowing into one at a T-junction. On the boulder strip facing each crossing there are five Chinese characters (泰山石敢当), meaning that the stone is protecting the village. During the rainy season, the rain flows from every siheyuan into the lanes, which also function as a convenient drainage system that funnels the water into Mishui River.

The delicate wood-like, tile-carved Filial Piety Monument (孝碑) is made with extraordinary technique and skill. The first thing that will catch your attention is the 6.7 metre tower on the bluestone foundation bed. On the top of the tower there are pantiles covering the eaves, with five ridges and six animal sculptures. Below the eaves are wood-like tile carvings and layer upon layer of brackets, beneath which lies a banner with Chinese characters (巾帼芳型) praising the power of women. The banner frame consists of carvings of a flying dragon, the mythical beast qilin and incense burners. Above the couplets on either side of the wall, there are two sculptures, each holding the Chinese character 寿 which represents longevity.

The Watch Home Building (看家楼) is a three-layer attic-style brick house located in the south of the village. The top of the building offers a wide view of the whole village. A hexagonal brick tower called Wenxing Pavilion (文星阁) on the southeast side of the village was once used to pray for good luck in imperial examinations. North of the village lies Miyang Stronghold (泌阳堡), built during the first year of Emperor Qianfeng's reign in the Qing Dynasty (1851). The stronghold has reputedly protected the village from attack numerous times throughout history.

**LIGHTLY DOES IT**

Local delicacies include sesame baked rolls (麻烧饼) and Dahongpao peppers (红袍花椒), which are often served together with a light broth (清汤).

After Dangjia Village became prosperous during the Ming and Qing Dynasties, the villagers not only built a lot of new infrastructure but also paid special attention to cultural accomplishments. In the halls and rooms of most siheyuans there are family maxims carved on the walls, encouraging people to learn and be moral. During the Ming and Qing Dynasties, almost half of the families in the village had members who gained official ranks.

Chinese New Year in Dangjia Village offers folk activities such as deity worshipping, ancestor worshipping and drum shows by school children. Lantern Festival (正月十五) lasts three days from the 15th of the first lunar month (usually falling in late January or Early February).

Inside a Dangjia Village Siheyuan

# Yangjiagou Village

## The Red Holy Land

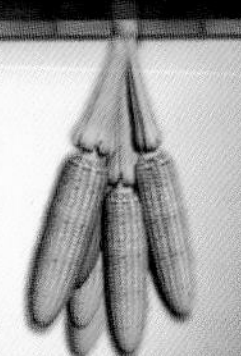

Yangjiagou Village marks the location ofvictory by the Chinese Red Army against the National Revolutionary Army in the northern Shaanxi battles and thus marks a pivotal moment in the history of the Communist Party of China. Nowadays, it has become a "patriotic educational base" and popular film location.

### Getting there

Yangjiagou Village, Yangjiagou Town, Mizhi County, Yulin City, Shaanxi Province.
Nearest City : Yulin.
陕西省榆林市米脂县杨家沟镇杨家沟村。
Take a train from Yulin Station(榆林站) to Mizhi Station(米脂站) (1 hour), and then get a taxi on to Yangjiagou Village (RMB20 & 10 mins).

Former residences of Mao Zedong and Zhou Enlai.

Yangjiagou Village is situated 25 km from the southeast Mizhi County. During the reign of Emperor Qianlong in the Qing Dynasty (1735-1796), the Ma (马) family moved to the area and later built the Fufeng Stockade (扶风寨) during the reign of Emperor Tongzhi (1861-1875). The private residences of the village are cave-style siheyuans (courtyards enclosed by rooms on all four sides). In 1947, Mao Zedong and his party stayed at the village for four months and transformed the Ma family residence into his personal headquarters, giving it the nickname "Little Beijing."

The site was originally called "Mao Zedong's Former Residence." In 1978, it was re-established as Yangjiagou Revolution Memorial Hall (杨家沟革命纪念馆). Main buildings include the former residences of Mao Zedong and Zhou Enlai as well as the former sites of the Central Political Department (中央政治部), Central Government Hospital (中央机关医院) and Xinhua News Agency (新华社旧址).

Private residences in Fufeng Stockade are mainly cave houses built on the mountains. Some are single courtyard buildings, while others are cave-style courtyard houses with four to six cave rooms. The most unique one is the former residence of Mao Zedong and Zhou Enlai (also known as New Yard, 新院). It was built at the hill of "Nine Dragons Mouth" (九龙口), and the building features many stone arches, gate towers and crenels. Eleven cave-houses are built with cornices and carving girders.

The well-preserved former site of the Chinese Communist Party's 1937 December Conference (十二月会议旧址) which took place at a time when China's fate hung in the balance, is a late Qing Dynasty cave-style siheyuan not far from New Yard. In the middle of the yard there are seven mountain-shaped half-timbered constructions. With five cave houses to the front and six cave rooms on the sides, the building functioned as the offices of Communist Party officials Ye Zilong and Wang Dongxing.

Located at the highest platform of Fufeng Stronghold, the former site of the Senior Military Conference (高级军事会议) has a gate with the Chinese characters for "Lecture Hall" written on it. On the east and west sides there are six cave rooms, which used to be Yangjiagou Fufeng Primary School (杨家沟扶风小学). In the courtyard stands the Ma Family Ancestral Hall (马氏宗祠), whose central hall is a mountain-shaped construction with eight hidden cave rooms. It is the only well-preserved late Qing Dynasty-style family temple and lecture hall in north Shaanxi Province.

Yangjiagou Revolution Memorial Hall was the place where Mao Zedong lived for the longest time when he was in north Shaanxi. Here Mao wrote 11 Communist masterpieces such as The Present Situation (目前形势) and Our Tasks (我们的任务.) On the 22nd of November, 1947, Mao Zedong and Zhou Enlai came to the village leading the People's Liberation Army. On the 21st of March, 1948, they crossed the Yellow River, to launch what can been seen as the final phase of their push for national power.

During the early years of Emperor Kangxi's reign in the Qing Dynasty (1661-1722), Ma Yunfeng established private schools to prepare family members for imperial examinations. During the Daoguang period of the Qing Dynasty (1820-1850), his successor Ma Jiale founded three private schools so that the children, friends and relatives of the Ma family, as well as children from other villages, could receive an education. All five sons and 11 grandsons from Guangyu Hall became officials, and 18 out of 25 great grandsons either received scholarly honours or an official rank, while three of them also went abroad for further study.

## COMRADE CAVES

Visitors can emulate Mao & co. and stay at local cave houses for about RMB20 per day. You can also test your revolutionary fortitude by trying local dishes such as pita soaked in lamb blood soup (粉汤羊血), donkey sausages (驴板), and "horse's hoof" shortbread (佳县马蹄). Local craft products include New Year woodblock pictures (木版年).



Fufeng Stockade is enclosed by walls and gates and contains many private residences, most of which are cave houses built in the mountains

# 东部沿海古村

# East Coast

## Ancestral Halls and Earth Buildings

# Tianluokeng Village

## Magnificent Earth Buildings

In Tianluokeng Village, five earth buildings sit on a wooded mountain. The layout of these buildings supposedly has a resemblance to Potala Palace in Lhasa (Tibet). The simile-prone Chinese have also described it as a "plum blossom on the earth" or a "flying dish" that has fallen from heaven.

### Getting there

Tianluokeng Village, Nanjing County, Fujian Province.
Nearest city: Xiamen..
福建省漳州市南靖县书洋镇田螺坑村。
From Xiamen take a train to Zhangzhou Station(漳州站) (2 hours). From Zhangzhou Bus Station(漳州汽车站) (a 6min walk from the train station) there are services to Shuyang Town(书洋镇) (about 1 hour). From Shuyang, you can reach Tianluokeng village by taxi or motorcycle (10 mins).

Inside an earth building of Tianluokeng Village

Tianluokeng ("Winkle Pit") Village has a site halfway up Hudong Mountain at a height of 787.8 metres above sea level. The village is located in the uphill part of Shuyang Town, 60 km from Nanjing County and 98 km from Zhangzhou City. Tanluokeng boasts square and round shaped constructions, the oval Zhenchang Pavilion (振昌楼) and a number of earth buildings.

Dahudong Mountain and the Dakedong Mountains surround the village on the east, north and west, while abundant terraces occupy the village's south. The village enjoys a pleasant natural setting and its earth building complex is regarded as the most magnificent in Fujian Province.

The oldest building in the village, Buyunlou (步云楼), was constructed in 1796, during the first year of the reign of Qing Dynasty Emperor Jiaqing. The newest building, Zhenchang Pavilion, was built in 1966. The village's earth building complex took a relatively long time to create, with the Jiaqing reign (1796-1820) being the earliest and most productive period. The famous group known as the "Five Earth Buildings" (五座土楼) have three-layers, all facing southwest. The first floor is the kitchen, the second the storehouse, and the third the bedroom. On each floor there are wooden passages connecting the doors. The Five Earth Buildings have been the home for the Huang clan (黄, a big Hakka family) for hundreds of years.

The main building material of an earth building in Tianlokeng Village is raw soil, which is combined with lime, fine sands, glutinous rice, brown sugar, bamboo and wood. The buildings are spaciously built for large families, and are well-protected from burglary, earthquakes, wild animals, fire and dampness. Good ventilation and lighting means that

The grand Earth Building Festival

they are warm in winter and cool in summer. The houses have a wooden structure with gradually thickening materials piled up by slab-stones. According to some specialists, the centre distances between the buildings in the village have applied the so-called "golden ratio", which was first studied by Pythagoras and Euclid in ancient Greece.

Hakka cuisine is relatively heavy and characterised by strong flavours. Popular local dishes include salty chicken (盐鸡), stuffed tofu (酿豆腐), pork braised in soy (红烧肉), five-spice roll (五香卷), pan-fried oyster (蚝仔煎), and tea rice (茶米). During Chinese New Year, villagers will make glutinous rice cakes (糍粑) in the hall for ancestor and god worshipping and to solicit a good harvest the following year. Around the winter solstice, villagers will make rice wine (米酒) out of new grains. This kind of rice wine is made from glutinous rice, clear spring water and red yeast rice.

"Zuo Da Fu" (做大福), a ceremony to welcome the God of the Land and the Buddha of Ziyunshan Temple (紫云山寺) back to the village, is the most exciting event in the village's social calendar, but is held only once every three years. During the ceremony (which falls in November or December - the last staging was in 2011), villagers will hold banners and flags, play the suo-na (唢呐, a Chinese trumpet) and bang drums to welcome the gods.

## GRAIN IN EAR

An especially good time to take pictures at Tianluokeng is during the "Grain in Ear" (芒种), one of the 24 solar terms of the Chinese calendar) festival. The festival usually falls in late June or early July. At that time, terraces near the earth buildings are filled with water and the mountain is often shrouded in mist. The Chinese New Year, when there are many folk activities, also makes for interesting photo opportunities.

The Five Earth Buildings, also known as "Four Dishes with One Soup", is a symbol of Fujian Province

Spectacular view of Tianluokeng Village's earth building complex

# Peitian Village

## Nine Halls and Eighteen Wells

Endued with beautiful landscapes and an important geographical position as well as the diligent spirit of its Hakka ancestors, Peitian Village offers visitors a treasure trove of Ming and Qing Dynasty Hakka vernacular architecture.

**Getting there**

Peitian Village, Liancheng County, Fujian Province.
Nearest city : Longyan..
福建省龙岩市连城县宣和乡培田村。
From Longyan Bus Station(龙岩汽车站), take a bus to Liancheng County(连城县) (2 hours) and get off at Pengkou Town(朋口镇), then continue to Peitian Village by mini-bus (RMB4 & 20 mins). Alternatively from Liancheng County Bus Station(连城车站), you can take a non-stop bus to Peitian Village (RMB20 & 1/2hour).

Peitian Village is situated in southwest Liancheng County and encircled by three streams and five mountains, the village is said to be embraced by "three dragons and five tigers". In 1344, the fourth year of Emperor Zhizheng's reign during the Yuan Dynasty, Wuba Silang, the ancestor of the Wu (吴) family, moved from Zhejiang to Peitian. Nowadays, there are over one thousand villagers here with the surname Wu. The village boasts no less than 21 Wu family temples, as well as 31 well-preserved luxurious residences, six private schools, four monasteries, two memorial arches and one ancient street.

The ancient Hakka people would pass along the old village street on their way to take imperial examinations in Tingzhou (an former preecture), and so the street has the

Enrong Memorial Arch, Peitian Village

nickname "Xiucai Street" (秀才街, denoting those who passed the imperial examinations at the County level.) Tea houses, traditional Chinese medicine stores, forges and traditional tofu and noodle joints fill the street, as well as antique shops and folk museums. The courtyards possess many well-preserved couplets from the Ming and Qing Dynasties. The one on the door of Zhide Residence (至德居) reads:: "Inside the court, beautiful orchids; outside the court, the bustling world" (庭中兰蕙秀，户外世尘嚣). In Dukun Mansion (都阃府), there is a well-known drawing called "Deer and Cranes in Spring" (鹿鹤同春).

Twenty-one temples line the two sides of the street. The temple gate towers are sumptuous with stone columns, carved beams, upswept eaves, red doors, colorful pillars, boards with golden characters, hollow-carved windows and screens, couplets, and wood mural paintings.

Due to the rainy weather of the south, the residences in Peitian Village were built by the Hakka people in the formation of "nine halls and 18 wells". Dafu Grand House (大夫第), also known as Jijin Hall, is an archetypal Peitan residence located at the southeast of the village. Starting in 1892, it took 11 years to finish building the house, which has 18 halls, 24 wells, 108 rooms and could contain 120 tables at feasts. The halls are connected by passages and separated by doors, a design suitable for both big families and clusters of smaller households. The upswept eaves, carving beams and painted pillars, windows and screens, as well as the decorated brackets, are all elaborately designed.

Official Hall (官厅), also called "Shiwei Mansion", has nine halls and 18 wells, surrounded by simple yet elegant fireproofing walls. Two stone lion drums sit before the front gate, while its five halls stand side-by-side to form an elegant sight under moonlight. Before the Communist Red Army headed north on its epic Long March (1934-1936), Official Hall was a headquarters for some of its generals, making Peitan Village one of the departure points of the Long March.

Yanqing Hall (衍庆堂), built during the Ming Dynasty, is similar in structure to Jijin Hall. The couplet on the door suggests that a successful marriage requires husband and wife to be well-matched in social and economic status. Inside the hall, you may chance upon a performance by Peitian folk bands comprised of traditional 10 Chinese wind and percussion folk instruments.

Visitors can have a look at the well-preserved stones for practicing martial arts in Jinshi Grand House (进士第), a site for learning wushu (Chinese martial arts) beside the village, and also at the martial arts school at Banruo Hall (般若堂).

Nanshan College (南山书院), which was built during the Chenghua period of the Ming Dynasty (1464-1487), is located at of the back of the village, surrounded by bamboos and trees. Many famous scholars have taught at the college ov.er the centuries. From the couplet on the gate tower which reads, "Streams like belts and mountains like pens, a house full of books and a homeland of fields" (水如环带山如笔，家有藏书陇有田), it is clear that the ancestors of Peitian Village paid substantial attention to both studying and farming.

## HAKKA JELLY

Peitian Village cuisine includes specialties such as sliced rabbit meat, (白斩兔), Liancheng white duck (连城白鸭). One must-try is Hakka rice jelly (米冻) which is popular during Chinese New Year. As the New Year approaches, villagers will start to make the rice jelly.

# Laifang Village

## A living Fossil of Hakka Architecture

With mountains behind and flowing streams in front, Laifang Village has been called another "living fossil" of Ming and Qing Dynasty-style Hakka ancient architecture.

**Getting there**

Laifang Village, Qingliu County, Fujian Province.
Nearest city : Sanming..
福建省三明市清流县赖坊乡
From Sanming Bus Station (三明汽车站) take a bus to Laifang Town(赖坊乡) (4hours) and then transfer to a bus heading to Laifang Village (40mins).

Laifang Village is situated at Dafeng Mountain beside Jiulong Lake, at the border of Qingliu County and Yong'an County. According to records of the Lai (赖) family, the village was built in 1022, the second year of Emperor Xianchun's reign during the Northern Song Dynasty, with Hakka people as the main villagers. The village features ancient residences, temples, streets, water systems and forts.

The original layout of the village is well-preserved, with Zhenwu Street, Loufangxia Street and Zhenanmen Street forming the main body and a large number of laneways branching off it. There are many temples and over 40 Ming

Laifang Village has sufficient ditches for water drawing, cleaning, and fire control

Cai Yinggeng

and Qing Dynasty-style ancient residences. Other impressive buildings include the Lai Family Ancestal Hall (赖氏祖庙), Cai Yinggeng (彩映庚), Hanlin Grand House (翰林第) and Dafu Grand House (大夫第), all of which have largely preserved their original designs.

The residences in Laifang Village were designed according to feng shui principles. The hall is usually built at the centre, constructed with a gate tower and rooms. In front of the hall there is a a patio, decorated by cobbles with patterns of flowers, coins and the yin-yang symbol. Ponds and lawns typically feature in front of the gate. The archetypal feng shui-inspired building is the Lai Family Ancestral Hall, built in the first year of Emperor Taichang's reign during the Ming Dynasty (1620).

The village is like a museum of Hakka village architecture, featuring the typical round-house-style Hakka courtyard, mansion-style buildings, watchtower-style buildings,"hanging-foot"-style buildings (吊脚楼) and so on. On the roof ridge, there are ornaments of mythical creatures. The decorated brackets and bracket arches are delicately made, reflecting the unique taste of the villagers. Together with the outstanding murals, colour paintings and carvings, Laifang Village is a veritable gallery of ancient residential decorative artworks.

The well-preserved irrigation system still functions in the labyrinth-like village. Two streams starting from the mountain at the back of the village are utilised ingeniously by designers, channelling into one stream which flows into every corner of the village. In the event of a sudden fire, villagers can put out the fire with the water from the stream by blocking the relevant outlet. The stream and the irrigation system are an important aspect of the lifestyle and culture of Laifang Village.

Laifang Village residences

## LION-DRAGON

Laifang Village celebrates traditional Hakka holidays such as the Lion-Dragon Festival (狮龙节), which is usually held in March, and the Torch Festival (火把节), which usually falls in July.

# Guifeng Village

## Cave in the Mountains, Paradise in the Clouds

Guifeng Village has attracted many writers and poets throughout the ages, leaving behind hundreds of priceless songs and verses. It may be a cliché, but strolling through the village is like stepping back in time – everything appears ancient, from the paths, streets and trees to the stories, tablet inscriptions and pictures...

**Getting there**

Guifeng Village, Youxi County, Fujian Province.
Nearest city : Fuzhou.
福建省三明市尤溪县洋中镇桂峰村。
Take a bus from Fuzhou West Station(福州西站) to Yangzhong Town(洋中镇) which is in Youxi County(尤溪)(about 2hours). At Yangzhong Town, transfer to a bus to Guifeng Village (RMB20 & 20mins).

Guifeng Village lies northeast of Yangzhong Town and is only 500 metres from the Jingfu Expressway. Surrounded by mountains and clouds, it has been honoured with flowery epithets such as "Cave in the Mountain" and "Paradise in the Clouds". Established in the seventh year of the Chunyou period in the Southern Song Dynasty (1247), at different times Guifeng Village was called Guiling, Cailing and Lingtou. As the village lies on an official path from Youxi to Fuzhou, in ancient times it was the only transfer station for high officials and noble lords, merchants and vendors, as well as watermen going to and from Youxi and Fuzhou. Its location brought Guifeng Village prosperity quickly, giving it the nickname "Little Fuzhou". Now 39 ancient dwellings remain, spread out along the village's three mountain slopes.

Built in the 32nd year of Wanli period of the Ming Dynasty (1604), the Stone Bridge Scenic Spot (石桥景区) is one of the "Eight Sights of Guifeng Village" and was called "Stone Bridge and Bright Moon" in ancient times. Near the bridge are four osmanthus trees, each with carved roots featuring one of four Chinese characters: "日", "月", "书" and "印" ("Sun", Moon", Book", and "A Seal" respectively.). The ancient stone path and bridges over the flowing water cast a beautiful reflection.

Overlooking Guifeng Villge from Liushizu Cuo

All paths in Guifeng Village are made of stone. Due to the rugged terrain and the short distances between each building, a large number of stones are used to

The Cai Family Ancestral Hall

The entrance to Guifeng Village

build revetments (energy absorbing structures), creating convenient alleys. Slabstone strips are paved on the road surface for each alley, forming a unique street pavement.

The style of the various residences in Guifeng Village is quite similar, consisting of a wooden structure, a courtyard, earth walls and a stone gate. On the gates are skillful carvings of human figures, landscapes, flowers, and birds. One relatively complete historic building is the Cai Family Ancestral Hall (蔡氏宗祠), which is located upstream of Stone Seal Bridge (石印桥). It was built after Cai Maoxiang returned home after becoming a "jinsh" (third-degree scholar from the imperial examinations) during the Ming Dynasty. Since then, it has become one of the most important memorial architectures for the Cai (蔡) family.

Tiandacuo (田大厝) was built in the Xianfeng period of the Qing Dynasty (1850-1861) and lies beside the mountain on the right side of the village. It is a mountaintop wood-structure building with three rows of buildings and double eaves. According to records, as the owner had an accident during construction, some parts of the building were not completed. However, in terms of artistry overall effect, Tiandacuo is regarded as one of the most outstanding buildings in Guifeng Village.

"Back Door Mountain" (后门岭) Residence, built in the 12th year of Emperor Qianlong's reign during the Qing Dynasty (1747), stands beside the mountain at the back left of the village. It is a two-row single-eave wood-structure building. On the central axis, there is the back hall, wing room, second hall and pavilion. On the left and right side there is the horizontal cuo .

The Stone Lion Compound (石狮厝) built in the Jiajing period of the Qing Dynasty (1521-1567) was named after its delicate stone lion. The compound is five rows long and three rows wide and is a mountaintop wood-structure building.

Louping Hall Big Compound (楼坪厅大厝) lies at the back of the village. It is a wood-structure building with two rows of buildings and was the childhood residence of well-known Fujianese businessman Cai Longhao.

The Cai Family Ancestral Hall (蔡氏祖庙) lies in the centre of the village. It is a two-row single-eave mountaintop wood-structure building and was the original base of the Cai family. Hanging in the hall are plaques with Chinese characters which say "Nine Peaks of Excellence" (九峰毓秀), "Jinshi", "Juren", "Number One Scholar", "Martial Arts Scholar" and "Five Generations Under One Roof" (五代同堂). The whole building is surrounded by a stone corridor. Behind the house there is a five-level flowerstand and two small wells on either side. The gurgling clear spring has the nickname "Eye of the Dragon" (龙眼).

## VIILLAGE CRAFTS

You can buy local craft products in Youxi County of the like of hanging trays, folding fans, small screens, hanging scrolls, root carving artworks, bamboo-weaving artworks and paper-cuttings.

# Xiamei Village

## Delicate Buildings, Lingering Aftertaste of Tea

Protected by mountains and nurtured by water, with its ancient street, ancient well, ancient port, ancient bazaar and simple folk customs, Xiamei Village is a classic southern Chinese riverside village. The well-preserved ancient residences from the Ming and Qing Dynasties line both sides of the 900-metre Dangxi Canal.

### Getting there

Xiamei Village, Wuyishan City, Fujian Province.
Nearest city : Nanping..
福建省南平市武夷山市武夷乡下梅村。
From Nanping′s Wuyishan International Airport, there are shuttle buses heading to the Wuyishan Scenic Area(武夷山风景区) (about 15min). .From Wuyi Mountain(武夷山市区) or Wuyi Mountain Holiday Resort(武夷山度假区) it is a 1/2hour local bus or taxi\ride to Xiamei Village.

Xiamei Village gets its name because it is located in the lower reaches of the Meixi steam. It stands 6 km east of downtown Wuyishan City and 5 km away from the Wuyi Mountain National Scenic Area. During the Kangxi (1661-1722) and Qianlong (1735-1796) periods of the Qing Dynasty, Xiamei Village was a prosperous tea market. Now,

The Zou Family Ancestral Hall integrates brick, stone and wood carvings

Xiamei Village still has more than 30 well-preserved ancient residences with Qing Dynasty architectural features and intriguing names such as the Zou Mansion's Young Lady Building (邹宅闺秀楼), the Fang Family Army Advisor's House (方氏参军第), Cheng Family Hermit House (程氏隐士居), Zhengguo Temple (镇国庙) and Tianyi Well (天一井).

Xiamei Village residences

The Zou (邹) family was originally from Nanfeng County in Jiangxi Province. The family's senior statesman  to Xiamei Village during the Shunzhi period of the Qing Dynasty (1643-1661) and lived on selling Wuyi Rock Tea. He invested in a 900-metre canal called Dangxi, which is connected with Meixi at the village entrance, forming a traffic network of rivers. He also invested in 70 houses on the southern and northern sides of the stream. A large number of arch bridges and slab bridges connect the corridors

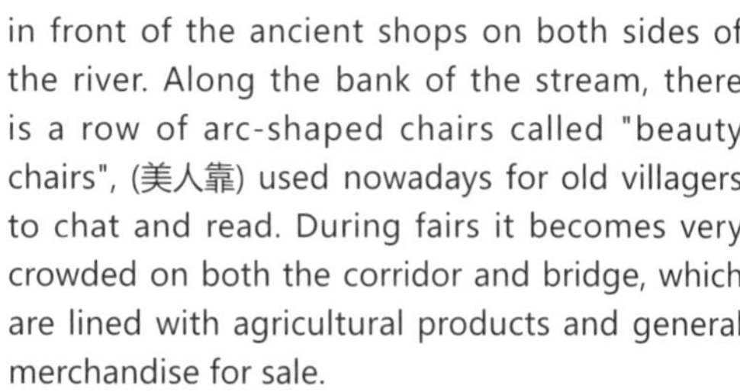

in front of the ancient shops on both sides of the river. Along the bank of the stream, there is a row of arc-shaped chairs called "beauty chairs", (美人靠) used nowadays for old villagers to chat and read. During fairs it becomes very crowded on both the corridor and bridge, which are lined with agricultural products and general merchandise for sale.

Xiamei Village's ancient architectural complex centres on residential architecture. For lighting, rain collection and ventilation, the houses feature a tianjing (天井, square inner courtyard). The exquisite Young Lady Building, study, garden, Buddhist prayer room and wing room all form a part of the distinctive style of the village' s ancient architecture. The door of each dwelling features vivid tile carvings which combine human images, flowers and birds, mountains and water. Most of the windows have carved panes. The four-door, six-door and eight-door windows all feature auspicious patterns of mascots, animals and plants on the lattices. The stone carvings on the base of the pillars and stone shelves in the dwellings are also colourful and exquisite.

## TEA THAT ROCK S

Xiamei Village's folk arts include paper-cuts and dragon dances. As the village is close to Wuyi Mountain, the dishes in this area are mainly delicacies and game from the mountains, and the village also offers Wuyi Rock tea (武夷岩茶等), a renowned Oolong tea with a fruity fragrance, which is grown in the rocks.

The Zou Family Senior Official Residence (邹氏大夫第) is the best kept ancient dwelling in Xiamei Village. The building's name comes from Zhou Maozhang, who was honoured as a Senior Official by Imperial Mandate. The residence has two halls and three main rooms with several wing rooms and studies. The back garden is a typical South China garden which features sights such as the Mirror and Moon Pavilion (镜月台), Goldfish Well (金鱼井), Game Platform (对弈台) and Stone Water Vat (石水缸).

Built in the 55th year of the Qianlong period in the Qing Dynasty (1790), the Zou Family Ancestral Hall is a fine example of an ancient dwelling which has been perfectly integrated with tile, stone and wood carvings. The main hall is open with wing rooms on either side and a theatre stage upstairs. The entrance screen is a wood carving gate displaying human images, life scenarios and village features, giving visitors a strong sense of the lifestyle and culture of the time.

Dali Lane (达理巷) lies before the gate of the Fang Family Residence (方宅门). It was built in the 20th year of Emperor Qianlong's reign during the Qing Dynasty (1755) and within arm's reach of the Fang Family Army Advisor's Residence. At the time, Zou, the wealthiest man in Xiamei Village, built his house so close to the Fang Family Residence that neither family could open their back doors, and neither were prepared to give in to the other. Fang later died while guarding the frontier beyond the Great Wall. Given Fang's sacrifice for his country, the Zou family decided to open a back door and build a 100-foot lane along the eastern fire wall. This later became Dali Lane, which means "being sensible and reasonable" (通情达理).



Xiamei Village still has more than 30 well-preserved ancient dwellings with Qing Dynasty features

# Lian Village

## The First Village of Jinshi in Fujian

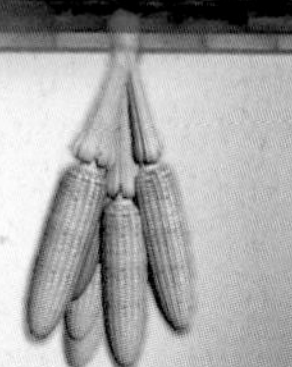

Lian Village is famous in China for its assocation with "incorruptible" official Xue Lingzhi and its beautiful landscape, featuring springs and pavilions, old camphor trees, tortoise and lion rocks and tidemarks and pools, as well as the grey Lian Mountain and flowing Lian Stream.

### Getting there

Lian Village, Fuan City, Fujian Province.
Nearest city: Fuzhou.
福建省宁德市福安市溪潭镇廉村
Take a high-speed train from Fuzhou South Station(福州南站) to Ningde Station (宁德站)(1hour) and then transfer to Ningde Bus Station (宁德汽车站) for a service to Fuan Bus Station(福安汽车站) (about 1hour). After you arrive at Fuan Bus Station, take one of the many buses to Zhouning(周宁) or Shancheng(山城), both of which services pass Lian Village (1/2 hour). Tickets for the Chen Family Ancestral Hall are RMB15.

Lian Village, originally named "Shiji Ferry", is located 15 km from downtown Fuan City and is known as the hometown of the first "jinshi" (third-degree imperial scholar) in Fujian, Xue Lingzhi. In honour of this famously honest jinshi, Emperor Suzong of the Tang Dynasty renamed Xue Lingzhi's hometown "Lian Village" ("Honest Village"). Cultural relics and historic sites in the village include the Masu Temple (妈祖庙), Chen Shuan's Residence (陈树安宅), Chen Zhusong's Residence (陈住松宅), "Intelligence" Spring (聪明泉), Xue Lingzhi's Former Residence (薛令之故居) and Linggu "Humble" Cottage (灵谷草堂), the place where Xue Lingzhi studied.

According to the Fuan County Annals, the ancient walls of Lian Village Castle (廉村古) are 1400 metres long, 3.6 metres thick and 4.4 meters high. It has six city gates named according to Confucian morality: Gate of Honesty, Gate of Loyalty, Gate of Filial Piety, Gate of Politeness, Gate of Justice and Gate of Faith. Nowadays, only the Gate of Loyalty (忠门) and the Gate of Filial Piety (孝门) are well-preserved.

Ancient architecture in Lian Village

The Lian Village defensive wall



In the south of the defensive wall along Yanxi (沿溪), a five-metre-wide ancient passage paved with cobblestones, there is a well-preserved ancient port which dates back to the Tang and Song Dynasties. It is paved with very large cobbles and extends toward the stream. According to records, the port used to "gather fishboats and fishing goods and connect all counties in Jianning Prefecture and the county towns and villages."

The Ancient Official Road (古官道) was used primarily for government official carriages. In the Lian Village Fortress, the grid-like roads have one or three polished stone slabs with inlaid cobbles engraved with wheat, wave and staircase motifs. The shape of a wheat ear represents a golden harvest; The shape of a wave represents unity; the shape of staircases represents promotion to a higher position.

Built during the Qing Dynasty, the "Five Jinshi in One Family" (一门五进士古民居) ancient residence still evokes the air of a literary household. The Chinese characters on the gatehouse mean "grand momentum and lofty ideals" (就日瞻云). The four Chinese characters inscribed on the plaque at the front door (古处是敦) is the prime directive of the family, encouraging their offspring to get along and be honest and simple. The inner couplets hung on the columns of the hall date from the Qing Dynasty (1644-1911.) On the left it writes, "Father is gracious and son is filial, so their duty is fulfilled" (父言慈子言孝职分当尽), while on the right it writes, "Books can be read and farmland can be ploughed, so the career is leisurely kept" (书可读田可耕事业悠存).

Ancient Official Road

There are five ancestral halls in Lian Village: Houhu Palace (后湖宫), Chen Family Ancestral Hall (陈氏宗祠), the First Chen Temple (陈氏长祠), the Second Chen Temple (陈氏次祠) and the Third Chen Temple (陈氏三祠). Built in the eighth year of the Zhengde period during the Ming Dynasty (1514), Houhu Palace was originally called "Moon God Ancestral Temple". The building comprises the gatehouse,

The theatre stage in the ancestral temple

theatre stage, courtyard and funerary temple. At the centre of the house there is a sculpture of Xue Lingzhi, above which is a plaque with four Chinese characters (覆载资生), which implies the meaning that officials should bring benefit to the common people. This is apparently what Tang Dynasty Emperor Taizong taught his son, the Emperor Gaozong of Tang. Nowadays, the students of Lian Village are still taken by their parents to Houhu Palace to make a wish in front of the Xue Lingzhi sculpture so that they can be successful in their exams.

Built during the transitional period between the Ming and Qing Dynasties, the Chen Family Ancestral Hall is is a three-room building comprising the main hall at the gatehouse (connected to the ancient theatre stage), two wing rooms at the back and a back wing room. Over the top of the stage stands the unique Prince Pavilion (太子亭). To this day, villagers still hold a ritual ceremony to worship ancestors at this pavilion during the winter solstice. An elder who enjoys suitable prestige will be selected as the leader of the ceremony and from the entrance of the temple he has to salute 360 times and be supported by his descendants. Sacrificial offerings such as whole pigs and lambs are placed in the middle of the back hall. The entire ceremony lasts from noon until the middle of the night and, villagers also enjoy singing shows and performances, which last for three days and nights.

The three ancestral temples of the Chen family store nearly 300 writings of famous and prominent individuals from various fields. One highlight is the Chinese character (廉) at the entrance which means "incorruptible". Upon closer inspection, you will see that the profound character is made up of pictures of a sun, a house, a couple, a round table and a moon.

Lian Village is also known as "Jinshi Village" and there are many stories such as "Five Jinshi in One Family", "Three Jinshi of Father and Sons" and "Three Martial Arts Scholar Brothers." The Xue and Chen families of Lian Village produced 17 jinshi during the 150 years between 1109 and 1259, and 33 jinshi overall. .

### PIES

Jiguang Pies (继光饼), a local specialty which have sesame fillings, are named for a Ming Dynasty general Qi Jiguang. There are two main varieties, Guang Pie (光饼) and Hang Pie (挂饼). Locals recommend dividing the Guang Pie along its edge into two pieces and inserting an oyster.

An ancient tablet from Lian Village

# Cheng Village

## A Mysterious Ancient Guangdong Kingdom

Cheng Village is situated on the southern slope of Wuyi Mountain in the north of Fujian Province. The old and quiet village is a veritable history book of the development of the ancient villages in the Wuyi Mountain region, an embodiment of the traditional culture of Chinese villages from the Ming and Qing Dynasties.

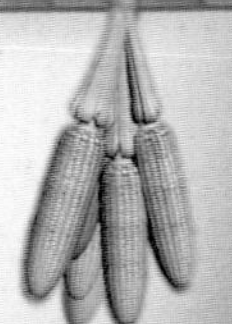

### Getting there

Cheng Village, Wuyishan City, Fujian Province
Nearest city : Nanping.
福建省南平市武夷山市兴田镇城村。
Take a taxi from Nanping's Wuyishan Internatational Airport to Wuyishan City Bus Station(武夷山汽车站) (15mins)and continue by bus to Cheng Village (40 mins). It is free to enter the village, but tickets to the Minyue Capital ruins(闽越王遗址) will cost RMB80.

Built in the Song Dynasty, Cheng Village was established almost a thousand years ago when the Zhao (赵), Lin (林) and Li (李) families decided to settle down in this region 20 km south of Wuyi Mountain. The remaining ancient constructions in the village include Guyue Gate Tower (古粤门楼), Huaixi Ford (淮溪首济), Baisui Archway (百岁坊), Xingfu Temple (兴福庙), ancestral temples of the Li, Lin and Zhao families, Jinshi House (进士第), Shen Pavilion (神亭0, Lanyuan Folk Residence (兰苑民居) and Tianhou Palace (天后宫).

The village is surrounded by protective walls with open gates and the streets are well organised, with three main streets paved with river gravels into the shape of an "H", and 36 winding and criss-crossing alleys. The drainage system is designed to be on both sides of the street, and water is cut from the river in the northwest

The ancient Minyue Capital ruins are the most complete Han Dynasty city ruins in South China

Local Han cuisine restaurant

divided into one main hall, two main exhibition halls, two corridors and a duplicate of Han Dynasty architecture. Many unearthed relics are exhibited here, evidencing the ups and downs of the Han Dynasty.

The Lin family of Cheng Village settled here over a thousand years ago and is the second largest family in the village. The Lin Family Ancestral Hall (林家祠堂) is a public place for ancestor worship, weddings and conventions. The Lin family offer visitors traditional foods and rooms to stay in and this has become a popular stop on the Wuyi Mountain tour.

Cheng Village locals have a reputation for longevity. The Baisui (100 years) Archway (百岁坊) was built in 1608 under the order of Ming Dynasty Emperor Shen Zong for the 100-year-old resident Zhao Xiyuan. The archway features four stone peaches representing longevity and has three arches supported by 12 columns with three layers of lift beams. It is the most complete Ming Dynasty wood-structure archway in north Fujian Province. During modern wedding ceremonies, villagers retain the tradition of carrying the bride through the Baisui Archway to bless her with longevity.

Guyue Teahouse (古粤茶座) lies inside the Zhao Family Ancestral Hall (赵氏宗祠). This is a good place to enjoy a cup of tea, listen to some local stories and savour the unique charm of the village.

then distributed across the village for the villagers' daily use. Ancient wells can be seen everywhere, and the well water is clear and slightly sweet.

The ruins of the supposed capital of the ancient Minyue (闽越王城遗址), situated one km southwest of Cheng Village, are the most complete Han Dynasty city ruins in South China. The city, which was buried for 1,000 years, consists of three hills running from east to west and a central area known as Gaohuping Palace (高胡坪王殿区). The residences of the aristocracy are situated inside the city while the government offices, folk houses, workshops and tombs are located outside. The bath in the palace is the oldest one in China, with a remarkably complete water supply and drainage system. Furthermore, it is evident from the 40,000 pieces of unearthed Han Dynasty relics that even as far back as 2,000 years ago, Fujian Province already possessed relatively advanced metallurgy, foundry and potting techniques.

According to historical documents, after Emperor Wudi of the Han Dynasty (41 BCE - 87 BCE) pacified the Minyue area, the original Yue villagers were forced to move to the Yangzi and Huai River regions, leaving Cheng Village abandoned for hundreds of years. The current Cheng Village was built on top of the old village of the Yue people.

The Minyue Capital Museum (闽越王城博物馆) is located southeast of the ruins. Inside the museum, the charts, texts, relics and duplicates reveal the hundred-year-long history of the Minyue Kingdom which existed more than 2,000 years ago. The museum is

## BASKET CUSTOMS

Many traditional customs are still observed in the village. The act of "handing in the rice basket" (接米斗) is one of them. Before a wedding, the bride has to hand in a gift from the groom – a rice basket – to her father or eldest brother. The bride will be carried by her mother's brother to the portable sedan chair with a pair of new shoes which have never touched the ground of her home.

# Jixia Village

## The Martial Arts Village

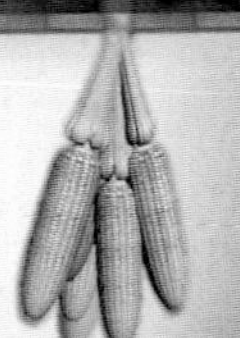

Jixia Village has a long history of nearly 600 years. The village has close bonds with Taiwan and is the homeland of the famous Qing Dynasty general Gan Guobao.

### Getting there

Jixia Village, Pingnan County,Ningde City, Fu Jian Province.
Nearest city: Fuzhou.
福建省宁德市屏南县甘棠乡漈下村
Take a high-speed train from Fuzhou South Station(福州南站) and get off at Minqing Station(闽清站)(40mins). Then transfer to a long-distance bus to Gantang County(甘棠乡) (about 2 hours). Jixia Village(漈下村) is a 10mins taxi ride from Gantang County.

In Jixia Village, most of the villagers living along the river are descendents of the Gan (甘) Family. This ancient village lies south of Pingnan County, 3 km from the 203rd provincial highway. Surrounded by the Feifeng, Maan, Niaogang and Wenbi Mountains, Jixia Village sits along a river which falls from the hills. The design of the village residences was based on the folk style of northeast Fujian Province but also borrowed ideas from the styles of Anhui and Zhejiang Provinces. The pattern of the houses resembles the shape of the Chinese character "臼" (mortar) and the wood carvings and clay sculptures they house are elegant. The village features many interesting spots, such as Siguo Pavilion (泥塑典雅), the Gan Family Ancestral Temple (甘氏宗祠), Feilai Temple (飞来庙), the Gan Family Ancestral Tombs (甘氏祖墓) and Yu Corridor (雨廊).

Jubao Bridge

The year Jubao Bridge (聚宝桥) was originally constructed is not clear, but anyway the bridge was rebuilt in the 33rd year of the Guangxu period in the Qing Dynasty (1907). Wooden columns support the bridge and on top there is a shrine, which makes it unique in Pingnan County. Meanwhile Hua Bridge (花桥) in the middle of the village, was built in

Ancient Gate Tower

the 41st year of the Kangxi period in the Qing Dynasty (1702) and is a flat bridge with three arches and eight columns. The two benches on the bridge can seat up to 50 people. There are beautiful paintings on top of the bridge, acts as something of a convention centre for the villagers, a place for them to discuss everything from family to global issues. .

Longji Temple (龙漈仙宫), also called Mashi Temple, is situated at the intersection of two streams. It was built in honour of Ma Xianniang, the founding mother of Longji, and was reconstructed in the third year of the Longqing period in the Ming Dynasty (1569). Built with earth and wood, the temple is square outside and round inside. The sunken panel and vaulted roof resembles an umbrella from the outside, with a bottle gourd made with lime-stone being the tip of the umbrella. The tiles are organised into eight parts, the walls are painted red and a tablet hangs in the middle.

Ming and Qing Dynasty folk residences line the two sides of the stream. The residence walls built with earth are mottled like an old book – but even though the papers have turned yellow, you can still feel the history hidden within.

The Ming Dynasty Ancient Gate (明代古城门) was built in the 5th year of the Tianshun period in the Ming Dynasty (1461) and is situated at the centre of the village, with Lin River and Hua Bridge in the west and Wenbi Mountain in the north. The gate tower is a two-storey building built with bricks, stones, earth and wood. The flagpole in front of the gate tower where illustrious ancestor, Qing General Gan Guobao held ancestor worshipping ceremonies is a local symbol.

The Gan Family Ancestral Temple was reconstructed in 1810 during the Qing Dynasty . Adopting a Ming Dynasty style, the temple was built with earth, wood, bricks and stones. The earth walls were painted red, and inside the hall there is a red ancestor shrine. The "fu" ( 福, "good fortune") tablet bestowed by Emperor Qianlong of the Qing Dynasty still hangs in the temple. The tablet is made of wood, thick and heavy, with gold writing gilded on a red background.

Jixia Village boasts a long history of martial arts, with every generation required to learn it. The practice of Hu Zhuang ("fake tiger") Boxing (虎桩拳) and Kung Fu is part of the local cultural heritage. Famous local martial arts styles include "Bench" Kung (凳功), "Hoe" Kung (锄头功) and "Pike" Kung (狼筅功). You can see lots of practice facilities like stone locks, stone eggs, race grounds and practice halls in the village. Every sixth month of the lunar calendar (usually July), villagers will carry statues out of the temples and perform ritual activities. Folk customs like the dragon and lion dance (舞龙舞狮), firework displays and firecrackers also attract villagers from other regions.

## CELESTIAL HORSE

Jixia Village's distinctive cultural traditions include the worshiping of celestial being Maxian (马仙) and holding winter gatherings, in addition to martial arts and opera. Celebrated local dishes include stewed chicken with sticky rice and herbs. (糯米炖母鸡). Peaches also grow around the village.

# Fuquan Village

## Calabash City

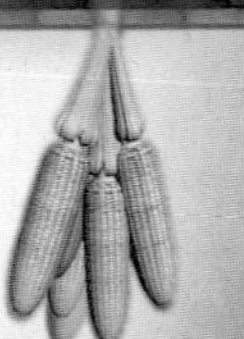

Fuquan, an ancient village filled with stories, exhibits distinctive features of both Fujian and Taiwanese culture.

### Getting there

Fuquan Village,Jinjing Town, Jinjiang City, Fu Jian Province.
Nearest city: Quanzhou.
福建省泉州市晋江市金井镇福全村。
You can reach Jinjing Town (金井镇) from any long-distance bus station in Jinjiang City（晋江市）(40mins). Jinjiang downtown city is just about 15mins riding from the Jinjiang International Airport. After arriving at Jinjing Town, take a motorcycle taxi to Fuquan Village (RMB6 & 10 minutes).

Fuquan Village faces Taiwan across the sea, with Quanzhou City 40 km to the north, and the Taiwan Strait to the east. The village. According to records, in 1387, the Governor of Jiangxia, Zhou Dexing, strengthened the coastal defenses and set up a coast guard under the direction of Emperor Zhu Yuanzhang. Zhou arrived at Fujian Province, conscripted one third of the young men to defend the coast against the Japanese pirates and moved the outposts to vital areas. That was the historical beginning of Fuquan Village. During the short-lived Guangqi period of the Tang Dynasty (885-887), troops were stationed at the village and developed the region. In the Song Dynasty, Fuquan became one of the biggest business ports along the southeast coast of China. It was also on the military frontline during Ming Dynasty battles against Japanese pirates.

The first thing you will see upon entering the village is the four big gilded Chinese characters on the gate (福全古城) which mean "Fuquan Ancient City". The village was built in the 20th year of the Hongwu period in the Ming Dynasty (1387) as a border town in the southeast coast of Jinjiang City. Throughout history, the coastal defense system comprising Fuquan, Yongning, Chongwu and Zhongzuo City successfully protected southeast Fujian Province against pirates.

Fuquan Village is shaped like a calabash and contains many criss-crossing roads. The ruins of the city walls still remain and the patterns of the streets have been maintained, while the well-managed ancient residences exude a definite charm under the sunlight and in the sea breeze.

This ancient village once had strong city walls, but most of the hard materials were removed from the walls during the 1958 Taiwan Strait Crisis and sent to the frontlines. Trees were planted for replacement, and as of today, only the ruins of the four city gates remain. North of Wuwei Tower (无尾塔) there is a big rock called "Yin Stone" (印石) and the tower and the stone are highly valued by the villagers because they are believed to be the keys to the village's feng shui. The west and north gate have been reconstructed. According to village rules which are strictly followed, weddings and funerals can only use the west gate and not the north gate.

The large number of temples and family residences is a characteristic of Fuquan Village. During the Kangxi period of the Qing Dynasty (1661-1722), Taiwan was under the jurisdiction of Fujian Province, so Quanzhou villagers sailed east across the strait to develop Taiwan. The temples and residences thus testify to the emotional tie between those villagers and their hometown. The He Family Residence (氏祖) was built in the Xianfeng period of the Qing Dynasty (1831-1861), after impoverished brothers from the family made some money in Taiwan and decided to build this building for the family. Meanwhile the Lin Family Temple (林氏家庙) and Lin Family Residence (林氏祖厝) were donations of Taiwan businessman Lin Honglu.

West Gate of Fuquan Ancient City

**MYTHS**

Fuquan Village is a place of myths and legends, such as those associated with the stone turtle (石龟) in Chengtian Temple (承天寺), and praying for rain from the Earth God (土地庙祈雨).

Built during the Ming Dynasty (1368-1644), the Jiang Family Temple (蒋氏家庙) and the former residence of Jiang Dejing (蒋德璟故宅) are situated in Northgate Street (北门街t). The former residence of Jiang Dejing used to have five courtyards, two patios, two wing rooms and a garden. Unfortunately, they were all burnt down and the halls which exist today were rebuilt in the Qing Dynasty.

Inside the village there is a hill called Yuanlong Mountain (元龙山) from which visitors can see the East China Sea. Yuan Long Mountain used to be an observatory during wartime, and in the days of peace it was frequented by many scholars to write poetry and inscriptions. Around the hill there is a well for military use, a well for forging weapons and a pool for water control.

Fuquan Village has an old saying which claims that its "finger-guessing game, strong liquors and music are unbeatable". Court music spread to the south during the Tang (618-907) and Song (960-1279) Dynasties and was named "southern music". Soldiers stationed in Fuquan Village during the Ming Dynasty used this kind of music to express their homesickness. Other local folk arts include performances featuring drums and trumpets, marionettes and hand puppets, as well as lively paper art.

Zhuzi Temple (朱子祠) and private schools were set up in the village in ancient times to develop education and most of the villagers remain well-educated. According to records, during the Ming and Qing Dynasty, more than 20 locals successfully passed the imperial examinations. Education is still a priority in the village and many overseas residents with local ties have sent back money to help develop the village's education system.

# Luxiang Village

## The Ancient Village of Taihu Lake

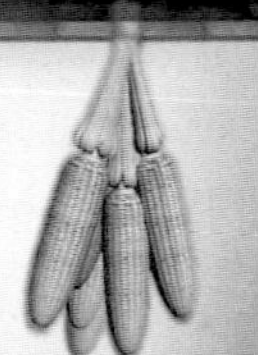

Luxiang Village is located at the back of East Mountain beside Taihu Lake. Nearby attractions include Hangu Mountain Park, Gongli Island, Hualong Pool and Wangao Tomb. The village is particularly known for its beautiful scenery which resembles a landscape painting.

### Getting there

**Luxiang Village, Wu County, Jiangsu Province.**
**Nearest City: Suzhou.**
**江苏省苏州市吴县吴中区东山镇陆巷村。**
**Take a #20 bus from Suzhou City Train Station (苏州火车站), or a minibus from Suzhou South Bus Station (苏州汽车南站) to Dongshan Town(东山镇) (both services take about 1hour). Then take a minibus or pedicab taxi to Luxiang Dock (陆巷码头)( RMB 30 & ⊠ hour).**

Luxiang Village is situated 40 km from downtown Suzhou City. Built in the Southern Song Dynasty, the village fills an area of just 0.74 square km. Among famous talents to originate from this village during the Ming and Qing

Old residences

Archway at the entrance of Luxiang Village

Dynasties, was Wang Ao, the Prime Minister of the Zhengde period in the Ming Dynasty (1505-1521). Luxiang Village was named after Wang Ao's mother's family name Lu (陆).

There are 10 remaining Ming and Qing Dynasty buildings in the central group of village residences, including Huihe Hall (惠和堂), Cuihe Hall (粹和堂) and Suigao Hall (遂高堂). There are also 20 other ancient buildings such as Wanshan Hall (晚山堂), Jiansan Hall (见三堂), Mingfeng Hall (鸣凤堂), Dongshan Cottage (东山草堂) and Renhe Hall (仁和堂) and Huairen Hall (怀德堂). Luxiang Village's ancient architectural complex has the largest number and highest quality of well-preserved folk residences in the county.

The 500-metre-long Zishi Street (紫石街) is unevenly paved with 2-metre-long granite slabs. The street is old and quaint, and the stones are smooth and shiny after being stepped on for hundreds of years. On both sides of the main street are stone doorsteps, stores with fences, tea houses and restaurants. Three impressive archways, built to commemorate Wang Ao's successes, form a "T" shape on the east, south and north sides of the street.

Wang Ao's former residence, Huihe Hall, is situated in the middle of the village. The foundations were laid in the Ming Dynasty, and construction began in the Qing Dynasty. Made of nanmu wood, with flower shelves and corridors carefully set in every hall, Huihe Hall covers 3000 square metres and has five halls. On the central axis there is the gateway, sedan hall, grand hall, main building, women's building and back garden. The parlour, library, little garden and residential building are on the left axis, while the teahouse, kitchen and wing house are on the right. Huihe Hall features Wang Ao's paintings,

## TEA AND FISH

Luxiang is a popular film location and tourism is relatively well developed here. The Tea Culture Tourism Festival of Dongshan Town every March and the Folk Culture Tourism Festival every September are very popular. Visitors are also invited to try the "three white aquatic products" of Taihu Lake – Taihu white prawn (太湖白虾), Taihu whitebait (太湖银鱼) and Taihu white fish (太湖白鱼).

a sculpture room, a Ming and Qing Dynasty furniture exhibition room and Congshi Garden.

Wang Ao's carriage is still in the sedan hall through the first entrance. Though the wood has become rotten, the carriage remains grand. The library on the west side of the main building has a lively "Nine Dragon" tile carving (九狮图). At the centre of the library' s screen wall, there is a round carving iinscribed with the characters "丹风朝阳" (meaning "Red Wind, Rising Sun"). The delicate inscription and lively figures make it one of the finest tile carvings in the village. It is said that when Wang Ao resigned, the emperor presented him with the Nine Lions, which is the only example of this design to be found outside the Imperial Palace.

In the Ming and Qing Dynasties, after Wang Ao's illustrious career, the village subsequently produced one first place scholar, seven third-degree scholars and 16 second-degree scholars.

Dongting Mountain (洞庭山), which is divided into East Mountain and West Mountain, is rich in fruits and special produce. In the spring, you can drink fine Biluochun tea (碧螺春), enjoy plum blossoms, taste loquats and peaches and pick waxberries. On the top of the mountain there are some large rocks, among which there is one with a long footprint on it known as Immortals Stone" (仙人石).

Further west, deep in the tangerine groves, sits a mountain stream. At the origin of the stream, there is "Transforming Dragon Spring" (化龙泉). The scenery of the spring was once vividly described in a poem called "Transforming Dragon Pool" (化龙池) by Lu Yantui, a poet from the Qing Dynasty. Visitors can also head over to nearby Sanshan Island by boat from the "No. 1 Bay of Taihu Lake" at the entrance of the village.

Grooved storefronts and granite flagstones under the Huiyuan and Xieyuan Archways

# Mingyuewan Village

## Village of Slaves and Nobles

Mingyuewan Village, with a history of more than 2000 years, has a poetic name to go with its picturesque scenery. A quiet and unsophisticated ancient village south of the Yangtze River, it is the epitome of ancient civilisation in the greater Suzhou region, with thousand-year-old legends and stories of ordinary everyday people.

### Getting there

**Mingyuewan Village, Wuzhong District, Suzhou City, Jiangsu Province.**
**Nearest city: Suzhou..**
**江苏省苏州市吴中区西山镇明月湾村。**
**Take bus # 58, 69 or 91 from Suzhou to Xishan Shigongshan Bus Station (西山石公山站) (RMB4 & 2 hours). From the Bus Station, walk 1 km west along the Lake-side Tourist Road(湖滨旅游公路) to reach Minyuewan Village.**

Mingyuewan Village is situated 2 km west of Shigong Mountain. With Taihu Lake to the south and backed by green mountains, Mingyuewan Village acquires its name from its moon shape. It is also said that the name comes from the legend that the King of Wu State and his favorite concubine Xishi had once admired the moon here.

According to legend, Mingyuewan Village was already a village in the Spring and Autumn Period of the Zhou Dynasty (771 BCE to 476 BCE). At that time, there was armed conflict between two rival coastal states, Wu (吴) and Yue (越). Apparetly most of the villagers were enslaved war prisoners from the Yue State, and they had to provide food and services to the King of Wu State and his concubine Xishi when they

Small bridges and memorial archways by the lake in Mingyuewan Village

Ancient residential buildings and streets

travelled here. "Eyebrow-penciling Spring" (画眉泉) where Xishi allegedly used to put on her make-up still commemorates the legend in the village.

Built in 1770, Flagstone Street (石板街) also known as "Chessboard Street", is 1,140 metres long and paved by 4,560 blocks of granite. The sewer beneath the street can rapidly drain away rainwater, and gave rise to the saying, "You can walk in Mingyuewan Village in embroidered satin shoes after the rain." The old dwellings on either side of the street vary in height and have seasonal flowers and fruits planted around them. Ling Ruhuan, a poet from the Qing Dynasty, described that in Mingyuewan Village, "the houses are hidden deep in a forest of flowers, while the flowers are surrounded by mountains and the mountains encircled by waters".

Most of the extant residences in the village were built during Emperor Qianlong's reign in the Qing Dynasty (1735-1796). With fortunes made from successful businesses and agricultural produce, Mingyuewan's villagers built mansions and ancestral halls, with exquisite brick, wood and stone carvings and colour paintings. Among them, Yugeng Hall, (裕耕堂) built in 1799, was once a part of the Wu family's Zhanrui Hall before being purchased by the Deng family in 1943. Covering an area of 744 square metres, the hall comprises the east court and west court, which are linked by a common door. Each court has its own entrance hall, gallery, garden, study and wing rooms. A delicate gate house is decorated by full relief sculptures of characters in folklores, interspersed with auspicious patterns like the immortality peach, ganoderma (a type of mushroom) and purple clouds. The carvings of lotuses on the pillars are also impressively vivid.

The land beside the lake at the entrance of the village used to be common land and so it is called "A Land for All Families" (众家地). The lofty trees growing there made it difficult for vessels in Taihu Lake to locate the village when voyaging at night. To direct these vessels, villagers erected a tall mast with a big red lantern during the South Song Dynasty. At night, the oil-lamp inside the lantern is lit (similar to modern lighthouses) so the vessels do not lose way and return back safely. The original mast was destroyed by the Japanese army in 1939 and the present one was rebuilt in 2005.

The ancient camphor tree with a history of 1200 years is an important symbol of Mingyuewan

Residences nestling at the foot of the mountain by Sishan Lake

Minyuewan Ancestral Hall

Village. It is said that the tree was planted by Liu Changqin, a famous poet from the Tang Dynasty, when he went to Mingyuewan Village to visit a friend. With a 2-metre trunk and a 25-metre crown, this tree has been through many tribulations: one side of the trunk has been burnt and struck by lightning. The tree leans slightly east towards the village and casts a substantial shadow, making it the perfect place for boatmen and villagers to rest and enjoy the shade.

The ancient dock (古码头) under the camphor tree has historically been the major waterway connecting Minyuewan Village to the outside world. It is so old that there is no record of when it was actually built. With a total length of 58 metres and a width of 4.6 metres, the dock remains bustling with people selling and buying fish, repairing fishnets and loading and discharging goods.

The time when the original Moon Bridge (明月桥) was built also remains a mystery. The one that exists now was built in during the Republic of China period. Legend has it that 2,500 years ago, the King of Wu State and his concubine Xishi once admired the moon on this bridge, which is why it was named "Moon Bridge."

Moon Monastery (明月禅院) is also called Moon Temple. The three remaining halls were built either in the Qing Dynasty or the Republic of China period. Inside the temple there are shrines dedicated to Buddhist deities Maitreya and Guanyin, as well as the Town God, The God of War, and the Goddess of Silk. These statues of gods provide evidence of the way that distinctions between Taoism and Buddism were blurred in village religious culture. Situated near mountains and facing a lake, Moon Monastery offers a good spot to admire the lake and moon from atop the building.

With its long history and beautiful scenery, famous Chinese writers and poets like Bai Juyi, Pi Rixiu, and Lu Guimeng have left literary works praising Minyuewan village.

## NOBLE VILLAGE

Mingyuewan Village covers an area of 9 hectares, and upwards of a hundred families live here permanently. Deng (邓), Qin (秦), Huang (黄) and Wu (吴) are the major family names in the village, and most families are the descendants of aristocrats from the Southern Song Dynasty. The majority of them now make a living by growing flowers, fruits, Biluo green tea, and fishing at Taihu Lake.

# Guodong Village

## The First Feng Shui Village of South China

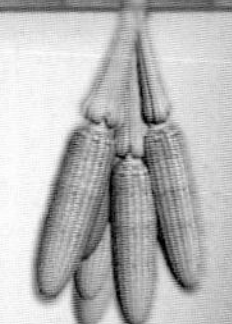

The 5-square-km scenic area of Guodong Village is filled with deep lanes, ancient residences, quiet ponds, tranquil valleys, steep cliffs, old forests, ancient bridges, pavilions, temples and walls. This serene village was once praised in an ancient poem as having "scenery as bright as the stars in the sky".

### Getting there

Guodong Village, Wuyi County, Zhejiang Province.
Nearest city: Jinhua..
浙江省金华市武义县武阳镇郭洞村。
Take a bus or train from Jinhua to Wuyi County(武义县)(about 40mins). After arrival at Wuyi County, from Wuyi Transportation Company Bus Station (武义县运输公司)take a bus to Guodong Village (RMB4 & 20mins).

Guodong Village is situated among mountains and valleys 10 km from Wuyi County. The earliest settler here was He Zhizhong, a prime minister of the Song Dynasty. In 1337, He's decedents designed the village according to the "Nei Jing Tu" (内经图, "Inner Landscape Diagram") preserved in Beijing's White Cloud Taoist Temple. Beside the village, two streams converge into one before meeting the green mountains in the distance. This terrific positive feng shui is one of the reasons why Guodong Village is known as the "First Feng Shui Village in South China."

Built in 1609, the He Family Ancestral Hall (何氏祠堂) is widely regarded as the best piece of Ming and Qing Dynasty architecture in Guodong Village. The three masts before the front gate were built for those who had gained official

Ancient residence in Guodong Village

positions and scholarly honours in ancient times. The shrine and partition board inside the hall with memorial tablets on them are relics from the Ming Dynasty. The podocarpus tree in the back hall with a lush crown and graceful shape is as old as the hall itself. The exquisite theatre in the hall is where performances were held on important festivals.

Built in the Chongzhen era of the Ming Dynasty (1627-1644), New Wuli Hall (新屋里) consists of three courtyards and 30 rooms, with eight windows featuring various wood carvings of auspicious and symbolic animals and creatures such as birds, phoenixes, lions, squirrels and fish. The brick carvings decorating the walls are exquisite and rich in scenery, folklore characters, coins and so forth.

It is said that Guodong Village's water gate (水口) is its spiritual heart; it is in fact a barrier at the entrance of the village to prevent invading enemies. Huilong Bridge (回龙桥) is located here. The original version of the bridge was built at the beginning of the Yuan Dynasty, but was washed away by flood. The one that stands now was rebuilt by villagers in 1721. A four-pillar stone pavilion called Pangui Pavilion (攀桂亭) was built on the bridge in 1754. A board inscribed with the Chinese characters for "Righteous Town" (义乡) can be found in the west of the pavilion. It was given by Magistrate Song Lanting of the Ming Dynasty to locals had bravely driven out local bandits. The bridge is one of the best places in the village to enjoy the picturesque scenery.

A 5-metre thick wall stands outside Huilong Bridge. In ancient times, villagers went in and out of town through the road which cuts through this wall. On the gate hangs a pair of inscribed couplets bearing Chinese words which say cryptically: "Scenery in Guodong eclipses time; time is forgotten in the cave" (郭外风光古，洞中日月长).

Dragon Mountain (龙山), 400 metres above

Streams flowing in front of village houses

## BAMBOO CRAZY

Guodong's villagers are bamboo masters: there are more than 10 kinds of local bamboo handiwork such as bamboo cups, bamboo pen holders and bamboo ashtrays. Meanwhile edibile delicacies include bamboo rice (竹筒饭), as well as the famous Xuan Lotus Root (宣莲), Jinhua ham (金华火腿) and fried bean curd in soy sauce (红烧老豆腐).

sea level, lies east of Huilong Bridge. With its steep cliffs, high peaks and pristine forest shrouded in heavy clouds, the mountain is called a "green pyramid" by locals because of its triangular shape. Giant six and seven hundred year-old trees can be seen everywhere in the forest.

Dawan Reservoir (大湾水库) lies deep inside the Guodong scenic area and is surrounded by mountains covered by lush bamboos. Every year the villagers trasport the cut bamboo to sell by assembling it into a raft which drifts through the reservoir to the village. This ancient way of transporting bamboo is a popular sight for many tourists.

Guodong Village claims to have produced altogether 146 scholars of various ranks from the village during the Ming and Qing Dynasties. With an average life expectancy of 85 years, the village is also famous for its longevity.

Apart from the scenic spots mentioned above, many other sites in Guodong Village are also worth visiting, such as the Memorial Archway of Chastity and Filial Piety (节孝牌坊), Wenchang Hall (文昌阁), Hailin Hall (海麟院) and Biefeng Pagoda (鳖峰塔), as well as an ancient water-powered trip-hammer (for husking rice).

Huilong Bridge surrounded by green trees

# Houwu Village

## The Poem of Hardships

According to a local tourist guide "If architecture is a three-dimensional poem, then Houwu Village is a poem composed for eight hundred years; if architecture is a silent song, then Houwu Village is a piece of music resonating with heavenly sounds and earthly emotions."

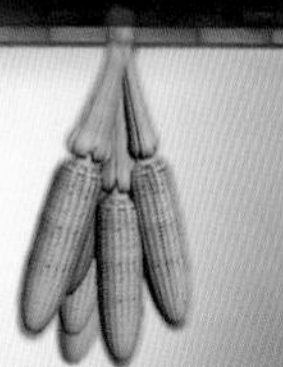

**Getting there**

Houwu Village, Yongkang City, Zhejiang Province.
Nearest city: Hangzhou .
浙江省永康市前仓镇厚吴村。
Take a train from Hangzhou to Yongkang Station (2hours). There are many direct bus routes from Yongkang Coach Station(永康东站) to Houwu Village (RMB3 & 1/2 hour).

Houwu Village is located in the south of Yongkang City and borders Jinyun County. In 1117, Wu Yangqin, the village's founding father, migrated here with his children from Xianju Bridge, making this a village where Wu (吴) is the most common surname. Furthermore, as its villagers were said to be honest and kind, the village was named "Houwu Village" (meaning "Honest and Kind Wu Family Village").

Lying against Jin Stream and facing Pin Mountain, Houwu Village features an intriguing layout of folk residences with grey bricks and black tiles. The buildings here were built in different dynasties, giving them varying characteristics – the buildings from the Ming Dynasty are of primitive simplicity; the buildings from the Qing Dynasty are sophisticated, intricate and elegant; the buildings of the Republic of China period are imposing and pragmatic. The wooden carvings on windows and lintels feature auspicious

The solemn Wu Yiting Ancestral Hall

designs such as "the fourth son of the Yang family visits his mother", "carp leaping over dragon's gate", "magpie standing on plum tree", and "nobility for generations".

Built in 1910, Sima Mansion, (司马第) the first mansion visitors see upon entering the village, contains three courtyards and 29 rooms. Several gates were built at the entrance: the first one is a two-pillar-and-three-storey gate house made of carving bricks. The second gate is crescent-shaped and the third gate is composed of one main door and two side doors, each bearing an inscription with Chinese characters which say things such as "Looking up to Erudition" (仰瞻山斗), "Mansion of Books" (书府) and "Forest of Volumes" (墨林). Poems are inscribed under the eaves. Wood carvings of historical characters, animals, plants and calligraphy cover a large number of windows and corbels in the first and second courtyards.

## FUN OF THE FAIR

Houwu Village boasts several temple fairs and lantern festivals. There are also local performances of Wu Opera (婺剧) and acrobatic routines such as Eighteen Bufferflies (十八蝴蝶), Eighteen Arhats (十八罗汉), as well as flag parades, human pyramids, and stilt-walking.

Built in 1468, Yanqing Hall (衍庆堂)) is the largest, oldest and best-preserved Ming Dynasty residence in the village. Comprising three courts, it contains a front hall with excellent ancient workmanship. All the columns of the hall are spindle-shaped with entasis (convex curve). The crescent beams are thin and high, and the beams and pillars are joined by T-shaped arches, crossing arches, brackets and hump-shaped arches.

Ping (Screen) Mountain Cottage (屏山精舍), also called "Shuyu Hall", was built some time before 1743 and features an arched gate house and brick carvings. The front hall contains heavy timbers and deep reliefs of animals on the brackets and beams, while the back hall and wing rooms have wood-carved shutters with Ming Dynasty characteristics.

Cuncheng Hall (存诚堂) is said to have been built during the Qianlong (1735-1796) and Jiaqing (1796-1820) eras of the Qing Dynasty by a father and a son, both of whom received scholarly honours. It is made up of 26 rooms. The first two courts are unsophisticated while the last court is exquisitely decorated. A 400-year-old camel-like cycas plant in the courtyard is one of the many highlights.

"Huai Well and Sweet Spring" (槐井醴泉) is situated in the old commercial street. "Sweet Spring Well" (醴泉井)

The walls of the village's ancient residences have witnessed the long his

is engraved on the walling crib, and the water in the well is crystal-clear. It is said that this octagonal well is as old as the village.

Ancestral Halls are another tourist attraction of Houwu Village. The extant ancestral halls, large and small, include the Wu Family Ancestral Hall (吴氏宗祠), Wu Yiting Ancestral Hall (吴仪庭公祠), Xiangyang Ancestral Hall (向阳公祠), Lishan Ancestral Hall (丽山公祠), Cengyi Ancestral Hall (澄一公祠), Jiufen Ancestral Hall (九份公祠) and Zhongde Hall (德忠已祠).

Wu Family Ancestral Hall was built in 1547. Apart from the brick gate house, the other parts of the building are reconstructions built during the Guangxu era (1875-1908) after the originals were burnt down by Taiping troops. The whole building comprises three halls. Scrolls of calligraphy and inkwash drawings are hung on the five gables on either side. With stone pillars and wooden beams, Xulun Hall (叙伦堂) in the middle contains five rooms. "Loyalty, filial piety, probity, righteousness" (忠孝廉节) is written on the gable wall.

Wu Gongyi Ancestral Hall, built in 1915, is one of the subordinate halls and consists of three courtyards in the front and three in the back. There is a wing room at each side and a four-pillar-and-five-storey gate house at the entrance.

Other ancient buildings scattered throughout the various streets and lanes well worth visiting include Juqing Hall (聚庆堂), Orchid Hall (兰花居), Liquan Well (礼泉井), Osmanthus Hall (桂花居), and South Town Hall (镇南殿).

Many residents of Houwu Village have made a name for themselves. In the second year of Emperor Deyou's reign in the Southern Song Dynasty (1275), local son Wu Jian was appointed Right Minister of the country. He went to negotiate with the Mongolians and was detained in Baoding, and before long he died in sorrow upon hearing the decline and fall of the Southern Song Dynasty. Wu Shi, a scholar, petitioned the emperor to recover lost territories. He dedicated himself to this task, leading an army on a northern expedition and achieving many victories. However, he was framed by Qin Hui, a notoriously sycophantic official, and became embittered by repeated banishment.



e village

# Yuyuan Village

## Longevity Village

Three hundred and ninety-five historic buildings dating back to the Ming and Qing Dynasties have been found in Yuyuan Village.

**Getting there**

Yuyuan Village, Wuyi County, Zhejiang Province.
Nearest city: Jinhua..
浙江省金华市武义县俞源乡俞源村。
Take a bus or train from Jinhua to Wuyi County(武义县) (about 1hour). Then take a minibus from Wuyi County(武义县) to Yuyuan Village(俞源村) (RMB25 & 40 mins).

Yuyuan Village is situated in southwest Wuyi County. Six hundred years ago, it was a village which frequently suffered droughts and floods as well as pestilence. According to historical records, Yuyuan Village's fortunes took an upward turn after Liu Bowen, an advisor of the first Ming emperor Zhu Yuanzhang, changed the layout of the village. In the 600 years since then, Yuyuan Village has allegedly never had one flood. The village's lucky reputation attracted the wealthy Yu (俞) family, which has made Yuyuan Village one of the largest habitations of the Yu clan in China. Given its reputation for longevity, the village has also been nicknamed "Longevity Village" (长寿村) since ancient times.

According to the Yu Family Genealogy, the layout of Yuyuan Village was designed by Liu Bowen "in accordance with celestial principles". An S-shape stream enclosing the paddy fields at the entrance of Yuyuan Village has the shape of a giant Yin and Yang Diagram. Eleven hillocks around the village together with the Taiji Yin and Yang Fish form the 12 signs of the zodiac and the 28 halls in the Eight Diagrams shape correspond to the 28 constellations. The "Seven-star Pool" (七星塘) and "Seven-star Well" (七星井) are distributed in the shape of the Big Dipper.

The theatre stage in the Yu Family Ancestral Hall

A corner of the ancient Shuangxi Lane

The first place to visit should be the Yu Family Ancestral Hall (俞氏宗祠), which was built in 1567. It has spacious and bright halls, tall and straight pillars and towering horse-head walls. Its damp courtyard, cobbled Taiji pattern and carving theatre stage, express the prestige of the Yu family at that time. In the side room, there is a large sand table illustration of Yuyuan Village, which makes it easier to comprehend its peculiar astrological layout.

Shengyuan Hall (声远堂) was buit in the second year of the Kangxi period of the Qing Dynasty (1663) and the whole hall contains 92 rooms. The antechamber is spacious and high, while the opisthodome is refined and peaceful. There is a marvelous wood carving in the antechamber, where the colour of the nine carps on the "beam of a hundred fishes" (百鱼梁) will turn to yellow, black and red as the season changes.

Yuhou Hall (裕后堂) was built in the 50th year of the Qianlong period of the Qing Dynasty (1784). With 120 remaining rooms and an area of 1,560 square metres, it is the largest ancient residence in the village.

Dongzhu Temple (洞主庙) lies at the foot of Jiulong Mountain at the end of the village. The 40-room temple can be divided into the main hall, quiet pavilion, wing rooms and affiliated rooms. All the rooms have exquisite shapes and clean and simple beds. However, during the Oneiromancy Festival (圆梦节, see below) these beds are far from enough... Villagers camp out on thousands of improvised beds which spill into the streets and lanes of the village, in the hope that the supernatural beings living inside Dongzhu Temple can grant them a "dream come true" (梦想成真).

## TIME TO DREAM

Make note of the local Dream Interpretation Festival which is usually put on twice each year, in February and August (the exact dates are based on the lunar calendar). Dream interpretation was a traditional Chinese form of divination practiced by Shamans (巫).

# Sanmenyuan Village

## Historical Drama Carved on Bricks

Sanmenyuan Village is a world of small bridges, flowing water and old-style residences. The cobble lane roads, brick and wooden ancient houses as well as the whitewashed walls and black tiles convey a strong sense of the ancient village.

### Getting there

Sanmenyuan Village, Longyou County, Zhejiang Province.
Nearest city: Jinhua.
浙江省衢州市龙游县石佛乡三门源村。
Take a train from Jinhua West Station(金华西站) to Longyou Station(龙游站) (about 1/2hour). Buses leave regularly from Longyou Bus Station(龙游汽车站) heading directly to Sanmenyuan Village (40 minutes).

Sanmenyuan Village is surrounded by mountains and has a stream passing through it from north to south. Since its mountain site was rarely affected by turmoil, the buildings in the village have largly preserved the features of Anhui Province dwellings from the middle and latter stage of the Qing Dynasty.

The Ye Family Residence (叶氏民居) was established in the 26th year of Daoguang period in Qing Dynasty (1846). It was built when local Ye Hetian returned home after becoming an official in the imperial government. Initially it had five main buildings, but now only three are left. The Chinese character inscriptions on the door say things such as: "irises and orchids come here" (芝兰入座), "Chinese redbud will be luxuriant forever" (荆花永茂) and "spring comes from the surrounding wall" (环堵生春). With an area of 4,500 square

Window carving from the Ye Family Residence

metres, the residence has a courtyard, garden and pool. The whole dwelling is representative of South China residences from the middle and latter stages of the Qing Dynasty.

The essence of Ye family architecture is its artistic brick carvings. At 56 centimetres long and 26 centimetres -wide, each of the 23 pieces of traditional Chinese opera embossments found in the residence depict scenes from Wu Opera, such as "Kill the Prime Minister Across the River", "Rainbow Barrier", "Baiyuan Teaches How to Play with Swords", "Liu Bei Proposes Marriage" and "Release Huang Zhong From Brotherhood".

These Chinese opera character figures have unusually big heads and small bodies, similar to the opera characters used in a puppet show. The discovery of the 23 pieces of ancient opera brick carvings provides strong evidence for the connection between Anhui Opera and Peking Opera, while also contributing valuable information about the the development of Wu Opera.

Ye Family Residence gate house

Once a volcano, Fanzeng Mountain sits beside the ancient village, 660 metres above sea level. The cone-shape volcanic vent on the top is like a gigantic rice steamer.

Two kilometers north of the mountain road lies the three-metre-wide Baifo Cliff Waterfall (白佛岩瀑). The 70-metre-long cascading waterfall is said to resemble a pendulous belt. Nearby attractions include Arhat Mountain (罗汉山), General's Peak (将军岭), Immortals Peak (仙人峰) and Dianyi Cave (点易洞). In the northeast corner, sits Stone Boat Mountain (石船山), which boasts vivid carvings of stone boats and stone figures.

On the 13th day of the first month of the lunar calendar (which usually falls in January or February,) Sanmenyuan's villagers hold "dragon lantern" and "lion" dances to drive out evil spirits and ask for good fortune.

Dwellings in Sanmenyuan Village

## ETERNAL POOL

"White Buddha" Cliff (白佛岩), with an elevation of about 700 metres above sea-level, is very steep. There is a natural spring pool called Ligu Well (里古井) two li (1km) rom the top of Baifo Cliff. It is said that this pool never dries all year round and the river snails living in it have no tails.

# Shen'ao Village

## Ming and Qing Dynasty Sculpture Museum

Shen'ao Village, the original home of the Shentu family, became famous in South China by virtue of its long history, unique geographic environment and cultural and historic sites. Every year, thousands of tourists are drawn to its serene paths, old ancestral temples and mottled grey walls.

### Getting there

Shenao Village, Tonglu County, Zhejiang Province.
Nearest city: Hangzhou..
浙江省杭州市桐庐县江南镇深澳村。
Buses leaving for Tonglu County(桐庐县) from any bus station in Hangzhou will pass Shenao Village(深奥村) (about 1 hour).It is a 5minute walk from the bus stop to the village.

Located on the southern bank of the Fuchun River, Shen'ao Village lies in the hills, north of Tianzi Hillock, in front of Lion Rock and behind Xuanshan Mountain. Yingjia Stream and Yangpo Stream flow to east and west respectively. The ancestors of the Shentu (申屠) family first moved here from Shentu Mountain in Fuyang in the early stages of the Southern Song Dynasty and later expanded into an influential clan. Today, most of the villagers still bear the Shentu name.

With a history of more than one thousand years, Shen'ao Village can be dated back to the last years of the Western Han Dynasty. Its 16,000 square-metre historic building complex is well-preserved, with a central area comprising 100 Ming and Qing Dynasty-style rooms.

In Shen'ao Village there is a 500-metre-long old street (老街) which runs from north to south. Under the road are

View of Shen'ao Village

sealed conduits, commonly referred to as "bays". (Shen'ao Village got its name for its deep bays.) On both sides of the street, there are buildings from the middle and latter years of the Qing Dynasty and the Republic of China period. In the village, there are traditional lanes such as Huangjia Lane, Houju Lane and Sanfang Lane, whose combined shape is supposedly like the Chinese character "非". A new street was built in 1980 which connects to the old street, and the street layout is now said to resemble the Chinese character "韭" (chives).

Shen'ao has many distinctive cultural sites such as Youxu Hall (攸叙堂), Shennong Hall (神农堂), Huaisu Hall (怀素堂), Gongen Hall (恭思堂) and Huaijing Hall (怀荆堂). Jiushi Hall (九世堂) and Rulin Hall (儒林堂) are the oldest. Qingyun Bridge (青云桥) in the east of the village was a key route from Tonglu to Fuyang. In the southeast of the village, there is a "War of Resistance Against Japan" monument (抗日纪念幢). In 1940, the 235 Corp of the Red Army's 79th Division blocked the Japanese invading army in Jingshan Mountain and thousands of people from Shen'ao and neighbouring villages joined the battle. The Japanese invading army eventually retreated in defeat but 156 anti-Japanese fighters died in the battle.

Villagers gathering at the entrance of an ancient lane

The mountain northeast of the village is often a cloud fairyland. On it lies Shennong Palace (神农殿), dedicated to the Buddhist godness Guanyin. Huangcheng Temple (黄程庙) is situated at the westnorthern corner of the village. It was once used to worship the local God of the Land for the eight surrounding villages. During the Lantern Festival and on other important dates, each village took turns to guard the temple and put on plays to thank and appease the gods. In 1954, the temple was converted into a grain supply centre, but it remains a popular place for festival celebrations

Tieliang Mountain (铁良山) has an elevation of 964.4 metres above sea level. From atop the mountain, visitors can enjoy a picturesque scene where the four reservoirs in the area appear like inlaid jades. The village also has a rippling spring which drips all year round, whistling pines and a 100-metre-high waterfall known as "Spray of the Old Dragon" (老龙喷水).

## WATER DRAGON

Highlights of the customs of Shenao Village include the Harvest Festival, (丰收节), Water Dragon Fair (水龙会),, lion dance and dragon dance. The traditional handicrafts include embroidery... and making toilet paper!

# 岭　南　古　村

# South of the Five Ridges

## Watchtowers and Hakka houses

# Pengcheng Village

## Birthplace of Generals

Dating back to the Ming and Qing Dynasties, Dapeng Fortress is the most complete coastal defence station in all of China. It boasts a magnificent city gate, elegant and well-preserved dwellings, deep and serene green stone lanes and several majestic general's mansions.

### Getting there

Peng Cheng Village, Da Peng Town, Long Gang District, Shen Zhen City, Guang Dong Province.
Nearest City: Shenzhen.
广东省深圳市龙岗区大鹏镇鹏城村
From downtown Shenzhen, take the #6 express bus line (机场6号快线) to Longgang district (1.5 hours) then get off at Yinhu Bus Station(银湖汽车站). Take a #350 bus onto Peng Cheng Village (about 2 hours). Alternatively the #364 bus from Futian bus station, or the Special Line #818 from Longgang, will also take you to Pengcheng Village in about the same time.

Pengcheng Village is located beside Daya Bay, Dapeng Peninsula, about 2 km from Dapeng town center, where the famous Dapeng Fortress (大鹏所城) is situated. Pengcheng Village is actually an amalgamation of seven natural villages, four of which belong to Dapeng Fortress. As a military fortress designed to defend against Japanese pirates, the village was established in the 14th year of the reign of Emperor Hongwu in the Ming Dynasty (1381).

Dapeng Fortress has gate towers, watch towers and a moat, all of which were renovated during the Qing Dynasty. The trapezoidal fortress has three main streets, namely Dongmen Street, Nanmen Street and Zhengjie Street, and the original structure is basically intact, with the East, West and South Gates particularly well preserved. Key constructions include a Granary (大鹏粮仓), the Generals Mansion (参将府), the God oF War Temple (关帝(庙), the Ancestral Temple of Marshal Zhao (赵公祠) and Tin Hau Temple (天后庙).

Side view of the East Gate of Pengcheng Village

Dapeng Fortress was once renowned for producing a string of famous generals such as Liu Zhong and Xu Xun from the Ming Dynasty, the renowned "five generals in three generations" of the Lai family and the "father and son generals" of the Liu

Pengcheng Village

family. With a dozen big generals in the Ming and Qing Dynasties alone, Dapeng Fortress is known to those around the area as "Generals' Village".

The mansion of the Zhenwei General Lai Sijue (思爵振威将军第) was built in the 24th year of the Daoguang period of the Qing Dynasty (1844) and is located 100 metres within the South Gate (南门). This Qing Dynasty mansion covers 2,500 square metres and is surrounded by spectacular walls over 3 metres high. The five big Chinese characters which say "Mansion of Zhenwei General" on the gate banner were written by Emperor Daoguang. A couple of stone lions and a pair of stone drums are placed in front of the gate to signify that this was the house of a military officer. The building is built with grey brick walls, red brick floors, wooden beams and stone columns, while the grey roofs are tiled in the shape of mountain tops. The eave boards and gilders are decorated with wood carvings of characters from folk tales, flowers, birds, plants and scenes from literary works.

The Lai family also owns four other general's mansions in Pengcheng Village. The one facing General Lai Sijue's mansion is the mansion of General Lai Shichao (赖世超将军第). In the main street lies the mansion of General Lai Yingyang (赖英扬将军第), and inside the West Gate (西门)

The mottled city wall is a reminder of the mighty presence this South China fortress once had

Atop the South Gate tower of Pengcheng Village

are the mansions of General Lai Enjue's first and fourth sons.

Dapeng Fortress is completely surrounded by villages of the Hakka people. Hakka houses tend to have steeple tops and a courtyard or patio, with wing rooms for people to live in. The eaves and ridges are straight like the northern official buildings and a contrast to the folk residences from Guangdong Province, which have upturned eaves and curved ridges. The interior decorations of Dapeng's folk houses share more similarities with traditional southern houses, such as the details of the floral ornaments, clay sculptures, lime sculptures and wood carvings.

The cylindrical Dragon Well Spring (龙井) is at the foot of Dragon Head Mountain (龙头山), 200 metres from the East Gate of Pengcheng Village (东门). The sweet spring water flows through the rock cavity from spring to winter and is said to be beneficial to health.

There are four bridges in Pengcheng Village. Dengyun Bridge (登云桥) is 160 years old and is situated at the west side of the village. It is 3 metres wide, 10 metres long and is built with granite stone strips. Local legend has it that the bridge will bring good luck to people who walk on it. Songyin Bridge (荣荫桥), with a history of 200 years, lies beside Sanjiao Pool (三角) in the east of Pengcheng Village. According to folklore, fortune goes to those who leave town through this bridge. Guankeng Bridge (官坑桥) is above the stream on the southern slope of Jiudun Mountain (九顿山). There is a high pier on both ends of the bridge. Fulong Bridge (福隆桥) is at the northwest side of the Pengcheng Village and the tablet with the bridge's name inscribed on it remains intact.

The unique folk culture of Pengcheng Village has made an important contribution to the development of Lingnan culture. Dapeng dialect, Dapeng mountain songs, Dapeng summer hats, the Da Peng Sea Festival and Dapeng fried sea urchins are all very famous.

**TASTY BITES**

Pengcheng Village ia a good place to try tasty Guangdong snacks such as yuan long pastries (元龙), tofu curd (豆腐花), steamed glutinous rice in bamboo leaves (粽子), glutinous turnip rice cakes (菜头角) steamed sponge cake (发糕), black tea fruit (红茶果) and fried meatballs (煎丸).

# Daqitou Village

## Home of "Wok-Ear" Residences

Quiet Daqitou Village is famous for its more than 200 Qing Dynasty "wok-ear" residences, which are arranged in a "chessboard" formation. These residences get their name from their big-tiled roofs and gables built with grey bricks into an inverted "U" shape .

### Getting there

Daqitou Village, Leping Town, Sanshui District, Foshan City, Guangdong Province. Nearest City : Guangzhou.
广东省佛山市三水区乐平镇大旗头村。
Take a minibus from Guanghou bus station(广州天河汽车站) to Datang (大唐)(RMB13 & 40 mins). Get off at the Lepingzhen stop(乐平镇), and then walk a few hundred metres to Daqitou Village. Alternatively, take a bus from Guangzhou provincial bus station(广东省汽车站) to San Shui Southeast bus station(三水西南车站) (about 50 minutes), then board a #613 bus to Daqitou Village (RMB6 & 35 mins).

Daqitou Village was once called "Zheng Village "and used to be the residence of Zheng Shaozhong (1834-1896), a Qing Dynasty Military Secretary and Commander of the Guangdong Navy. As the Empress Dowager Cixi apparently had a very high opinion of Zheng, she ordered the residences to be built for him and his family when he turned 60 in 1894. However, there is no one living in them now as their former residents have all moved to new houses nearby.

Daqitou Village covers an area of 52,000 square metres, including 14,000 square metres of ancient buildings. The folk houses, temples, family temples, mansions, drying yards, public squares and pools are all well-preserved.

Every house in the village has a slanted courtyard because the ground of the village itself is low in the front and high in the back. This design assists the village' s drainage system and there are holes every several metres

Unique "wok-ear" folk residences in Daqitou Village

in the narrow streets which lead to a water conduit underneath. Accordingly, the waste water from every residence can flow with the downward slope directly into the village pool and into the river.

The residential compounds in the village basically follow the same pattern: "wok-ear" (镬耳) residences with three rooms around a courtyard with a kitchen and corridors along two sides. The middle room is is divided by a wooden screen into a hall and a bedroom, above which there is an attic. The simple shrine in front of the wooden screen is for honouring ancestors.

The top of each work-ear wall forms an inverted "U" shape (resembling a wok), the main purpose of which is fire prevention. The work-ear walls were also called "Ao Yu" (鳌鱼, "Being Number One") walls, because they were thought to resemble the flaps of the ancient official headgear. Originally, this type of design could only be adopted by houses of government officials, but over time the style was gradually picked up by large families and businessmen for their own homes.

A corner of an ancient building in Daqitou Village

It is said that Zheng Shaozhong had lots of difficulties as an illiterate commander, and he obviously hoped that his descendants would be more knowledgeable than he was. The triplex Wen Tower (文塔) is supposedly like an upside down Chinese calligraphy pen. At the foot of the tower are two cube-shaped stones. The bigger one is a metre high and resembles an ink stone. The smaller one is like the seal, and the drying yard is supposedly the paper. Together they form a symbol meant to encourage later generations to study hard and become officials.

According to the folk customs of Guangdong Province, every villager has a duty to clean and tidy up the temples and gather during traditional festivals to worship their ancestors. Family members living outside the village will often also return home to attend these activities, or send money back to ask others to attend in their place.

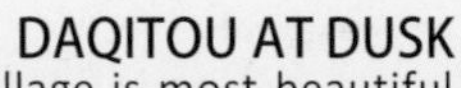

## DAQITOU AT DUSK

Daqitou Village is most beautiful after 4pm, when the dusk brings out the soft beauty of the curved “wok-ear” gables. If you ask the gatekeeper to open the second door of the Zheng Family Ancestral Hall, the setting sun will usually shine through the first and second doors, providing a good opportunity for photos.

# Bijiang Village

## Gold Building on Bijiang River

Bijiang Village, situated on the lower reaches of the Yangtze River, boasts a rich historical legacy and is well-known for its splendid buildings, including the Gold Building and the Mud Building.

### Getting there

Bijiang Village, Beijiao Town, Shunde District, Foshan City, Guangdong Province.
Nearest City : Guangzhou.
广东省佛山市顺德区北滘镇碧江村。
Take a #252 bus from Foshan's Chancheng District(禅城区) from Dengzhou Park(登洲公园) or #231 or 231[S] from Shunde Bus Station(顺德客运总站), both take about 1 hour. The buses from Guang Zhou to FoShan should pass by Bijiang Village(碧江村) (RMB15 & 1hour).

Located 11 km north of Daliang City, Bijiang Village was built in the Song Dynasty. It was one of the four biggest market towns in Shunde County during the Ming and Qing Dynasties. Famous local produce include paper art and marinated bamboo shoots. Today, Bijiang Village is one of the biggest transfer stations for goods en route to Guangzhou.

The flourishing economy, education and culture of ancient Bijiang Village have bequeathed to its descendants a rich architectural legacy. Records of the Xianfeng period of the Qing Dynasty (1850-1861) wrote: "The temples are important, the clan temples are magnificent; some cost hundreds of pieces of gold". Other remaining heritage sites in the village include the Gold Building (金楼), Mud Building (泥楼), Office Holder's Residence (职方第), Mutanggong Temple (慕堂苏公), Five Hall Temple (五间祠), Suxng Street Ancestral Hall (泰兴大街祠堂) and Deyun Bridge. (德云桥).

The buildings in Bijiang Village have mostly retained their architectural features, such as rammed earth walls, oyster-shell walls, mill stones and wok-ear gables. As for decorations, there is everything from wood, brick, stone and lime carvings to murals. The Bijiang Gold Building is the most famous local house, a showcase of wood carvings which also houses calligraphy and paintings of Qing Dynasty celebrities and Ming and Qing Dynasty furniture. The wall carving in the back garden is known as Bijiang Village's version of the famous 12th century panoramic painting by Chinese artist Zhang Zeduan entitled "Along the River During the Qing Ming Festival".

Bijiang Gold Building was built as a library for Su Piwen during the Jiaqing (1796-1820) and Daoguang (1820-1850) periods of the Qing Dynasty. The two-storey construction derived its name from its many wood carvings decorated

with gold foil. The building exhibits a variety of engraving styles, including shallow, deep and relief sculptures along with line, and hollow carvings and glass inlays. The precious materials of the wood carvings are teak, rosewood and mahogany. The back garden has many highlights, from the Buddha bamboos to the greenstripe bamboos, from 100-year-old longans to the 200-year-old crape myrtle.

Three wells were built in the wooden building: one in the courtyard, one in the main hall and one caisson on the top. According to the Chinese five elements theory, wood is suppressed by fire, and fire by water. As such, the wells in the courtyard and main hall are for fireproofing and cooling, while the caisson on the top has five bats carved on it, with the symbolic meaning "five blessings descend upon the house".

The Mud Building is a local residence next to the Gold Building. Its two side corridors were rebuilt by the owner who studied abroad in the first half of the 20th century. Some western architectural elements were also added, such as archs and columns. The Office Holder's Residence  is well-preserved, and it represents the Guangdong folk houses of the Pearl Delta in the latter years of the Qing Dynasty.

Mutanggong Temple has three rows of halls. The main structure remains intact and the decorations and design are satisfying. The tablet above the main hall was handwritten by Yu Youren, the patriarch of the Kuomintang (Chinese Nationalist Party).

### GOLDEN BEAUTY

It is said that after Dai Peiqiong, the goddaughter of the Empress Dowager Cixi. married Su Piwen, the vice director of the military department, she stayed with him in the Gold Building. From this story came a saying: “Keeping a beauty in a golden house" .

Yiyu Book House (亦渔遗塾) is a late-Qing Dynasty private school. It is situated in Sanxing Alley (三兴巷) in the centre of the village and connects two one-storey houses with "mountain-style" roofs (山式平房) and small courtyards inside. Its foyer, stone tablets, brick and lime carvings, murals, fences, corner doors and wood screens are all well-preserved.

Since the Song Dynasty, Bijiang Village has been famous for the academic accomplishments of its residents, producing many scholars who passed the imperial examinations. During the War of Resistance against Japan, communist intellectuals like Ye Jianying, Guo Moruo and Shen Yanbing all visited and spread the spirit of revolution to teachers and students in the village.

A corner of Bijiang Village

# Daling Village

## Oyster Shell Walls

The stone streets of Daling Village are lined with western-style buildings, old houses with oyster shell walls and green foxtails waving in the wind...

### Getting there

Da Ling Village, Shi Lou Town, Pan Yu District, Guang Zhou City, Guang Dong Province.
Nearest City :Guangzhou..
广东省广州市番禺区石楼镇大岭村
Take Guangzhou's Line 3 metro to Shiqiao Station(市桥站) in Pan Yu City（番禺市）. Walk 5mins to the Shiqiao Bus Station(市桥汽车站), then take a bus heading to Lianhua Shan(莲花山), and get off at Shilou Town(石楼镇)(RMB3.5 & 40mins). From Shilou Town, walk or charter a motorbike to Daling Village RMB 2 & 10mins).

Located in northeast Panyu District, Daling Village was founded in the first year of the Xuanhe period of the North Song Dynasty (1119) and is one of the oldest villages in the area. Once called "Pushan Village", it was founded by the Xu (许) family, though Chen (陈) is now the most common surname in the village. With Pu Mountain in the front and Yudai River in the back, Daling Village is actually an agglomeration of five natural villages. An ancient tower sits at the southwest corner of the village, which also has plenty of stone bridges, temples, tower gates, archways, granite alleys, old trees and oyster shell walls.

The five white stone streets in Daling Village were built in the 23rd year of the Guangxu period of the Qing Dynasty (1897). The upper street (上街) is paved with five white stone slabs and is 400 metres long. The original red stones were later reused in the lower street to build a 630-metre dike. Several old houses along the alley have been demolished, but some traditional houses with grey brick wok-ear walls remain well preserved, including Old Woman's House (姑婆屋).

Over the winding Yudai River rests Longjin Bridge (龙津桥), made of red sandy gravel and built in the Kangxi period of the Qing Dynasty (1662-1722). It is a two-hole arch bridge with dividing ridges on both sides of the pier to prevent ships from crashing and to reduce water swells. There are 16 balusters and 15 ripping fences on both sides with Ming Dynasty-patterns such as "Carp leaping through the dragon's gate" in the centre and Chinese inscriptions like "Dragon Ford" (龙津) in the middle of the bridge. At the west end of the bridge there is a statue of a westerner on his knees, holding up a plate. Meet Dragon Bridge (接龙桥) is another stone bridge from which visitors can watch ducks swimming

on the Yudai River below. Along the river live a number of Dan people, who generally reside in coastal provinces such as Guangdong and Zhejiang, and typically rely on fishing to make a living. Here they occupy the floating boats on the Yudai river and the thatched cottages known as "maoliao" (茅寮) along the shores.

Facing Longjin Bridge, the Big Pavilion (大魁阁) was built in the 10th year of the Guangxu period of the Qing Dynasty (1884). The top is a shaped like a hexagon, the ridges are curved and the tower spire is a green glaze gourd about 20 metres high, pointing towards the sky. A trumpet hanging on the top of the Dakuige was allegedly used as a broadcast station during the Cultural Revolution.

The many temples of Daling Village include the Chen Family Grand Temple (氏大宗祠), Jinshi Temple (进士公祠), Bless River Temple (佑江公祠), and the Near Bay Temple (近湾公祠). Among the most magnificent is the ancestral hall of the Daling Chen Family, known as Xianzong Temple (显宗祠). Built in 1522, the temple has three columns and three rows of halls. At the front, there are four "lotus bracket" (莲花斗拱) arches. On the door stones are carvings of westerners in foreign costumes, which are extremely rare and suggest that the Chen family had been involved in foreign affairs.

Under the hundred-year-old linden tree rests the oldest and most intact temple in the village – Two Hall Temple (两塘公祠). Most of its walls are built from oyster shells which make the temple warm in winter and cool in summer. The building technique involves threading the shells together with iron wires, then using lime mortar or shell slurry to fix them. Windows and skylights made from oyster shells transmit light and help maintain privacy. Another interesting fact about the temple is that there are many bulletholes on the roof as it used to be an important stronghold during the War of Resistance against Japan. Above the door, there is a cultural revolution era portrait of Chairman Mao.

The "Pushan Spring" (菩山第一泉) under the foot of the mountain northeast of the village is a natural clear mountain spring filtrated by sand. In the old days, scholars and the wealthy used the spring water to brew tea because of its sweet flavour. In 1958, the spring was blocked but villagers re-dug it and used a 10 centimetre pipe to bring water to the roadside for passers-by to taste.

## BOUNTEOUS WELL

The white granite well known as Shajingqi (沙井气) was built in the Qianlong period of the Qing Dynasty (1735-1796.) The well apparently never dries, and according to locals, the water is fantastic for brewing tea and boiling rice, which will not go bad the next day even in the hottest days of summer.

"Big Pavilion" in Daling Village

# Nanshe Village

## Lotus Shades and Willow Branches

Nanshe Village is surrounded by large farm fields and small hills populated by lychee trees. The rectangular pond in the centre of the village comprises four connected pools. With residential alleys built perpendicularly to the edges of the pond, the landscape of the village is said to resemble a clasped hand.

### Getting there

Nanshe Village, Chashan Town, Dongguan,Guangdong Province.
Nearest City: Shenzhen.
广东省东莞市茶山镇南社村。
Take a High-speed train from Shenzhen Luohu Railway Station(深圳罗湖汽车站) and get off at Shilong Station (石龙站) (40mins), than proceed to Nanshe Village by taxi (RMB40 & 1/2 hour).

Nanshe Village is located south of the Dong River between two mountains – Horsehead Mountain and Zhanggang Mountain. Most villagers belong to the Xie family (谢), whose history could be traced back to the Southern Song Dynasty. By the end of the Ming Dynast, locals had built a wall around the village and erected four gates and 17 towers for protection. Nowadays, only a few sections of the wall and towers remain.

The extant ancient architectures in Nanshe Village are mostly within the ancient walls, although there is also a God of War Temple (关帝庙) and a nunnery (尼姑庵) outside the east gate. The walls of the ancient buildings are made of carefully selected red sandstone strips and black bricks and the wooden, stone and calcic sculptures within are generally of high artistic merit. The scale of the traditional Ming and Qing architectures in the village is considerable: 30 ancestral halls, 3 temples, more than 250 ancient folk houses, over 40 ancient wells and 36 ancient tombs (one within the block of ancient buildings and 35 outside the walls).

Some of the public buildings, in particular the ancestral halls, embody the commercial and profit-making culture of the village. Many of the ancestral halls are shaped like the mouth of a bugle, getting smaller and smaller as it approaches the back of the hall. This design is a physical

Ancient folk residences systematically arranged on the edges of the river

representation of two Chinese proverbs: "Receiving the wealth of the world" (广纳天下财) and "Getting more for less" (进多出少). Typical representations include the Xie Family Ancestral Hall (谢氏大宗祠), the Long Life Ancestral Hall (百岁坊祠), Land God Temple (社田公祠), Xieyuqi Family Temple (谢遇奇家庙) and the God of War Temple.

Built during the 34th year of the reign of Emperor Jiaqing of the Ming Dynasty (1555), Xie Family Ancestral Hall is regarded as the main ancestral hall of Nanshe Village. The south facing building is located on the northern shore of the pond in the centre of the village. Covered by a hill-shaped roof, the ancestral hall comprises three main rooms and three dooryards. It is a building with splendid size, structure and decoration and a solemn place for villagers to worship their ancestors.

The Long Life Ancestral Hall was also constructed during the Ming Dynasty, and has a traditional layout comprising three buildings connected by three dooryards. The hall is also covered by a hill-shaped roof. A stele made in 1595 which reads "Record of the Long Life Ancestral Hall" (百岁翁祠记) is currently preserved inside the hall. The base of the stage and the stele are decorated with classic Ming Dynasty-style red-stone sculptures.

Zizheng Residence (资政邸) was the residence of a successful candidate in the highest imperial examinations of the Qing Dynasty named Xie Yuanjun. Though only two buildings of the big dwelling have been preserved, its former prosperity can be sensed from the exquisite coloured lintels and the flower and bird sculptures on Chuihua Door in the middle of the hall, which include a vivid peacock tail and phoenix head stretching out of the branches.

Hundred year Hall (百岁坊) was constructed during the reign of Emperor Wanli during the Ming Dynasty (1592-1598). It was built by the local feudal government to celebrate the longevity of villager Xie Yanjuan and his wife, both of whom were over a hundred years old.

The Xie family of Nanshe Village highly valued the size of the lintel on their doors. A pillar set in front of the Xie ancestral hall, is inscribed with the names of successful candidates from imperial examinations to serve as an inspiration for future generations. During the Ming and Qing Dynasties, nine locals are recorded as having succeeded in the examinations.

## LYCHEE PICKING

The surrounding lychee woods are a good place for visitors to experience the beauties of nature. Around the time of the Qing Ming Festival (usually in April), the flowers of the lychee trees will blossom, creating an alluring aroma. In summer, the lychees will ripen and villagers will climb up the trees to collect the fruit.

Ancestral hall in Nanshe Village

# Tangwei Village

## A Walled World of Ancient Dwellings

Village names in the Dongguang area generally have the suffix "wei" ("walled"). Tangwei Village is one of the largest and best preserved of these walled villages in the Dongguang region, providing valuable references for the study of local customs, civilisation and architectural styles.

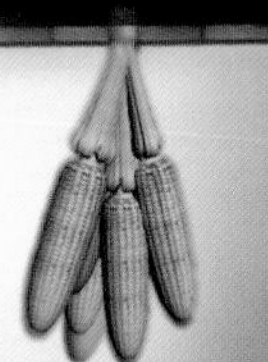



**Getting there**

Tangwei Village, Shipai Town, Dongguang, Guangdong Province.
Nearest City: Dongguan.
广东省东莞市石排镇塘尾村。
Take a bus from Dongguang South Bus Station(东莞南城汽车站) to Shipai Bus Station(石排汽车站) (50mins), and then a minbus to Tangwei Village (about 1 hour). Alternatively, from Dongguan South Bus Station board a service to Zhangmutou Bus Station(樟木头车站) (1hour), then transfer to a #87 bus and get off at Shipai Garden(石排公园) ( 5 mins), than walk 5mins to Tangwei Village.

Built during the Ming and Qing Dynasties, Tangwei Village was laid out to fit the natural slope of the mountain. Three ponds in front of the village wall – one big and two small – are said to resemble a crab shell and two crab pincers. The two ancient wells nearby are regarded as the eyes of the crab. The symbolic crab is considered by villagers as a tutelary spirit that has guarded the the village for hundreds of years.

Well-preserved historic sites in the village include 286 ancient residences, 21 ancestral halls, 19 studies, 10 wells, 4 walled-gates and 28 gun turrets. One distinguishing feature of the village's residences is that most of them are connected to either studies or ancestral halls.

The original gates and gun turrets of Tangwei Village were built in the Ming Dynasty but have been continuously repaired over the years. Constructed as the

Scenery of Tangwei Village

boundary of the village, the well-preserved wall of Tangwei Village is 860.8 metres long, 5 metres high and 0.35 metres wide, with a red stone base and a black-brick wall body.

Of the four gates on the wall, the East Gate (东门) is the largest and has a plaque inscribed with the Chinese phrase "Xiu Ba Dong Nan" (秀把东南, meaning "Prosperity of the Southeast"). Along the wall are 28 gun turrets of varying sizes named after 28 different stars. The wall, walled gate and gun turrets formed a strong defensive unit.

The network of alleys in the village is said to look like the Chinese character "井" (a well). Seven main alleys cross the village from south to north, and four horizonal ones run east to west. At the end of the reign of the Qing Dynasty Emperor Guangxu (1875-1908), a rich gentleman named Zhizhong Li replaced the original red stones of the alleys with granite and expanded them beyond the wall. One of the alleys was reconstructed to go straight to Shilong Harbour from the North Gate, though only 300 metres of the original 10 km remain.

Built during the Ming Dynasty, Li Family Ancestral Hall (李氏宗祠) contains five doors, two living rooms and three yards.

Jing Tong Ancestral Hall (景通公祠) originally built in the middle of the Qing Dynasty, was the ancestral hall of Jing Tong, who was the 10th "Shizu" 世祖. ancestor) of the village founder. The rooms and interior are famous for their delicate carvings on the beams.

Mei Ancestral Hall (梅公祠), built during the reign of the Emperor Daoguang in the Qing Dynasty (1820-1850), was the ancestral hall of the 12th Shizu. It preserves memorial tablets of ancestors from the 10th Shizu of the Ming Dynasty to the 22nd Shizu of the Qing Dynasty. It also contains a statue of local deity the Shenkang King (神康王).

Protect Virtue Hall (守善堂) is an ancestral hall which is connected to a residence and was built during the reign of Emperor Guangxu in the Qing Dynasty (1875-1908).

The Baoqing School House (宝卿家塾) was originally an ancestral hall and residence combo, but during the Republic of China period it was converted into a family school.

10 ancient wells in Tangwei Village provided water for public and private use. The wall of the wells were originally black brisk with red stone, but in the latter years of Qing Dynasty the red stones were replaced with granite.

### SHENKANG KING

From the first to seventh of the seventh month of the lunar calendar (uually August), large scale celebrations are held annually in Tangwei Village to celebrate the birth of local deity the Shenkang King. The event (康王诞) has a history of more than 300 years.

# Cuiheng Village

## The Birth Place of Sun Yat-sen

Cuiheng Village is a pleasant village famous for being the birthplace of Chinese revolutionary and the Republic of China's first president, Sun Yat-sen.

### Getting there

Cuiheng Village, Nanlang District, Zhongshan, Guangdong Province.
Nearest City: Guangzhou.
广东省中山市南朗镇翠亨村。
Tourist buses and regular #12 route services leave from downtown Zhongshan to the Memorial Museum of Sun Yan-set(孙中山纪念馆) (about 1.5 hours). The entrance fee for the Memorial Museum of Sun Yan -set is RMB20, except on March 12, May 18 and November 12,when entrance is free of charge.

Considered a way bigger draw than the poetic setting of Cuiheng Village is the village's Home of Sun Yat-sen Memorial Museum (孙中山故居纪念馆), which enables visitors to experience the birthplace of China's first republican President, Sun Yat-sen and the historic and social environment he grew up in.

Located beside the Ghuangzhu Highway (from Guanzhou to Zhuhai), Cuiheng Village is situated 17.6 km from Zhongshan's city center, about 100 km south of Guangzhou and 30 km north of Macau. The Pearl River separates the village from Shenzhen and Hong Kong, while the green wooded Wugui Mountain sits in the west.

The village was established by the Cai (蔡) family during the Kangxi era of the Qing Dynasty (1661-1722). Because of the scenic location of the village, which sits beside both a river and a mountain, the village was named "Cuiheng – "Cui" for the Cai people who established it and "Heng" for its beautiful landscape. The name implies that everything should go smoothly for the village.

Cuiheng Village offers a number of historic sites – the residence of Yang Yin (杨殷故居), the residence of Lu Hao Dong (陆 皓 东故居), the tombs of Lu Hao Dong (陆皓东墓) and Sun Chang (孙昌墓), Cui Heng Inn (翠亨宾馆), and Sun Yat-sen Memorial Middle School (中山纪念中学).

The village's main tourist attraction is however the Home of Sun Yat-sen Memorial Museum, which features the former home of Sun Yat-sen and Sun Yat-sen Memorial Hall; sculptures of Sun Yat-sen listening to stories about the Taiping Rebellion; and even the place where Sun supposedly tested explosives!

Completed in 1892, the former home of Sun

Yat-sen was designed by the great man himself. It is a two-storey house which broke from the traditional design of houses in the village at the time. The house combines both the style of traditional Guangdong tile-roofed houses and western residential features, a fitting and rare combination of Chinese and Western culture. The house is surrounded by a small yard and on the right side of the gate is a stone plaque with an inscription of four Chinese characters which say "Home of Sun Yat-sen" (孙中山故居), written by Sun's wife Song Qingling. The second storey of the house is Sun Yat-sen's study where he wrote the famous A Letter to Li Hongzhong, in which he implored the Qing government to save the country and its people.

In 1956, a park was built in front of Sun's former residence. To mark the 100th anniversary of Sun' s birth, an Exhibition Centre (辅助陈列) was established in 1966, and it now attracts thousands of tourists every year.

## IN MINIATURE

A "Mini Zhongshan City" (中山城) has been built in Cuiheng Village and exhibits the regional culture of Zhongshan as well as architectural styles of other countries. The miniature city has become a popular spot for film and TV shoots.

During Sun's childhood, he worked with his father every day as they cultivated their 2-acre farmland. This land, formerly known as "Dragon Field" (龙田) is now part of the 60 acre site of the Cuiheng Village Agricultural Exhibition Centre. (翠亨农业展示区). In the right corner of the field is a row of typical South China three-roomed rural tile-roofed houses. Inside the houses are pictures and sculptures of Sun's family and village locals. The centre is a good place to learn about the unique agricultural practices of the Pearl River Delta of China.

The village also houses a Cuiheng Residential Exhibition Centre which introduces how locals of different social backgrounds lived during the Qing Dynasty.

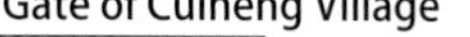

Gate of Cuiheng Village

Sun Yat-sen Memorial Hall

# Zili Village

## The Watchtower Museum

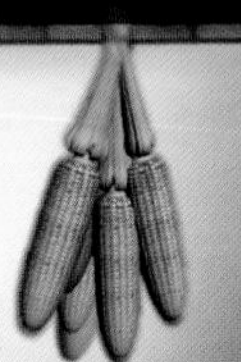

There is a local saying that goes, "You haven't really been to Guangdong unless you've visited the watchtowers of Kaiping", and the best watchtowers of Kaiping are in Zili Village. In 1920, due to frequent floods and bandits, many watchtowers and residences were built under the sponsorship of Overseas Chinese or compatriots in Hong Kong and Macao.

### Getting there

Zili Village, Tangkou District, Kaiping, Guangdong.
Nearest City: Zhuhai.
广东省开平市塘口镇自力村。
Take a bus from Zhuhai's Gongbei Bus Station(拱北口岸) to Kaiping Yici Bus Station(开平义祠客运总站), (about 1.5 hours). From Kaiping, take another bus to Magang Town(马冈镇),and get off at the intersection leading to Zili Village ( 1 hour). Then take a motor bike taxi towards the watchtowers (about 2 km).

Zili Village is situated about 12 km to the east of Kaiping City. The village is a union of three natural villages, of which An Village and Li Village founded in the Xianfeng era of the Qing Dynasty (1850-1861) are the oldest. Later during the reign of Emperor Guangxu (1875-1908), a new village named Heanli was established, and during the early years of Republic of China period (1912-1949) another village split out and was named Yonganli.

Currently there are about 15 well-preserved watchtowers and traditional residences in Zili Village. The most famous of the (mostly early C20) residences include Shuming Stone House (数铭石楼), Yesheng House (叶生居庐) and Guansheng House (官生居庐). These buildings feature a combination of western and local architectural styles created by Overseas Chinese and local villagers during the early decades of the last century.

Heanli (合安里), the area where most of the watchtowers are located, is just past the banyan tree at the entrance of the village. Two rows of traditional black-bricked folk houses with tiled roofs run along the front. The grey sculptures on the wall and the traditional murals on the house gates exhibit scenes from local history. The oldest watchtower is Dragon Victory House (龙胜楼), which was built in 1919, while a group of five watchtowers built in 1948 is known as Zhan Lu (湛庐).

From the field, a stone alley runs to the back of the village. Dozens of watchtowers and Western-style building are scattered in this area. The design of the watchtowers is quite varied, with some having four storeys and others six. The decorations are relatively simple on the lower parts of the barbicans, but spectacular on the upper parts. The watchtowers were used for defending local houses from bandits. Originally, locals used stones and water to defend



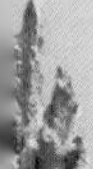

Watchtowers under a blue sky

themselves but later began using the guns brought back by the Overseas Chinese.

The watchtowers feature many details which combine elements of Western and Chinese cultures. The gate of Guansheng House, for example, is made of imported steel but inscribed with the Chinese character "fu" ("福", meaning "good fortune") and other reliefs in a rococo style. These European design elements were brought to the village by the Overseas Chinese.

One particular watchtower is also a house for family activities. The six-storey Mingshi House (铭石楼) belongs to the big family of Fang Runwen and it is widely regarded as the most beautiful watchtower in the village.

Inside Mingshi House there are four large pictures (each about a metre in heightl) of Fang Runwen and his three wives hung on the front wall of the main room. The dress and the facial expressions of the four people in these portraits exemplify their social status and education, and the portrait is a testimony to the "quiet polygamy" of many traditional Chinese families of the time. Rooms from the second to fourth storeys belong to the sons of Fang Runwen. The fifth floor houses a family shrine with dozens of memorial tablets dedicated to ancestors of the family. The shrine is carefully designed and again contains some European elements. On the sixth-floor watchtower is an arbor with green vitreous tiles. The six columns and arch of the arbor is reminiscent of those seen in ancient Rome. Though a little strange, it again typifies the blending of Chinese and Western cultures seen throughout the village.

Shengju House (生居庐) is slightly smaller than Mingshi House. Rumour has it that the builder of this house stored lots of gold in the walls. The wall has apparently been struck by lighting twice, as gold is said to attract lightning.

Zili Village sees itself as a cultured place and claims a number of scholars and literary figures such as: Chen Baisha, the only scholar from South China to go to the Confucius Temple in the Ming Dynasty.

### TROTTERS

Zili Village is a good place to sample some authentic dishes of the Kaiping area, such as pig's feet (猪手), ginger chicken (杀姜鸡), soft-boiled lamb (秘制白切乳羊) and so forth.

Watchtowers standing in the woods

# Xiema Village

## The Horse-shaped Village

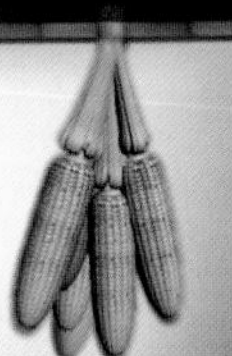

Xiema Village ("Rest Horse Village") is surrounded by water and hills. The history of the village has been traced back almost 700 years to the Yuan Dynasty.

### Getting there

Xiema Village, Shengtang District, Enping, Jiangmen, Guangdong Province.
Nearest City:Zhuhai.
广东省江门市恩平市圣堂镇歇马村。
Take a bus from Zhuhai's Gongbei Bus Station(拱北口岸) to Enping Bus Station(恩平汽车站) (1.5hours). Take the bus to Dongchen Town(东成镇) and get off at the stop for Xiema Village(歇马村)(1/2hour).
An alternative would be to take a bus from Gongbei to Kaiping Yici Bus Station(开平义祠客运总站), (about 1.5 hours).From Kaiping, a taxi to the village should cost about RMB40 for the 9km ride.

Xiema Village is located on the banks of the Jingjiang River. The village has many tourist attractions, including Men's Alleys, Women's Alleys, Lizhi Park (励志园), "Mysterious Field", (神秘村场), Xuanwu Altar (玄武坛), the Stele Forest (功名碑林) and the Jingjiang River itself.

This ancient village was laid out according to Chinese feng shui principles and is said to resemble the shape of a horse. The "head" of the horse is said to imply that the village would produce heads of govenment, while the "tail" implies the village would produce wealthy merchants. The village's drainage system and ponds are seen as the organs of the

Women's Alley in Xiema village.

horse.

The 14 large and 14 small alleys of Xiema Village are full of historic charm. Traditionally, only men could use the big alleys and women the small ones, which is why they have been nicknamed Men's Alleys (男人巷) and Women's Alleys (娘女巷) by locals. Every alley contains ditches (visible and invisible ones) for draining dirty water. The 2-metre-high walls are made of marble covered by black bricks. The grey roof ridges and eaves feature sculptures of dragons and phoenixes.

Lizhi Garden, built during the reign of the Emperor Daoguang in the Qing Dynasty (1820-1850), is surrounded by flowers and thick trees. The layout of the buildings, corridors and study rooms were all carefully designed. The east wing room is a study room, elegant, clean and bright, and filled with many books. The west wing room is a gallery, preserving famous works of ancient scholars, including Tang Bohu, Zhao Mengqing, and Hai Rui. The original scholarly garden was destroyed, and the current garden is a reconstruction based on the former design.

Xiema Park (歇马公园), built in 2001, is surrounded by trees. On the right side of the gate stands a 150-year-old longan tree that is 7 metres tall with many small holes on the trunk. Despite its age it is still verdant and can produce lots of fruit. The Changguan Memorial Building (昌官纪念楼) standing in the east of the garden

The Eight Flag Poles of Scholarly Honour

The Lizhi Platform of Xiema Village

## HOT SPRINGS

In the area around the village there are several places worth visiting, such as Jinshan Hot Spring in Naji Village (金山温泉) or Stone Village (石头村约), about 30 km from Xiema Village.

is an entertainment venue for the villagers. The garden also contains steles which record the past fame and successes of the villagers.

The Stele Forest was established during the Ming Dynasty and features the Eight Flag Poles of Scholarly Honour (八大旗杆夹), Juren Road (举人路), the Imperial Order Stele (皇帝敕命碑), the Stage for Educating Children (教子地台), and the Statue of Confucius (孔子塑像), The steles name every candidate from the village that passed the imperial examinations until the exams were abolished at the end of the Qing Dynasty. Nowadays, all the steles stand on the banks of the Jingjiang River, encouraging the current village residents to study hard and strive for success.

Xiema Village has a long history of physical education. The two 200-kilogram weight stones for practicing martial arts set at the village gate were reputedly made by legendary the monk, Yiquzhi. Jiang Wenliang Ancestral Hall (翁梁公祠), built in 1629, was once an ancestral hall and is now the location of the village's sports association for seniors.

Xiema Village was well-known throughout history for the number of first-place candidates in the provincial official examinations. During the Ming and Qing Dynasties, Xiema Village reportedly fostered more than 680 prestigious scholars, explaining the large number of sites in the village associated with study.

The Stele of Scholarly Honour

# Qianmei Village

## Chaoshan Architectural Miracle

Qianmei Village offers a distinctive blend of Chinese and Western style architecture, old Chaoshan folk-customs and the graceful feel of the olden days. The village is also known as the former home of famous businesman, navigator and local benefactor Chen Xihong, and the site of Chen Cihong's Former Residence, which is regarded by many as the epitome of Chaoshan culture.

### Getting there

Qianmei Village, Longdu Town, Chenghai District, Shantou City, Guangdong Province.
Nearest City: Shantou.
广东省汕头市澄海区隆都镇前美村。
From Shanto's Jieyang Chaoshan Airport(揭阳潮汕机场) take a bus to Chenghai Bus Station(澄海汽车总站) (about 1 hour), then change to a #8 Bus on to Qianmei Village (RMB 3 &1/2 hour).

Qianmei Village had two peak periods of prosperity. The first was when ancestor Chen Tingguang made a fortune after becoming an official during Emperor Yongzheng's reign during the Qing Dynasty. The second was during the late Qing Dynasty and early Republic of China period, when Chen Cihong's family and other enterprising locals first got rich in outheast Asia and then made significant financial contributions to their ancestral hometown.

The ancient village contains large quantities of undamaged buildings from the late Qing Dynasty and early Republic of China period, covering a total area of more than 30,000 square metres. The grand Chen Family Ancestral Hall (陈氏祠堂) is a highlight, attracting visitors by virtue of its uniqueness and history. The old walls and well-preserved wood and brick carvings and porcelain clay demonstrates the distinctive style of Overseas Chinese architecture of the time. The lintels of dozens of mansions are engraved with Chinese characters meaning "Imperial Academy House" (翰林第) or "Senior Official House" (大夫第), a testimony to the large number of high officials and noble lords who returned to the village after making their fortunes at the imperial court.

Typical of residences in this area, Chen Cihong's Former Residence combines Chinese and Western elements. Built in the second year of the Xuantong period in the Qing Dynasty (1909), it has survived several generations. With an area of 25,40 square meters, it comprises Langzhong House (郎中第), Longevity House (寿康里), Virtue House (善居室) and Sanlu House (三庐宅), totalling 506 rooms. The overall pattern mixes Western and traditional Chinese-style pavillions, terraces and open halls. It is said that there used to be a servant in charge of opening and closing the doors and windows in the Chen house. Every morning, he would open each window, and by

Inside Chen Cihong's Former Residence

the time he had opened all the windows in the house it would be time to start closing them again.

About 200 metres from the complex is a stream which curves southward and surrounds the house in line with the principles of "auspicious water" (吉水) and "left green dragon" (左青龙) in feng shui philosophy. In the east of the former residence there is a spacious paddy field with an open view. In the past one hundred years, no houses have been built on this field so as to preserve the feng shui pattern.

Virtue House is the largest and most well-preserved house among all the houses in Chen Ciying's Former Residence. With an area of 6,861 square metres and 202 rooms, construction began in 1922 but it was not completed until 1939, when the Japanese army invaded Shantou. The decorations on the doors and windows of Shanju House are an outstanding combination of Chinese and Western cultures. The main gateway was designed in the stone-carving style of Chaoshan tradition, while the gateways in the alleys mostly feature Western enamel bricks. The column base, column shaft and column cap of the columns in the building are made up of one building stone, which is in contrast to China's traditional column style.Chaoshan gold lacquer wood carving has long had a solid reputation for its strong local style. In Virtue House, the wonderful wood carvings with feng shui patterns, decorative patterns and traditional auspicious characters, birds and animals are distributed throughout the front hall, middle hall and each courtyard.

Yongning Stockade (永宁寨) to the north of Chen Cihong's Former Residence is the place where

The main hall of Chen Cihong's Former Residence

The restaurant in Chen Cihong's Former Residence

the Chen family made their fortune. With an area of 10,333 square metres, it was built by Chen's ancestor Chen Yanguang in the 10th year of the Yongzheng period in the Qing Dynasty (1732). It is called "Yongning" (永宁, literally "Eternal Peace") because their ancestors hoped it would be forever peaceful. One side of the village wall is high and the other three are lower. All walls, which are extant, are made from mud but they look firm as rocks. In front of the stockade are protective irrigation canals, ditches and ponds. The clear water in the pond reflects the distant Lotus Mountain in good weather.

With an area of 1,700 square metres, the Cultural Garden (文园占地) has 23 rooms and five halls. The garden has been opened to students of art schools from Guangzhou and Shantou and as far away as Beijing.

The "Wish Longevity" ancient screen (祝寿古屏) kept in the Cuinan Ancestral Temple of Family Chen (陈氏翠南祖祠) is the earliest of the four screens preserved in Chenghai District, highlighting the combined arts of calligraphy, painting and carving. The screens are family relics used by families to educate their descendants about the history of their ancestors.

In addition to Chen Cihong's Former Residence, Qianmei Village has a number of other attractions which are worth a look if you have time, such as the Chen Cihong Family Museum (陈慈黉家史馆), the Sculpture of the Red Boat (红头船雕塑), Chaoshan Opera House (潮汕戏曲馆), Puppet House (木偶馆), Gongfu Tea House (工夫茶馆) and Chaoshan Handwork House (潮汕工艺礼品馆), all of which exemplify the traditional folk art culture of the Chaoshan area. The village also puts on displays of Chaoshan-style dancing called "Double-Biting Goose Dancing" (双咬鹅).

### "LION HEAD" GOOSE

In and around the Qianmei area there are Cantonese restaurants and stalls with a large variety of dishes. The can't-miss foods include the famous "Lion Head" Goose (卤狮头鹅) and "Pig Head" rice dumplings (猪头粽).

# Nangang Gupai Village

## The Thousand-year-old Yao Residences

From the snaking mountain road, to chic "hanging foot houses" with meshed bamboo staircases, and barns with cattle pens below and food stores above, every aspect of Nangang Gupai Village reveals much about the lifestyles of the ancient Yao people, one of the oldest and largest minority groups in Guangdong Province.



### Getting there

Nanganggupai Village, Sanpai Town, Liannan Yao Autonomous County, Qingyuan City, Guangdong Province.
Nearest City: Guangzhou.
广东省清远市连南瑶族自治县三排镇南岗古排村。
Take a bus from Guangdong Bus Station to Lianzhou (连州) (3 hours). At Lianzhou County Bus Station (连县汽车站) transfer to a shuttle bus to Nanganggupai Village (1 hour).

Nangang Gupai Village lies 20 km from Liannan Town and was built in the Song Dynasty, with a history of more than 1,400 years. At present, it is one of the oldest and best-preserved Yao (瑶) stockades in the country. The streets in the stockade are in an orderly grid pattern, while the primitive hillside dwellings are simple and trim.

The scenery of Yao Mountain is distinctive. As it is a Karst lava zone, many rocky mountains rise abruptly out of the ground, with towering peaks and grotesquely jagged rocks, over which rosy clouds slowly rise through purple smoke like mist. The poet Wei Qiu once described the sight as "Skyscraper stalagmites and celestial islands" (摩天石笋神仙岛). It is a place with rivers and an immense forest full of twittering birds and fragrant flowers.

The picturesque scenery of Nangang Gupai Village.

Yao residences are thickly dotted throughout of Nangang Gupai Village, layer upon layer on the hills. As each house is built on a slope, the roof at the front of the house is usually at the same level as the base of the house in the back..

Above the second mountain gate in Nangang Gupai Village is a plaque inscribed with the Chinese

characters "南岗" (meaning "Southern Post"). Inside lay the Yao residences, which are closely connected to each other and made from black bricks and grey tiles, exuding a quiet and united colour tone. Both the roads and steps of the Yao stockade are paved with irregularly shaped stones and connected through a series of stone steps. More than 300 buildings in the stockade are connected to each other.

Although some are delapidated, the residences remain imposing. Even Sanzhou Mountain (三州山), which offers a view of three provinces (Lianzhou, Wuzhou and Jingzhou, belonging to Guangdong, Guanxi and Hunan, respectively), pales in comparison to the grandeur of the stockade. In the middle of the stockade, there are wide stone steps which form the "central square" (中心广场), the place where the Yao people would congregate for big celebrations or events

The Yao stockade is known as the home of many festivals such as the Ploughing Festival in April/May (开耕节), the Fresh Delicacy-tasting Festival in June/July(尝新节), and the Singing Festival in July/August (开唱节). (Exact dates each year are based on the lunar calendar.) Held in Autumn (generally mid-October), the Shuagetang Festival (耍歌堂, effectively a harvest festival) is one of the biggest folk gatherings in Liannan Yao Nationality Autonomous County . There should also be opportunities to see the long-drum dance (长鼓舞表演) which has been passed on from generation to generation.

A corner of Nangang Gupal Village

## ALL ABOUT RICE

Glutinous rice cakes (糍粑), green bamboo rice (竹筒饭), and rice wine (米酒) are all authentic Yao specialties. If you feel like a walK, then the Observation Tower (观景台) on the hillside opposite the village offers spectacular views.

A Yao residence in Nangang Gupai Village

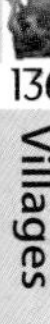

# Dalu Village

## The Guangxi Village of Couplets

Dalu Village's greatest material legacy is the three hundred-plus pairs of couplets from the Ming and Qing Dynasties, which reveal much about local culture and clan philospohy. The village has been called "The First Village of Couplets in Guangxi" due to the rich content of the couplets, many of which are concerned with things such as cultivating one's moral character, governing a family, and serving the country.

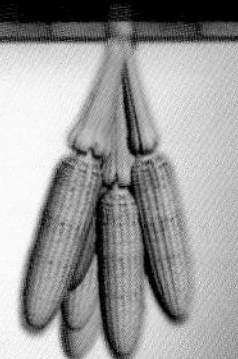

### Getting there

Dalu Village, Fozi Town, Lingshan County, Qinzhou City, Guangxi Zhuang Autonoumous Region.
Nearest City: Nanning.
广西壮族自治区钦州市灵山县佛子镇大芦村。
Take a train from Nanning Station to Qinzhou East Station(钦州东站) (about 2hours). From Qingzhou Bus Station(钦州客运站) take a bus to Lingshan County(灵山县) (RMB22 & 1 hour). and then continue by pedicab taxi or normal taxi to Dalu Village ( RMB12 & 15mins).

Dalu Village, also known as "The Village of Lychees", lies 8 km from the eastern suburbs of Lingshan County. The village has a history of over 400 years. Wu Biqi, a poet of Hengzhou during Qing Dynasty, described the scenery of Dalu Village as: "Charming peaks stand beyond the stream girding the houses. In the evening mist, cranes return to the pine forest. The setting sun shines on a little pavilion, and the square pond with its reflection of red lychees".

Dalu Village possesses a rich cultural heritage, numerous old trees and a strong ecological environment. The villag's old residences of the Lao (劳) clan from the Ming and Qing Dynasties consist of nine clusters. At present five clusters are accessible to visitors, namely the Wok-Ear (镬耳楼) House, Sanda Hall (三达堂), Double Blessing Hall (双庆堂), the East Garden Villa (东园别墅) and Prosperous Spring Hall (富春园). The threee hundred pairs of couplets created in and handed down from the Ming and Qing Dynasties are hung up on the gates and pillars of the various buildings. .

Wok-Ear House is also called Simei Hall and is the original residence of the Lao family. The layout of the building resembles the Chinese character "国" (meaning "country") and comprises front gatehouse, main house, auxiliary houses,

From a distance, Dalu Village is like a landscape painting

Simei Hall of Dalu Villiage

lower houses, corridor and walls. Construction began in the 25th year of the Jiajing period in the Ming Dynasty (1546). The architecture of the houses, with their complex functional structures, embodies the values of the patriarchal system. The couplets hung on the houses also reflect the strict discipline of that time. For example, the couplet hung on the four eave-columns of the ancestral temple reads: "We should do good for our kind and brothers and be tolerant to protect our descendants". Similarly, the couplet hung on the four columns reads: "Being industrious and frugal is the best way to manage a family, and being harmonious and tolerant is the right way to conduct oneself in society".

Sanda Hall, constructed in the Kangxi period of the Qing Dynasty (1694-1719), was the original residence of the second oldest child of the Lao family. The name of the building carries the meaning of being moral, capable and wise. The corresponding title of Simei Hall was granted to the ancestral temple that was inhabited by the oldest child of Lao family at that time. The couplets hung in Zhang Guiyu Hall are elegant. For instance, the couplet on the outboards of four water columns reads: "The rising sun and orchids and sweet osmanthus trees indicate the spring breeze".

The East Garden Villa was constructed in the 12th year of the Qianlong period of the Qing Dynasty (1747) by Lao Zirong, an eighth generation descendant of the Lao family. The French-style old buildings exemplify the idea of a scholary family, embodied by the overall layout, exquisite decorations, precious cultural relics and peaceful atmosphere. The architectural style and couplets are also said to reflect Lao Zirong's honest temperament and broad mind. For example, the couplet in the upper study reads: "The virtue of patience is as deep as the mirror and long consideration makes beautiful writing".

Double Blessing Hall was constructued in the sixth year of the Daoguang period in the Qing Dynasty (1826) by Lao Changfu and Lao Changyou, brothers of the tenth generation of the Lao family. The bulding's name is said to mean:: "the older brother gets rich and the younger brother is safe; talent and morality are equally important." The hall possesses an independent gate linked with numerous passageways, making it both comfortable and convenient. Additionally, the exquisite cavvings on the house decorations, eave decorations, chairs, beds and appliances all reveal the importance the family placed on style.

## VILLAGE FESTIVALS

On the 14th day of the seventh lunar month (usually August), people of the Gui clan will eat eggplant porridge to show that "they will never forget the virtues of their fathers". However the temple fair (岭头节), which usually falls in October, is the most popular festival in Dalu Village. At this time, locals will gather under the old tree behind the Wok Ear Tower and don masks to perform sacred folk dances, beat on long drums and perform the traditional "Lingtou dance" (跳岭头) in the moonlight.

# Xiushui Village

## Birthplace of Scholars

Xiushui Village showcases not only ancient buildings from the Ming and Qing Dynasties, but also a cultural and educational tradition that has been flourishing for over a millenium. A large variety of inscriptions bestowed by emperors and officials at all levels are preserved in the in the village, making it a museum of Chinese culture and education.

### Getting there

Xiushui Village, Chaodong Town, Fuchuan Yao Autonomous County, Hezhou City, Guangxi Zhuang Autonomous Region. Nearest City: Nanning.
广西壮族自治区贺州市富川瑶族自治县朝东镇秀水村。
Take a train from Nanning Station(南宁站) to Hezhou Station(贺州站) (about 8 hours). .Take a bus from Hezhou Bus Station(贺州东站) to Fuchuan County(富川县) (RMB16 & 2 hours) and then another bus from Fuchuan County to Chaodong Town(朝东镇) (1/2 hour). From Chaodong Town you can take a remodeled "tractor taxi" to Xiushui Village (RMB10 & 5 mins).

Founded during the Tang Dynasty, Xiushui Village is located in the southeast of the Xiaohe Ancient Track (潇贺古道). It is in a region bordering Guangdong Province, Hunan Province and Guangxi Autonomous Region. With its back against Southwest China and with Guangdong Province, Hong Kong, Macao and Southeast Asia to its south, Xiushui Village is perfectly situated in the middle of the Huzhou-Guilin tourist zone.

Xiushui Village is actually an area consisting of four natural villages, namely Shuilou Village, Anfu Village, Bafang Village, and Shiyu Village. It is famous for possessing the largest ancient residential cluster of the Ming and Qing Dynasties in all of China, with popular tourist attractions like the Temple of No. 1 Scholar (状元庙), the Tree of Love (心心相印树), Mao Family Ancestral Hall (毛氏宗祠), and the Rusifu Theatre (如斯夫戏台). These old residences of the village are generally so unadorned that it is hard to imagine that generations of high-ranking officials used to live there. However, the unsophisticated beauty of the brilliantly curved eaves, the moss-covered wells, and the many horse tethering stones provide reminders of the prosperity this historic village once enjoyed.

A corner of Xiushui Village

Mao Family Ancestral Hall is the first building visitors will see upong entering the village. The building enshrines memorial tablets honouring ancient ancestors. In the main hall stands a tall statue of Mao Zizhi (a scholar who topped the imperial examinations) in a sitting posture, dressed in a red official suit and holding books in his hand. The pictures on the wall tell stories of how Mao Zizhi studied hard to receive the title of "No.1 Scholar" (状元) from the emperor. In the hall also stands a unique "No.1 Scholar Pavilion", featuring a carving of "two dragons playing with pearls" on the ridge in the middle of the roof. The four corners of the roof are curved towards the sky, resembling an eagle about to take fight, and implying that generations of talents in the village have soared their way to glory.

It is said that the gates of Mao Family Ancestral Hall and other scholars' houses are all 1.25 to 1.55 metres in width, which is exactly the width between two shafts of a carriage in the Qin and Han Dynasties. Even now, wheel-shaped stone drums and stones in the shape of a half-wheel can be found at both sides of some gates, and the frame and threshold of the gate resemble an ancient carriage. According to the Genealogy of the Mao Clan, such a design aims to remind descedants of the hardship endured by their ancestors in travelling here and building the village. Among all the gate houses, "Jimeifu" (吉美孚) stands out, exhibiting a westernised design that is considered rare in Fuchuan County. The vaulted roof is not covered by any tiles, and the wall is covered by white and grey papers.

An archaistic archway named "Flat Expanse" (坦川) stands at the front of the bridge before the Celestial Mother Temple (仙娘庙). Behind the archway lies Celestial Mother Well (仙娘井), which is shaped like a full moon. With crystal-clear water, it apparently never runs dry nor overflows. The temple beside the well was built to commemorate the female ancestor Lady Huang, a heroine whom by legend led an insurgent group to fight against bandits. Opposite to the temple is the elegant Tachuan Theatre (塔川庙戏台), featuring vivid and lifelike carvings of a dragon's head and lion's body and a colour painting of "The Eight Immortals Crossing the Sea.".

Built in the Kaiyuan era of the Tang Dynasty (712-756), Xiushui Village has a history of more than 1300 years. The first settler Mao Zhong was a second-degree scholar who was was appointed prefectural governor of Hezhou City.

## XIUFENG RESTAURANT

Xiufeng Restaurant (秀峰饭店) at the entrance of Shiyu Village provides rural food with similar spicy flavours to Hunan cuisine, and with options for all budgets. Specialties include dried pork (腊味) and wild vegetables (野菜).

Subsequently, Xiushui Village produced one "No. 1 Scholar" (during the Song Dynasty (960-1279) and twenty-six second-degree scholars Apparently, the reason Xiushui Village has brought up so many scholars lies partly in the Xiaohe Ancient Track (潇贺古道), which not only facilitated trade and logistics of goods but also enhanced the exchange of information and personnel. This allowed outside scholars to teach inside the village and local villagers to venture to the outside world to pursue studies, take examinations, take official positions and conduct businesses.

A "convex-shaped" theatre (凸”字形古戏台) opposite Mao Ancestral Hall stands in the shadow of a hundred-year-old camphor tree. On traditional festivals such as Spring Festival, the second day of the eighth month of the lunar calendar and the eighth day of the ninth month of the lunar calendar, grand operas such as Gui Opera (桂剧) and Caidiao Opera (彩调剧) are performed on this ancient stage. The eighth day of the ninth month of lunar calendar is the birthday of their oldest ancestor. On this day, performances are held all night long, and festivities continue from nightfall to dawn.

A range of grey mountains lie in the distant northeast outside the village. Against the setting sun and misty sky, they are said to look like a giant lying on his back. Villagers with the surname "Mao" (毛) believe they are from the same clan as the Mao family in Shaoshan in Xiangtan City, Hunan Province, the birthplace of Mao Zedong. Apparently, the ancient bridge on the Xiaohe Ancient Track suddenly collapsed the night before Mao Zedong passed away, adding a touch of intrigue to this legendary village.

# Gaoshan Village

## Ancestral Hall Culture in Guangxi

Walking along ancient paved lanes; taking in the aroma of rural cooking mixed with the special fragrance of burnt straw and the sound of crowing cocks and barking dogs – visiting Gaoshan Village is like taking a trip to a moment in history when people lived a simple, primitive life unencumbered by the everyday stresses of the modern world.

### Getting there

Gaoshan Village, Community Committee of North Yulin District, Yulin City, Guangxi Autonomous Region..
Nearest City: Nanning City .
广西壮族自治区玉林市玉州区城北街道办事处高山村。
Take a train from Nanning Station(南宁站) to Yulin Station(玉林站) (about 3 hours) and then transfer to Yulin North Coach Station(玉林城北汽车站) (1 hour). Take a bus bound for Xiaoping Shan County(小平山乡), and get off at Gaoshan Village ( about 1.5 hours).

Built in the Tianshun era of the Ming Dyasty (1457-1464), Gaoshan Village has a history of 600 years. With Darong Mountain to the north, Jinma Mountain and Wenbi Mountains to the east, Hanshan Mountain to the west and Qingwan River to the south, it is situated 5 km north of Yulin City. Even though it is not high above sea level, the village is named "Gaoshan" (meaning "high mountain") because it has never been flooded. The village is a historical and cultural tourist destination and its main draws are equally its large cluster of ancient buildings, long history of academic culture and beautiful rural scenery.

Gaoshan Village has a rich cluster of architectures representative of the ancestral hall culture of Guangdong and Guangxi Provinces. The village still features 13 ancient ancestral halls from the Ming and Qing Dynasties, 60 ancient residences, 150 buildings, nine ancient fire-brick lanes, and other ancient architectures such as wells, stages, stone tablets and ramparts. Most of these structures are perfectly preserved.

Ancient residential buildings in Gaoshan Village

Ancient buildings in the village usually have outer walls made of grey bricks, inner walls pasted by lime and containthree, four or five courtyards. The "ladder-like wooden doors" (推笼) unique to Guangdong and Guangxi and screens combining feng shui, aesthetic and ethical functions can be found almost in very house. The murals, wood and stone carvings and clay figures inside the houses are exquisite and lifelike. All interior structures, decorating patterns and scrolls in the houses articulate advocacy of ancestry, feudal ethics and scholarly honors and also embody the wish for fortune, prosperity, longevity and flourishing families.

The layout of Gaoshan Village is comb-like, which is commonly seen in Guangdong and Guangxi Provinces. Single houses are rare; most houses, facing south or east, are neatly and scientifically built in lines and connected to each other by lanes. A house is built around an axis, which represents a family, and the courtyard represents the extended family. Such a design demonstrates the Chinese tradition of having extended families living under the one roof.. The seven big clans in the village are the Mou (牟), Li, (李), Chen (陈), Zhong (钟), Feng (冯), Zhu (朱) and Yi (易) clans.

The Mansion of Scholar Li Bamou (李拔谋进士第) and the Former Residence of Mou Rizhu (牟日铢故居), both of which face east, feature tall main buildings, deep courtyards and densely-built rooms. The front parts of the houses are spacious and interspersed by delicate screens.

The deep and narrow Qingyun Lane

The gate of Mou Shaode Ancestral Hall

There are usually two or three courtyards, and each courtyard comprises a hall, rooms, wing-rooms and side-rooms. The upper hall was the place where the patriarchs of the family discuss events and worship ancestors. The middle hall was used as an office, and the side hall was used for receiving guests. The upstairs hall acted as a well-stocked study and the wing-rooms were where family members lived.

Throughout history, great importance has been attached to education and learning in Gaoshan Village, and generations of famous talents have been cultivated here. As such, Gaoshan Village is yet another "Village of Scholars". A school named "Dutuibo" (独堆坡书房) was established in the village in 1574, and after that each clan raced to open their own private schools, primary schools and advanced schools. By the end of the Qing Dynasty there were 15 schools in the village.

To the east of Gaoshan Village there is a tourist zone with an eco-agriculture theme, (农业观光体验区) comprising a thousand-metre-long corridor of fruit and vegetables, gardens of flowers and bonsai, a rural barbecue area and public bathing spot.

## PERFECT DAY

It is worth allowing A full day to visit all the ancient buildings in Gaoshan Village. The village folk song troupe (高山村山歌队) gives regular performances and there are also some other cultural activities like on-the-spot paper-cutting and tea-making.

# 中原古村
# Central Plains
## Stockades, Temples and Dragons

# Luotian Village

## Ancient Village with Graceful Gardens

Located on an ancient commercial route connecting the counties of Anyi, Yongxiu, and Wanbu with Nanchang, Luotian Village was a flourishing market town that was also once a key stop on the pilgrimage route from Jiujiang, Yongxiu and Anyi to Wanshou Palace in the Western Mountain (Xishan).

### Getting there

Luotian Village, Shibi Town, Anyi County, Nanchang City, Jiangxi Province.
Nearest City:Nanchang.
江西省南昌市安义县石鼻镇罗田村。
From Nanchang's Hongcheng Market Bus Station (洪城大市场汽车站) take a bus heading to Anyi County(安义县) and get off at Wanbu Town(万埠镇) (about 1.5hours). From Wanbu Town your best option is to take a taxi onto Luotian Village (罗田村) (about 16km).

Luotian Village has a history of more than 1,120 years. It was founded when Huang Kechang from Luotian County escaped here during wartime and decided to name the place after his hometown. The village has four gates and is divided into 10 parts along family clan lines. Its delicate residences, simple but elegant brick, stone and wood carvings and ancient stone streets are still clearly visible today. The sub-street drainage system is also still the same one built by the village's ancestors.

Three metres wide and over 400 metres long, Luotian Village's well-preserved ancient main street was built with a deep sewer. During the village's golden age, there were over one hundred businesses in the street, such as wineries, pharmacies, gold and silver shops, pawn shops, oil shops and candle shops. Anyi Kaipa (安义楷杷), a Luotian Village delicacy made from loquat fruit, is a yummy and inexpensive local snack. However, visitors may notice that the guards, merchants and folk art performers in the village are mostly children and the elderly, as locals of working age generally tend to work outside the village.

Particularly famous sites along the main street include the Jiang Family Forge (江氏铁匠铺), the oil and noodle stores of the Du family (杜家油面店) and the Huang Family Mill (黄家磨坊). The well-preserved Shidafu Grand Residence (世大夫第) was built by wealthy merchant Huang Xiuwen in 1762. The residence is half-timbered, with "horse-head" fire walls on both sides and various styles of courtyards. Inside this grand complex, visitors can find four lanes, schools, rooms for servants, ancestor-

## TANG TREE

Outside the village stands a thousand-year-old camphor tree planted back in the Tang Dynasty by ancestor Huang Kechang. The tree is the largest and the oldest camphor in Nanchang County, and it would take six people to encircle its vast girth.

Front Street

worshipping halls and dining halls in each house, beautifully built in the typical layout of villages in the Jiangnan area.

Shidafu Grand Residence was a private little world, functional and dainty and with a dining hall covering over 200 square metres, a private school for descendants, stock houses, rooms for servants, rice milling rooms, feed lots, drying yards and so on. The central hall is called Qixu Hall (启绪堂), connecting Xuyi Hall (叙彝堂) and Xuanhua Hall (宣化堂) on the left. On the wooden windows of the back hall there is a carving of 100 bats, called"Hundred-Bat Picture". The bats are vividly realised in various shapes.

Luotian Village is also known as "Longevity Village" (长寿村) and boasts 10 ancient wells. Situated at the southern end of Shidafu Grand Residence is Shoulkang Well (寿康井) which means "long life and health". Over 12 metres deep, with a square mouth and constructed with stones in mortise-tenon connections, the well vividly shows the pictographic origins of the Chinese character "井" (well).

Shidafu Grand Residence

# Liukeng Village

## A Village for the Ages

Surrounded by mountains and streams, Liukeng Village is equally well endowed with peaceful cobblestone lanes, simple yet elegant Ming and Qing Dynasty architectures and wood carvings and marvellous works by famous calligraphers and painters.

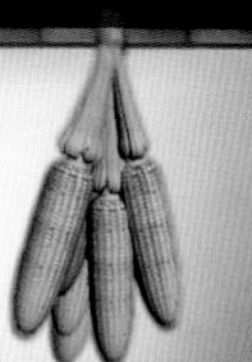

### Getting there

Liukeng Village, Niutian Town, Le'an County, Fuzhou City, Jiangxi Province..
Nearest City: Nanchang./
江西省抚州市乐安县牛田镇流坑村
Take a bus from Nanchang Long-Distance Bus Station(南昌长途汽车站) to Le'an County Station(乐安县新车站) (2hours). From Le'an County it takes one hour to Liukeng Village by regular bus, with services at 8:40 and 15:00 everyday (RMB30).

Liukeng Village is located at the transition zone from the mountains to the low hills of west Le'an County. Established during the latter years of the Tang Dynasty of the Five Dynasties and Ten Kingdoms period (923-937), the village is famous for its splendid traditional architecture and unique layout.

In the middle of the Ming Dynasty, villagers of Liukeng laid seven streets in an east-west direction and one in a south-north direction. Clansmen lived in different streets according to their relationships and set gate towers in the lanes. Walls were built between each tower to connect them. There are more than 260 ancient buildings and structures in the village which date back to the Ming and Qing Dynasties, including studies, memorial arches, wells, pavilions, wharves, old bridges and towers. Historical higlights include Shuishen

Scenery of Liukeng Village

## SPRING FESTIVAL

A good time to visit Liukeng Village is during the period from the second day to the 15th day of the first lunar month (late January or early February), as the village will feature many unique folk activities like Nuo Dance (傩舞), the Heyang Lantern Show (何杨灯会), Bodhisattva Parade (游菩萨) and so on.

Shanhu Residence (水绅山笏宅), Zhenjun Pavilion (真君阁), Yangshan Temple Grand Theater (仰山庙大戏台), Zhenqing Tomb (振卿公墓), Dong Fanchang Couple Tomb (蕃昌夫妇合葬墓), and Huanzhong Ancestral Temple (环中公祠).

Most ancient buildings in the village are simple half-timbered houses with two doors and one patio. Villagers paid much attention to building decorations, including exquisitely rendered wood, brick and stone carvings and colourful ink paintings. Masterpieces include the Ming Dynasty-style mural painting and brick carving of "Sparrow, Deer, Bee, Monkey" in Huaide Hall, representing nobility and fortune, because of their similar pronunciations in Chinese. Another highlight is the carving of "Qilin Looking at the Sun", engraved on the screen wall facing the gate of Yongxiang Hall (永享堂). In addition, there are 682 tablets spread among the various halls and hundreds of couplets adorning the village's many doors.

Built in the latter years of the Ming Dynasty, the residence of Dong Sui (董隧故居0, a famous official and master of Neo-Confucianism, is situated in the middle of Central Lane (中巷) and forms an architectural complex of 18 residences. Another interesting attraction is the rectangular Dabin Grand House (大宾第) located at the crossing of West Central Lane and Shashang Lane (沙上巷), which is a building complex known as "a village inside a village".

Many private schools were founded in the village from the early years of the Song Dynasty to the end of

Liukeng is famous for its magnificent traditional architectures and unique village layout.

the Qing Dynasty. During imperial times, the village produced a "number one scholar" (ie. zhangyuan) in arts and one in martial arts, as well as 34 jinshi and 78 juren. Five memorial arches were built in 1034, the first year of Emperor Songrenzong's reign in the Jingyou period, to commend five members of the Dong family for their success in the imperial examinations. Though nowadays only footstones remain, there are many other testaments in the village to the honours of the past.

Built in 1164, the second year of Emperor Xiaozong's reign in the Longxing period of the Southern Song Dynasty, Zhuangyuan Building 状元楼) stands beside Qipan Street (棋盘街) on the west bank of Dragon Lake (龙湖), the highest point of the village. It was built as a two-layer half-timbered construction to memorialise the number one scholar of that year, local hero Dong Deyuan. Above the lintel of the door is a tablet with Chinese words for "Zhuangyuan Building" written by famous Confucian scholar Zhu Xi. The spot in front of the tablet offers stunning views of misty Donghua and Meiling Mountains in the distance and a lake reflecting the tall old trees and houses of the village.

Hanlin Building (翰林楼) is situated at the east exit of Xianbo Lane (贤伯巷). The top of the building offers views of Wujiang River in the front and clusters of ancient residences at the back. It was built to protect the village and to commemorate Dong Yan, an official of the Hanlin and Imperial Academies of the Ming Dynasty.

Liukeng Village is regarded by many as an embodiment of Chinese feudal society. Various family trees are preserved in the village's 58 temples. There are three family trees from the 10th year of the Wanli period of the Ming Dynasty (1581) and over 20 family trees dating back to the Qing Dynasty. In the Big Ancestral Hall (大宗祠), which is known as the "Old Summer Palace" of Liukeng Village, visitors can see five granite columns of 8 metres in height and 0.7 metres in diameter. Wudang Pavilion (武当阁), built in the Ming Dynasty, is located at the point where the various streams of Liukeng Village converge, about 1 km north of the village. It is a complex building dedicated to Taoist, Buddhist, and other deities in a single temple. Tuntian Temple (屯田公祠) was built during the reign of Emperor Kangxi in the Qing Dynasty (1661-1722) and is the largest well-preserved temple in the village. With many imposing stone columns, the temple looks solemn and dignified.

# Tianbao Village

## Boat-shaped "heavenly treasure"

Established during the Tang Dynasty, Tianbao Village (literally "Heavenly Treasure Village") is situated 23 km north of Yifeng County. Shaped llke a boat, the village is surrounded by mountains and a natural moat.

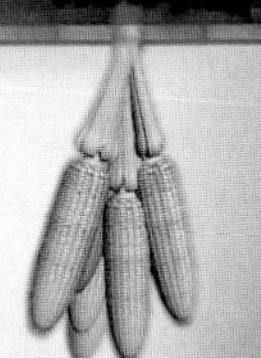

### Getting there

Tianbao Village, Yifeng County, Yichun City, Jiangxi Province..
Nearest City: Nanchang..
江西省宜春市宜丰县天宝乡天宝村。
From Nanchang Long-Distance Bus Station (南昌长途汽车站)take a non-stop bus to Yifeng County (宜丰县) (3 hours), and then continue to Tianbao Village in Yifeng County by taxi (1/2 hour).



Tianbao Village is surrounded by a 2500-metre-long moat which flows east to west and courses through the nearby mountains. West of the village is Tengjiang River, and in the north stands the magnificent relics of its 1490-metre-long ancient city walls. Inside the village, there are 170 well-preserved Ming and Qing Dynasty-style residences, 48 lanes and various small ditches forming a network for traffic, drinking water and washing.

Upon entering the village, visitors will be met with an evocative scene of old camphor trees and ancient buildings, a reflection of its past prosperity. The traditional buildings include temples, pavilions, official halls, folk houses, memorial arches, pagodas and monasteries . The exterior walls of these buildings are made in a "mountain" style (风火山墙), while the insides feature wooden structures with a column and tile construction or lifting beam, or both. The buildings are rich with wood, stone and brick carvings and all kinds of decorated doors, windows, gate towers and stone blocks, a testimony to the ingenious designs of the village' s ancient architects.

Season Temple

In the ancient residences, the front doors are constructed in the styles of "mendang" (门当) and "hudui" (户对).Mendang refers to wood or brick carvings on the door lintel or on either sides of it, parallel to the ground and vertical to the lintel. This symbolises the wish of families to continuously give birth to boys. Hudui refers to a pair of drum-shaped stone blocks at the door, which are believed to be able to deter evil spirits. There are two kinds — the round one is for officials and the square one is for officers. According to ancient Chinese architectural aesthetics, a residence with a hudui must also have a mendang. As such, the two terms are often used together, and "Mendang Hudui" eventually became a common term used to describe a marriage which was regarded as a "good match".

Season Temple (四季公祠) is the largest and the best-preserved temple in the village. It was built in 1585 by Liu Jizhao from the sixth generation of the Liu family. The temple has a well-designed shallow courtyard in an official-hat shape, which prevents water from gathering in the yard. There are five pictures in the temple which exhibit the ancient ideals of "studying hard", "five sons passing imperial examinations", "two phoenixes flying to the sun" (representing a peaceful life, hopes and dreams), "unicorn delivering child" and a pine crane (symbolising longevity).

Once grand and magnificent, the Liu Family Ancestral Hall (刘氏大宗祠) now only has a decorated archway with beam made by wood without any iron nails. Baoben Hall (报本堂) is the place for worshipping the ancestors of the Liu family. It is said that one could "rise step by step in life" (步步高升) by walking up the stairs of this hall.

Peigen Vocational School (培根职业学校)is the very first modern vocational school in Jiangxi Province. It is a western style building built in 1919 by Liu Huacheng, who was the first of the Liu family to be influenced by the "May Fourth" movement which called for modernisation.

Baoben Hall

Of the 48 ancient wells in Tianbao Village, 36 are still in use. Yuanbao Well (元宝井0, with its sweet and clear water, is said to be able to make its drinkers come first in exams. The village also boasts what is known as the "Green Treasures" – 46 ancient trees, each with a girth diameter of over 2 metres. Throughout history, Tianbao Village is said to have given birth to 10 jinshi (third-degree scholars) and 76 juren (second-degree scholars).

## VILLAGE OF HOTTIES

Since ancient times, the girls of Tianbao Village have always been recognised as great beauties, giving rise to the saying: "Wanzai is famous for firecrackers, Liuyang for umbrellas and Tianbao for girls" (万载的爆竹浏阳的伞，天宝的妹子不用拣).

# Jiajia Village

## Village of Officials

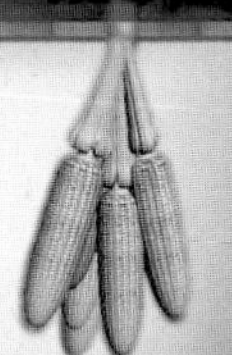

With its pleasant rural scenery, beautiful Luquan Lake and comely hot spring villas, Jiajia Village is a great place for relaxation which also boasts an impressive collection of ancient architectural complexes .



### Getting there

Jiajia Village, Xinjie Town, GaoAn, Yichun, Jiangxi.
Nearest City: Nanchang City.
江西省宜春市高安市新街镇贾家村。
Take a bus from Nanchang Long-Distance Bus Station(南昌长途汽车站) to Gaoan City (高安市)(2 hours). From Gaoan City there are many bus routes heading to Huibu town(灰埠镇)(40 mins), and then take a taxi to Jiajia village (about 15mins).

Built during the Song Dynasty, Jiajia Village (literally "Jia Family Village") is one of the most well-preserved classical Jiangnan-style (south of the Yangtze River) ancient village architectural complexes. The lanes in the village are paved by green stones and run between more than 300 ancient residences, of which around 140 date back to the end of the Yuan Dynasty and the beginning of the Ming Dynasty. The residences can be grouped into ancestral halls, rain pavilions, main halls, wardrooms, parlours and dwellings. There are also 18 academies for classical learning, nunneries, temples and Taoist temples. In the south of the village is the Seven-Storey Jade Tower (七级玉塔) a symbol of the cultural prosperity once enjoyed by the Jia family in the Sheshan area. The inside of the village features an abundance of sculptures, paintings and calligraphy artworks, while the outside offers beautiful pastoral sceneries.

The village's architectural complex and gardens are divided into two main areas: "inside the pass" and "outside of the pass". Three of the nine original pass gates are still in use today. In the event of an emergency, the villagers will lock the gates, making it difficult for outsiders to enter the village. Within the pass gates, the criss-crossing green stone streets and lanes make the village resemble a giant maze.

On the right side of the village gate is a palace built onto a mound, known as the "dragon vein" (龙脉). Since ancient times, families with newborn babies would deposit soil here to wish for good fortune, and over the years this became a mound. The villagers' faith was apparently not misplaced: during the Ming and Qing Dynasties, Jiajia Village produced more than 140 scholars.

There are still many classical learning academies in the village. The four best preserved ones are Mingyuexuan

Village gate

Village dwellings

Academy (明月轩书院), Wanyuexuan Academy (皖月轩书院), Helu Academy (鹤鹿书院) and Wenchang Academy (文昌书院).

Happy Love Hall (怡爱堂) is the oldest residence in the village. A dual-channel archway is built in a crescent moon style, while shrines for family tablets beside the stack door reflect architectural styles from both the Ming and Yuan Dynasties. The village was initially established by Jia Jiliang, the owner of Happy Love Hall. During the second generation of Jiajia Village, the number of high officials reached a peak, giving the village the reputation of "Village of Officials", a moniker which has stuck over the succeeding centuries. The wardrooms were built as courier stations for nearby officials and it was also the local government office. Cifu Hall (赐福堂), which was built at the beginning of the Qing Dynasty, offers the most typical wardroom architecture with its Confucian idea of placing more emphasis on the inside as opposed to the outside. In the courtyard, four Chinese characters which are translated to say blessing (福), emolument (禄), longevity (寿) and luck (喜), are carved into the green bricks. The hall also features wood and stone carvings using the techniques of round cutting, empty carving and high relief. The gables are all built with 1.5 metre granite bars, which are stable and help make the building intruder-proof. The gables and back walls have many auspicious stone inscriptions and decorations including deer, phoenixes, bats, the "Eight Diagrams" (八卦) and so forth.

In the incense-wreathed room of the gorgeous mansion of Jia Xin hangs a large portrait painting and biography of this illustratious official. The smooth tiles inside the rooms are still in good condition, making it hard to believe that they have been in place for hundreds of years.

The Jia Family Clan Hall (贾氏宗祠) is located in the centre of the village. It is built in the Sijin-style (四进, which literally means "four entances") architecture, with the Rain Pavilion (雨亭), Worship Pavilion (拜亭), Bedroom (寝宫) and Guanyin Hall (观音堂) located on the north-south axis. This symmetrical design principle is seldom seen in the clan halls of the Jiangnan area. The hall was built more than 100 years earlier than the time Matteo Ricci from Italy introduced the principles of geometry to China. In the past, clan halls were used as important places for discussion, or giving out rewards or punishments in the village. Nowadays, they are used for announcing village rules and for holding celebrations. Village officials and merchants who live outside of the village will return home each year for the Qingming ("Tomb Sweeping") Festival and gather in the clan hall, talk with locals and describe the splendid world outside the village to them.

Jiajia Village's religious legacy combines Confucianism, Buddhism and Taoism. There are many temples and old pagodas in and around this ancient village. In the south of the village there is the Seven-Storey Pagoda (七级浮塔), Xiannong Temple (先农庙) and a bamboo forest.

Panoramic view of Jiajia village

## PAWN SHOP

The village's former pawn shop (当铺) has a unique architectural style. Every window is on the roof, which was considered most convenient for scrutinising pledges. In the past, the pawn shop's door frame and roof were embedded with golden embroidery. The front courtyard has no drain, because the pawn shop owner hoped his wealth would never “flow away”.

# Meipi Village

## Village of Movies

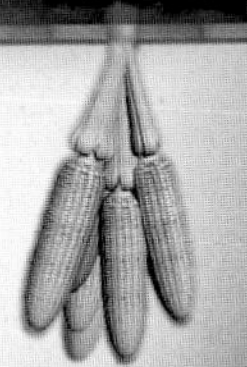

Located beside beautiful Fushui River, Meipi Village is a mysterious ancient village renowned for its proud history, classical building complex and amazing sculptures and artworks from the Ming and Qing Dynasties.

### Getting there

Meipi Village, Wenpi Town, Qingyuan District, Ji'An City, Jiangxi Province.
Nearest City: Nanchang City..
江西省吉安市青原区文陂乡渼陂村。
Take a high-speed train from Nanchang Station(南昌站) to Ji'An Station(吉安站) (RMB40 & 2hours). Transfer to a service to Qingyuan Bus Station(青原汽车站) (about 1.5hours), and then take another bus to Meipi village ( RMB30 & 1/2hour).

Meipi Village dates back more than 1,000 years to the early years of the Later Tang Dynasty (923-927). Almost all of its residents share the family name Liang (梁). The village has preserved 367 ancient residences, four academies of classical learning, one old pavilion, four archways and more than 20 old clan halls and temples. Lots of film directors have been attracted to Meipi Village by its grand architectural complexes, earning it the moniker "The Village of Movies".

Pitou Street (陂头古街) is the village's commercial street from the era of the Ming and Qing Dynasties. From Longevity Palace (万寿宫) and the granary (义仓) to Fushen Temple (福神庙), it is easy to imagine the bustling activities that once took place here. The street, with its 108 stores and 600-metre length, is also a key location for shooting historical Chinese TV dramas. The centre of the street is paved with green stones, while the sides are paved with cobbles. The houses, archways, plaques, couplets, pillars, walls, and even the calligraphy works from the Ming and Qing Dynasties which adorn them, are all well-preserved. Attractions along this street and its surrounding lanes include Jieshou Hall (节寿堂), Xiaoyou Hall (孝友堂), Mingqing Academy (明新书院), Jingde Academy (敬德书院), Sima Hall (司马第), Qigong Clan Hall (启公祠), Hongqing Hall (洪庆堂) and so forth.

Hanlin Mansion (翰林第) covers an area of 1,200 square metres and has 37 maroon-coloured stone pillars. On each of the pillars there is a couplet, and each of the couplets start with the Chinese characters "Yong Mu" (永慕, "perpetual yearning") thus giving it the nickname "Yongmu Hall".

There are two 600-year-old camphor trees called "Couple Trees" beside Hanlin Mansion. According to local legend, the two trees looked to be withering at the beginning of the last century. However, during the revolutionary period,

Guomindang executioner Zhang Huizan was caught and executed here by the revolutionary army and his head was hung on the branches of the right camphor tree. It is said that the trees began to revive after this.

Longevity Hall (万寿宫) is now a primary school. The plaques on the archways on both sides are inscribed with Chinese characters which read "No night" (天不夜) and "Bright forever moon" (月常明).

On the ceilings of Qiuzhi Hall (求志堂) are two amazing pictures called "Hundreds of the Young" (百少图) and "Hundreds of the Old" (百老图), which feature, respectively, 100 young persons and 100 old men, each portraying a different posture and expression.

The village also features the former residences of famous figures such as Mao Zedong, Zhu De, Peng Dehuang, Huang Gonglve, Zeng Shan, and Mao Zetan. The slogans written by the Red Army during its revolutionary days in Meipi Village can still be seen on the walls of many buildings.

There are several memorial arches in Meipi Village, such as the village gate's "Old Locust" Mansion Archway (古槐第牌坊), the archway-style "More Options" screen wall (多留余地), and the two "Chastity Archways" (处贞节坊) representing a mother and a daughter. Two filial piety Festival Halls (节孝祠) are situated at the back of each Chastity Archway. Apparently the daughter died before she got married, so her archway was closed and filled with bricks. The Chinese characters 冰清玉洁 on the top of the archway mean "as clean as ice and as pure as jade".

Meipi Village's 28 ponds symbolise that the village is guarded by 28 stars in the sky. The water channels under each pond are connected with each other and the water levels of each pond would automatically adjust in different seasons.

Locals of Meipi Village celebrate two Lantern Festivals. One is on the 15th day of the first month of the lunar calendar (early February), while the other is on the first day of the second month (late Febr)uary or early March). During the festivals, the Dragon Dance will be put on.

### MONKEY AND PALS

The Caiqing Show (彩擎表演) is a unique tradition in which the children of Meipi village play roles from the Chinese classic Journey to the West, such as The Monkey King, Sun Wukong (孙悟空); Pig, Zhu Bajie (猪八戒); and disaster-prone pilgrim Tang-Sanzang (唐三藏).

Wenchang Pavilion

# Pixia Village

## Red Village Under the Camphor Tree

Hidden among old camphor trees and with the beautiful Fushui River flowing by, Pixia Village has an air of mystery about it. To the east is a camphor tree which has another umbrella-shaped tree growing inside of it. According to villagers, this unusual tree resembles a pretty girl standing on her husband's shoulder, looking into the distance and showing off her beauty.

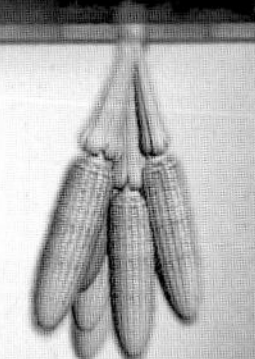

### Getting there

Pixia Village, Futian Town, Qingyuan District, Ji'An City, Jiangxi province . Nearest City: Nanchang..
江西省吉安市青原区富田镇陂下村。
Take a high-speed train from Nanchang Station(南昌站) to Ji'An Station(吉安站) (RMB40, about 2hours). From Ji'an Station (吉安站)it is a 5 minute walk to Qingyuan Bus Station(青原汽车站), from where you can take another bus to Futian Town(富田镇) (about 2 hours), and then walk 10mins to Pixia Village.

Established during the Tang Dynasty, Pixia Village is located on the west shore of Fushui River and has a history of more than 1,000 years. Ninety percent of the villagers have the surname Hu (胡). Today there remain 36 well-preserved ancestral halls, four archways and 18 old wells, among which Nanming Well (南明井) is considered the most distinctive. Old camphor trees grow abundantly inside and outside of the village.

Pixia Old Street (陂下古街) has a length of about 100 metres and was laid down 180 years ago in the Qing Dynasty. Dye houses, grocery stores, wine shops and medicine stores occupy either sides of the once-properous street. Anren

Dragon Dance

Pavilion (安人亭) was built at around the same time. This loft-like pavilion was constructed by villager Hu Shaoting for the homeless and poor widows and orphans. According to local tradition, to ensure their future security, Hu families must walk across Anren Pavilion when holding weddings or funerals. This custom continues today.

Although now dominated by the Hu family, Pixia Village was once a multi-surname village. In the early days, each family with the same surname would build its own closed lanes. Occasional neighbourly tensions are implied by the bullet holes in the walls of some of the houses. As the population increased, the entire village was closed off with walls, leaving only four gates: "Welcome Dragon" Gate (迎龙门), "Morning" Gate (朝天门), "Long Fortune" Gate (延福门) and "Dragon River" Gate (龙川阁).

Hu Huang, the Hu family ancestor, has a plaque dedicated to him from Emperor Renzong of the Song Dynasty as praise for his outstanding military exploits. Emperor Daoguang of the Qing Dynasty also wrote a plaque in Hu's honour, and this plaque can still be seen on the Welcome Dragon Gate.

Built during the Wanli period of the Ming Dynasty, Dunren Hall (敦仁堂) is the clan hall of the Hu family in Pixia Village. The hall has significant Red Army associations. Deng Xiaoping arrived here in the spring of 1930 to spread the army's revolutionary message. Between the 22nd and 27th of March that year, Mao Zedong also held a conference inside this clan hall. A Red Army school was opened in the back part of this building and Red Army supremo Zhu De even stayed here to impart his military knowledge to the men of the Red Army.

Many other sites in the village also have a historical Red Army association , such as Zhuyin Hall (竹隐堂), Zhisheng Hall (志笙堂), Tanbin Hall (潭滨堂), Pixia Academy (陂下书院) and Lenin Platform (列宁台). Several battle trenches can still be seen inside the village and the slogans of the Red Army on the walls can still be made out.

## NEW LANTERN FESTIVAL

The "New Lantern Festival" (下元宵) was first held in Pixia Village on 24 February 2009 and includes dragon dance, lion dance, and "lanterns on the river" (放河灯) which is rare in China. Meanwhile the "Calling the Boat" (喊船) activity, which involves hundreds of villagers, has a history of 1,000 years and is a unique custom to Jiangxi Province.

Former address of the Soviet Government in southwest Jiangxi Province

Grand old architecture

# Yanfang Village

## "Trees Inside Village, Village Inside Trees"

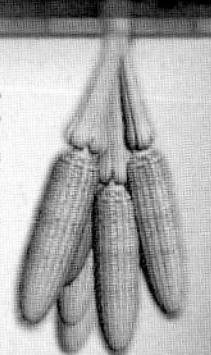

Peaceful Yanfang Village is situated beside Ganjiang River. With few tourist crowds, visitors can take leisurely strolls along its ancient streets and enjoy the village's unspoiled charm, from the beautiful rural scenery, ancient buildings and vines on old brick walls to the tangled weeds on the ground and the duckweed floating on the ponds.

### Getting there

Yanfang Village, West Bank of Ganjiang River, Jishui county, Ji′ An, Jiangxi..
Nearest City: Nanchang..
江西省吉安市吉水县赣江西岸
Take a high-speed train from Nanchang Station(南昌站) to Ji'An Station(吉安站) (RMB40, about 2hours). From Ji'An Station (吉安站) walk about 5minutes to Qingyyuan Bus Station(青原汽车站)), and take a bus to Jishui County(吉水县)(RMB 7, 1/2 hour). Upon arrival in Jishui County, take a #2 bus and get off after passing the Jishui bridge(吉水大桥), then take a taxi on to Yanfang Village (about 10mins).

### LOOKS FAMILIAR?

Shuimu Qinghua Archway ("水木清华") in Yanfang Village is nearly identical to the one in Beijing's famous Qinghua University, though the former is 50 years older.

Founded in the middle of the Southern Song Dynasty, Yanfang VIllage contains over 160 clan halls, academies and dwellings from the Ming and Qing Dynasties. Nearly a thousand luxuriantly green camphor trees extend from the beginning of the village to its end. The style of residences in Yanfang Village is the typical Luling (庐陵) dwelling style, which can be further divided into single buildings and complexes. The single buildings include Dafu Mansion (大夫第) and Zhou Sima Mansion (州司马第), while the complexes include "Twenty Ridgepole Compound" (二十栋大院), Zizheng Mansion (资政第) and Linfeng Courtyard (麟凤院).

The village's red stone lintels feature carvings of people, stories, flowers, couplets and calligraphy. Unusually, the old residences of Yanfang Village have no open inner courtyards. Instead, villagers installed what are known as "sky eyes" (天眼) on the roofs to provide lighting and ventilation.

Clan halls are the most important public buildings in Yanfang Village. The Yan (鄢), Wang (王) and Rao (饶) families each have their own family clan halls. In front of the large Wang family clan hall (三槐第) there is s a 22-metre screen wall. Old archways are another feature of Yanfang Village. Some of the 19 well-preserved archways feature exquisite reliefs, while others are connected with a linked courtyard. The sculptures are usually concerned with people and their stories, auspicious animals, precious plants and rare birds.

Yanfang Village is also abundant in officials' mansions such as Zhou Sima Mansion, Dafu Mansion and Zizheng Mansion. During the Ming Dynasty, many officials in the royal courty came from Jiangxi Province, prompting the saying: "Half of the officials come from Jiangxi". This reputation actually encouraged villagers to purchase more official positions (a custom which was accepted in ancient China).

# Bailu Village

## Madam Wang's Village

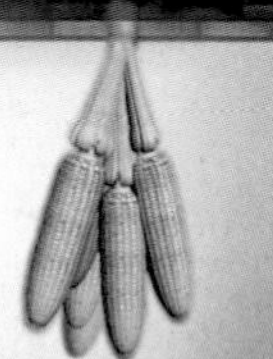

Baílu Village boasts the first and only female ancestral temple dedicated to a woman in China. Sitting beside a mountain and along the Luxi stream, the village is shaped like a crescent moon.

### Getting there

Bailu Village, Gan Town, Ganzhou City, Jiangxi Province..
Nearest City: Ganzhou.
江西省赣州市赣县白鹭乡白鹭村。
Take a train from Nanchang Station(南昌站) to Ganzhou Station(赣州站) (about 5hours). After arriving at Ganzhou Station, take a 1/2hour taxi ride to Ganzhou East Bus Station (赣州东汽车站)from where there are many buses heading to Bailu Village (about 1 hour).

Bailu Village is situated north of Gan County in the Hakka midland area, south of Jiangxi Province. The four main streets of the village form the Chinese character "丰" ("feng", which means "harvest"). With Longgang in the south, Wangping Mountain in the north and five foothills extending behind the village, this area is known as "Wulong Shanxing" (meaning "mountain shaped like five dragons").

Southern Jiangxi Province was the first stop in the migration of Hakka ancestors to the south and is regarded as the cradle of Hakka culture. Since the Southern Song Dynasty, almost the entire village has shared the same ancestor and hence the same family name – Zhong (钟). The village contains 69 exquisite gate towers and nearly 60,000 square metres of ancient architecture. Their gorgeous wood, stone and brick carving works reveal a rich folk culture.

While the ancient buildings of Bailu Village have eroded over time, much remains to be seen. Sanyuan Palace is now the hall of the township government. The first entrance is for the the main gate and the theatre stage (戏台), while the second leads to pavilions and the back entry to a Bodhisattva shrine (菩萨). Shizi Street (十字街) was formed in the first year of the reign of Emperor Hongzhi in the Ming Dynasty (1488). It was originally Bailu Village's old embankment but later became a residential area.

The most notable of the many clan halls in Bailu Village is the Clan Hall of Madam Wang (王太夫人祠). In ancient China a man's worth was thought to be superior to that of a woman, and so a clan hall featuring a woman's name is extremely rare. Madam Wang was the wife of minister Zhong Yuchang during the Qing Dynasty. Throughout her life she was involved in building many granaries to provide food for the less fortunate, so people built this hall in memory of her. The hall has two entrances and a wide courtyard. The grand "Bazi"gate tower (八字楼) is wider than all other gates in Bailu Village. The sculpture above the gate is especially exquisite and features a unicorn, tortoise, phoenix, bat, calabash and ganoderma. Upstairs was a granary for storing millet, while the downstairs was a school for the poor. During famines, this courtyard was used to make free porridge. It is no wonder that the Clan Hall of Madam Wang continues to be regarded as a holy place in the minds of many villagers to this day.

Located at the foot of the mountain west of Bailu Village, Huilie Clan Hall (恢烈公祠) is a colossal building which was built by Zhong Yuchang during the Qianlong period of the Qing Dynasty (1736-1795) and comprises three elegantly connected buildings. In addition to halls and pavilions, there are gardens and rockeries, though significant parts the building were destroyed by the army of Shi Dakai in the Qing Dynasty, with only the western wing preserved. Inside the first remaining buiding, Baozhong Hall (葆中堂) and the middle building Youyi Hall (友益堂) the passages and corridors are like a maze. In the courtyard there are two 300 year-old podocarpus trees. One is male and the other is female. The thick and strong male has only blossoms but no fruits, whereas the graceful female is has only fruits but no blossoms...

Shichang Hall (世昌堂) is the clan hall of the Zhong family. This building that stands today was rebuilt in the 1940s according to its original structure and position. The plaque above the main door is inscribed with Chinese characters for "Shichang Hall", while the plaque above the middle door is inscribed with the words "Clan Hall of the Zhong Family". In the broad square outside the building a carving of the "Eight Trigrams" of Taoist cosmology (Bagua) can still be seen.

Late Ming Dynasty Hongyu Hall (洪宇堂) is located on the left side of Shichang Hall and was a branch clan hall for the Zhong family. It is regarded as one of the more unique clan halls in all of China. There is a wooden archway in the south side with two huge wooden pillars holding up the structure while in the middle are two thick wooden gates. The ceiling is designed in the rare brackets and column style, which is commonly known as a wooden "bird's nest" (雀巢). The gate tower has colourful decorations and exquisite sculptures of flowers and auspicious birds.

Nowadays, Bailu Village is known as a repository of Hakka culture. The village's special Hakka dwellings and ethnic customs have attraction the attention of many domestic and foreign tourists and academics.

## HAKKA CUSTOMS

Many Hakka customs of southern Jiangxi Province can be experienced here, such as making sticky rice cakes (打黄元米果),"robbing the sedan" (抢打轿), and "burning the tile pagoda" (烧瓦塔).During the autumn harvest season there is a Taro Festival (芋头节), where locals will roast taro balls (烧芋头丸) and sample other dishes such as taro dumplings (芋包).

The dwellings and picturesque countryside scenery of Bailu Village

# Zhangdian Village

## Home Village of Zhang Liang

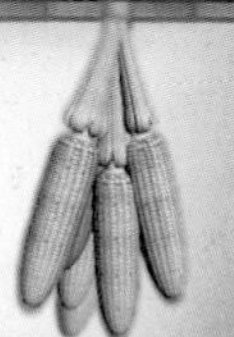

Stone tools unearthed from this area indicate that human activity existed here more than 5,000 years ago. This village was named "Zhangdian Village" after the legendary"Three Kingdoms" era strategist Zhang Liang, whose five generations of forefathers had served the Han state during the Era of Warring States.

### Getting there

Zhangdian village, Li Kou, Jia Town, Pingdingshan city, Henan province.
Nearest City: Luoyang
河南省平顶山市郏县李口乡张店村。
Take a train from Luoyang Station(洛阳站) to Pingdingshan Station(平顶山站) (about 2 hours). From Pingdingshan Long-Distance Bus Station (平顶山长途汽车站) there are direct bus routes to Zhangdian village (about 1hour).

### GODDESS STONE

On Zhangzhai hill (张寨山) there is a Goddess of Mercy Stone (观音石), which is supposedly where the Goddess Guanyin listened to Zhang Liang playing his flute, until the stone eventually took on her likeness.

Portait of Zhang Liang

Born during the Western Han Dynasty, Zhang Liang was instrumental in overthrowing the Qin Dynasty and developing the Han Dynasty.

Up to 80% of the villiagers in Zhangdian Village have Zhang (张) as their surname. The village has produced 12 governors, such as Governor Zhang Yueshun in the Ming Dynasty. A rock unearthed from the village contains an inscription from legendary strategist Zhuge Liang from the Three Kingdoms period, which was written as a dedication to the Temple of Zhang Liang, aka Liuhou Temple (留侯祠).

The main buildings in Zhangdian Village include the officer residences from the Ming Dynasty. Of these, Qing Xi Officer Residence (清西官宅) has 44 rooms, while Qing Xi Yousheng (清西酉盛) has 10, Qing Bei Yi He (清北义和) has 16, and Qing Hua Gate (清东官宅) has 12. Unfortunately, Zhuangdian Village has been struck by the effects of time. Its five gates and 15 gate towers no longer exist, and only fragments of the village walls remain. The Temple of Zhang Liang (Liuhou Temple has also been damaged.

As officer residences, the buildings of Zhangdian Village are magnificent and well-structured. Wood sculptures can be found in nearly 30 different spots and feature more than a thousand designs, such as "lion playing with silk ball", "24 examples of filial piety', "pine and crane deliver longevity", "the Four Immortals" and so forth. There are also nearly 400 brick and stone sculptures scattered throughout the village.

To the west of the village by the Zhi River there is a stretch of deep water called "Bathe Horse Lake" (滤马潭). This is said to be the place where Zhang Liang bathed his horse. The "Horse Running Valley" (跑马沟) is said to be the place where Zhang Liang trained his horse, while Noble's Horse Valley (侯马沟) is said to be the place he fed his horse!

# Linfeng Stockade

## Red Stone Stockade of the Central Plains

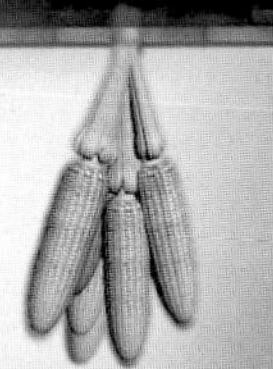

With red walls, a green moat, green reeds, white flowers and colourful birds, Linfeng Stockade is like a painting, earning it the reputation of "The First Red Stone Stockade of the Central Plains".



### Getting there

Lin Feng village, Tangjie Town, Jia County, Pingdingshan city, Henan province.
Nearest City: Zhengzhou.
河南省平顶山市郏县堂街镇临沣寨。
From Zhengzhou Long-distance Bus Station(郑州长途汽车站) there are many direct routes to Jia County (郏县) (2hours). After arriving at Jia County, you can take a taxi directly to Linfeng Village(临沣寨) (about 20mins).

Linfeng Stockade was built in the latter years of the Ming Dynasty and rebuilt in the first year of Emperor Tongzhi's reign in the Qing Dynasty (1862). Situated beside the North Ru River, the stockade is a typical low-lying ancient village surrounded by acres of reeds and bamboo. Lingfeng Village has more than 10 extant Ming and Qing Dynasty courtyards and more than 100 sites of ancient architecture, ancient walls, moats, gates, ancestral halls, temples, wells, bridges and tombs. Village highlights include the Ancient Village Museum and Zhu Zheng House.

The walls of Linfeng Stockade cover an area of about 70,000 square metres. Built from the pure-coloured redstone, the wall is about 1,100 metres in circumference, more than 6 metres in height and contains 800 battlements.

There are three gates in Linfeng Stockade, set in three directions according to Taoist bagua (the Eight Trigrams). The northwest door is called "Linfeng" because of the Linfeng River, which is also the source of the village' s name. On top of the gate hangs a redstone plaque with the Chinese characters for "Linfeng". Beneath, on the two elm packed, rusting metal doors the inscriptions "First Year of the Tongzhi Reign" (同治元年) and "The Year of Ren Xu" (岁

Ancient village walls and gates

在壬戌) - each indicating the year 1862 - are still legible.

Linfeng Stockade has a fire-preventing water tank on each gate, as well as gun holes set at various levels. Outside the gates there are flood gates and a hidden passage to drain water to the outside. These were well-designed and easy to use for both defense and attack. Beyond the village walls there is a 1,500-metre moat wrapped around the village. By the south gate, Feng River joins the moat, which nicely sets off the redstone walls.

A corner of Linfeng Stockade

Zhu Family Courtyard Residence (朱家大院) is divided into three houses. The second oldest of three brothers, Zhu Zhen Nan built the Residence in the 11th year of the Daoguang period of the Qing Dynasty (1830). The house features tall roofs and elegant window frames, and on the lintel of the east-west wing rooms are family mottos such as "be kind-hearted" (迁善), and "make up for mistakes" (补过). The Residence of the eldest Zhu brother, Zhu Zigui, was built four years later. The house has three inner chambers – the main building, east wing and west wing – all of which are two-storey brick buildings. Black bricks and tiles offset the emblems of golden corn beneath the eaves. The house also has a embroidery room for young women (小姐的绣楼). In the east of the courtyard lies Zifeng House (朱紫峰的宅院), the residence of the third Zhu brother, who was the governor in charge of the transportation of salt. Built 14 years after the second residence, it has a tall gate, beautiful brickwork, wood and stone carvings and paintings, giving it the honorific title of "Best House on Ru River's South Bank". With its tall gate, beautiful brickwork, wood and stone carvings, painting, and numerous tethers for the horses, Zifeng House makes it clear how prominent and prosperous the Zhu family was.

Village residences in Linfeng Stockade

## GOOD FENG SHUI

From a feng shui point of view, Linfeng Stockade is tops as it faces water on both sides and lies low in the land land. The layout of the gates are in accordance with the Eight Triagrams of Taosist cosmology (bagua), and from above the village is said to be shaped like a boat.

# Dayuwan Village

## Village of Potters and Poets

Surrounded by small streams, Dayuwan VIllage features a winding bluestone path, blocks of old houses, blue stone walls, black tiles, alleys, ancient wells, a stone mill, mottled wooden booths, old murals, wood and stone carvings and plaques.



### Getting there

Dayuwan village, Mulan Town, Huangpi district, Wuhan, Hubei province.
Nearest City: Wuhan.
湖北省武汉市黄陂区木兰乡大余湾村。
From Wuhan Tianhe International Airport(武汉天河国际机场), or from any long-distance bus station in Wuhan, take a bus to Huangpi District (黄陂区) (40 mins). After you have arrived at Huangpi District ,take a bus heading to Mulan County(木兰乡) ( about 1hour), and then a cab to Dayuwan Village (about 1/2hour).

Dayuwan is situated in the northwest corner of Huangpi District about 40 km from the city of Wuhan. The village has preserved more than 20 alleys and more than 50 Ming and Qing Dynasty stone buildings.

Dayuwan Village embodies the ancients' respect for nature. Mulan Mountain is regarded as nature's masterpiece, with the Mulan Gorge looking like a 10 km-long artist's eco-valley. Dayuwan Village sits on the south-east side of Mulan Mountain by the southern mouth of Mulan Gorge and this unique setting was incorporated into the overall planning of the village.

The archiectural style, stone and wood building techniques seen in Dayuwan Village are similar to the style common to north Jiangxi Province. The world of the ancient houses was once described in a folk song about the village: "Front wall surrounded by water, back wall surrounded by mountains, large yards hold small yards, small homes hold the rooms, a hundred families in the village, living in twenty alleys, and all houses are connected, indoor there are many carvings and the front verandah is painted".

The overall layout of residential buildings in Dayuwan Village reflects the Confucian spirit which guided family life and work .

The ancient houses in the village were based on the "three-yard model" (三

合院形制) consisting of three main buildings, two wing houses and a courtyard. There are several antiquities in the houses, such as an age-old straight-backed chair, a carved drum skin screen and even yellowed thread-bound ancient books on a bookshelf, as well as a spinning wheel passed down through the daughters-in-law of several generations.

In other village homes, visitors can see an old comb dowry, heavy inkstone units, ancient scales, ancient containers and blue and white and printed porcelain. Dayuwan village is well known for its artisans such as carpenter, painters, masons, and especially potters. Indeed the village had a saying of "four potters out of ten men" (十汉四窑匠).

In the house of villager Yu Chuansong (余传松家), there is a large carved wooden bed, built in the Ming Dynasty. Made from an extremely valuable rosewood, the top part is a carved dragon and phoenix with the legendary Eight Immortals, (八仙) while the bed frame features engravings of lifelike insects and fish.

With a traditional agricultural economy and society, the people of Dayuwan Village are said to believe in the life concept of "farming to get rich, studying to get honour" (耕可致富，读可荣身). In addition to basic agricultural village labour, they planted flowers and trees, landscaped gardens, and wrote and sang songs and worked from sunrise to sunset.

The village also boasts a proud academic history, and cites distinctions such as "three prefecture heads in one family" and "four governors in five generations".

Village street

Ancient residence interior

During down periods in the agricultural calendar, locals sing and perform dramas together and parade the dragon lantern. The Chinese New Year period in late January or early February is particularly lively, with households pasting couplets and playing with firecrackers, while others sing and play drums during marches. The villagers here are also reputed to be fluent at reciting classical poetry

One lasting village tradition is to place books out in the sun. When the rainy season arrived, villagers would take their ancient books, paintings and letters out into the sunlight to prevent mildew. During this time, it is said that the collective smell and yellowing colour of the paper fills the alleys, providing a spectacular scene enjoyed by locals and visitors alike.

### VIEW FROM THE TOP

The summit of Mulan Mountain (木兰山) is a good place to get a panoramic view of Dayuwan Village.

# Gunlongba Village

## The Tujia Village

Gunlongba ("Rolling Dragon Dam") Village is mostly populated by farmers from the Tujia ethnic minority. The village contains one of the largest and best-preserved collection of Ming aand Qing Dynasty ancient buildings in the area, with many connected brick paths, old trees and bamboo, and a harmonious backdrop of mountains and water.

### Getting there

**Gunlongba village, Cuijiaba Town, Enshizhou city, Enshi State, Hubei province.**
**Nearest City: Enshizhou.**
**湖北省恩施州恩施市崔家坝镇滚龙坝村**
**Buses heading from Enshizhou City(恩施市) to Cuijiaba Town(崔家坝镇) will pass Gunlongba Village (about 1/2 hour).**

Gunlongba Village lies 2 km from the Yaque Village Market and 40 km from the city of Enshi. Seventy percent of the 200 ancient buildings in the village are regarded as well-preserved. Leading local attractions include a ruined pagoda (宝塔), the Xiang Family Ancestral hall (向氏老祠堂), antique furniture, plaques and other ancient relics.

Gunlongba Village is situated on a plain between mountains, a geographic feature commonly seen in villages in west Hubei Province. Jianlong River and Yangyugou River flow from north and south sides respectively through the village. The water of Jianlong River is yellow, giving it the nickname "Yellow Dragon", while Yangyugou River is known as "Blue Dragon" because its water is clear ("blue" in many dialects of Chinese is pronouned identically to "clear"). The village is also surrounded by various mountains, including Blue Dragon Mountain, Saddle Mountain, the Five Peaks, Pagoda Mountain and Tiger Mountain.

The species of the seven 500-year-old trees in Gunlongba Village are Pteroceltis (commonly known as "candy tree" as its fruits are sweet and edible) and Ginkgo biloba.

The extant Ming and Qing Dynasty ancient buildings of the village are mainly located in three areas: Maukan Mountain (茅坎山), the Zhong Village area (中村) and at the foot of Tiger Mountain (老虎山). Most of the residences are made from fire bricks and contain stone yards, a hall, studies, side houses, barns and fire pits. Some residences feature exquisite stone and wood carvings, including traditional auspicious designs of dragons gusting flames, lions playing with a silk ball, tai chi fish, a monkey holding a peach, a magpie playing with plum flowers and even scenes from the Chinese Ming Dynasty era classic, Journey to the West .

Village residence

The vast complex known as Long Street Residence (长街檐屋) comprises three stone gates, three entrances, nine front rooms, eight back rooms, eight side rooms, four yards and a back garden. With the exception of some of the demolished side rooms and pavilion hall and the rebuilt central door, the building is regarded as well preserved and still feature lively sculptures on the stone doors, drums and watert tanks as well as unique carvings on the doors and windows.

Stone Lion Residence (石狮子屋) is a wood-brick building with three houses situated about 200 metres from the main group of ancient buildings in the village. The central house has a stone door decorated on either side with a stone lion head. In front of the door sit two stone lions built in the 18th year of the Daoguang period of the Qing Dynasty (1837 ), thus giving the residence its name.

The buildings of Xiang Cundao Residence (向存道屋) by the foot of Tiger Mountain are located 50 metres from Stone Lion Residence. It is an imposing structure which demonstrates the custom for extended families to reside under one roof in feudal China. With the exception of some partially collapsed rooms and a few halls damaged by fire, the building is well preserved.

There are more than 30 tombs in Gunlongba Village. Maokan Mountain Tomb (茅坎山墓) is the largest and the earliest burial was 360 years ago. Although some burials took place during the Ming Dynasty, many tombs were rebuilt during the Qing Dynasty, predominantly in the Xianfeng (1850-1861), Tongzhi (1861-1875) and Guangxu (1875-1908) periods. The tombs come in all shapes and sizes. Some are rectangular, round or pointy, while more elaborate ones may be shaped like a house or a tiger's head.

## ADVENTURES WITH PIRATES

According to local records, the Xiang family of Gunlongba took a leading role in the fight against Japanese pirates, and was praised for defending the motherland's territorial integrity.




Old trees and ancient architecture in Gunlongba Village

# Lianghekou Village

## Tujia Village in the Mountains

The landscape of Lianghekou Village evokes poetic conceptions of the Chinese countryside with folk residences dotted around vast green fields. Due to its many heritage sites, the village is also an important exhibit of the history of folk art and folk culture in China.

### Getting there

Liangkou Village, Shadaogou town, Xuan En County, Enshi District, Hu Bei Province. Nearest City: Enshizhou.
湖北省恩施州宣恩县沙道沟镇两河口村
Take a bus from Enshizhou to Xuan'en County (宣恩县) (2 hours). From Xuan'en County, take a minibus to Shadaogou Town(沙道沟镇), (RMB15 & 1hour)., then transfer to a local bus to Liangkou Village (about 1hour).

In ancient times, Lianghekou Village was situated at the territorial border of the land belonging to the so-called "Wild Miao" minority. Currently, there are more than 1,300 villagers and 80% of them belong to the Tujia minority. The village is known for its amazing views — two mountain chains extend southwest from the east with the Longtan River passing between them, while wooden folk residences are scattered over the luxuriant green of the mountain slope like in a landscape painting.

According to archaeological research, the Old Street (盐花古道) of Lianghekou Village was once an important part of the ancient path between Hunan Province and Hubei Province which flourised during the Song Dynasty. A Communist government barracks also was set up in the street in 1935.

Several groups of diaojiaolou (吊脚楼, "hanging foot houses") can be found in the village. Peng Family Stockade (彭家寨) sits in the center, with three others (belonging to the

Bridges of Peng Family Stockade

Zeng, Wang and Tang families) scattered around it, supposedly like a moon surrounded by three stars. Other houses of different sizes such as the Fu Family Stockade (符家寨) and Ban Liping (板栗坪) are distributed along the Longtan River.

The Peng Family Stockade, built on the slope of the mountain, is famous for the beauty of the construction, design and contour of its diaojiaolous. In front of the Shuifu Temple (水府庙), built in the 57th year of the Qianlong period of the Qing Dynasty (1735-1796), there is a stone stele inscribed with the history of the village, including the development of its social system, patriachal values and beliefs.

Every house in the village has its own inner space which stretches out in the shape of a fan and usually comprises three rooms – two living rooms separated by a kitchen in the middle. Such residences are called Tujia Corner Houses (土家转角楼). Tujia Corner Houses are supported by a column in the middle of the house. The part that connect two bedrooms together is the roof covering, called "dragon spine" by locals and is used for distributing rain water on the roof.

Lianghekou Village is well-known for its strong local folk culture, especially dance and other arts such as stilt walking. The various styles of dancing include Clamshell Dance (蚌壳舞) and Carriage Lantern Dance (车灯舞), while dances which display particular dancing skills include Dragon Dance, Lion Dance, Monkey Dance and so forth. The music which accompanies the Copper Bell Dance (宝铜铃舞) includes delightful local tunes, sad songs of girls leaving home for marriage and soft tunes of night birds . The dance, accompanied by gong and drum is regarded as a valuable reference for the study of Tujia culture.

Scenes of Lianghekou Village

Girl in Tujia costume

The history of Xieshou Dance (摆手舞) can be traced back to ancient times, and it is still performed by local men and women, accompanied by a big drum (大堂鼓) and big gong (大锣). Originally an activity for entertaining and worshiping gods the dance movements are joyful and the music is pleasant and filled with simple lyrics.

Local delicacies that are worth trying include oil-tea wine with wheat (油茶包谷酒), preserved ham (泡菜土腊肉) and "Ba Ba" fish (粑粑鱼).

### EXPERT EMBROIDERS

Lianghekou Village women are said to be experts in emboidery and can emboider flowers on shoes and shoe pads. There is a local saying that goes: “Girls who learn emboidery when they are 12 will marry well" (女儿十二学绣花，长大能找好婆家).

# Zhangguying Village

## Village of Dragons

Founded in the Ming Dynasty, Zhangguying Village is located at the foot of Bijia Mountain in the east of Yueyang Distrct. Zhangguying Village, with its beautiful landscape and its artful composition, is a blend of traditional architecture, folk customs, patriachal values, agriculture and scholarship.

### Getting there

Zhangguying Village, Zhangguying Town, Yue Yang District, Yueyang, Hu Nan Province.
Nearest City: Changsha.
湖南省岳阳市岳阳县张谷英镇张谷英村。
There are direct buses from Changsha Bus Station (长沙汽车东站) (situated nearby to Changsha Train Station) to Zhangguying Village (2.5hours).There are also buses to the village from Yueyang Bus Station (岳阳汽车站)(a 5mins walk from Yueyang Train Station(岳阳站)) - the journey takes about 2 hours.

It is said that Zhangguying Village's founder Zhang Guyng, a feng shui expert from Jiangxi Province, moved to the area in order to protect his family from the dangers of war. As a feng shui master, Zhang ascertained the village to be a good place for living after cautious examination.

The layout of the ancient village looks like a half moon. A tai chi diagram hangs on the lintel of the gate of the main house, ensuring the safety and wealth of the village. There are two big ponds on the right and left sides of the gate. The ponds are used as fireproofing mechanisms and are known as the "eyes of the dragon". Weixi River, with its many twists

View of 24 dooryards and 24 central rooms with 422 rooms of the Dangdamen Residence

and turns, cuts across the village. Forty-seven stone bridges have been built on the river and are connected to the walls of the houses. A long black-bricked corridor was paved along the edge of the river. Inside the corridor, tai chi diagrams are inscribed on the beams and there are delicate pictures of deer carved on the roof. There are also many other decorations on the windows or walls including pictures of birds, ferocious beasts and plum blossoms.

Though Zhangguying Village has been affected by the passage of time, it has, more or less, maintained its original structure and appearance. Dangdamen (当大门), Wangjiaduan (王家塅) and Shangxinwu (上新屋) are houses which contain some of the best preserved gates and yards in the village. Each of the differently sized gates and yards are connected to an entrance hall, meeting room, ancestral hall, and many wing rooms. The formation of the rooms and inner yards resembles the Chinese letter "井" (a well), and from afar, it looks like the village is full of them.

Built in 1573, Dangdamen Residence is located in front of the Longxing ("Dragon Shaped) Mountain (龙形山), and is thus known as the "mouth of the dragon". There is a stream in front of the gate with two stone bridges, which are regarded as the moustache of the dragon. Inside the house, the 24 central rooms 24 dooryards and 422 living rooms occupy a total space of 9,200 square metres. The layout of the house is like an open fan. The cultural square in front of the gate of the house is a place where villagers gather to perform dragon or lion dances or conduct meetings. There are two stone-roads on the square, inscribed with many auspicious Chinese characters such as "Fu" (福), the character for "luck". The idea is that by walking on the roads, the passer-by would bring luck home with them.

The Dragon Pearl Stone (龙珠石) lies before Dangdamen and is regarded as the mouth of the dragon of Longxing Mountain. The stone, which is 3 metres in diameter, supposedly looks like a pearl. According to legend, there were two giant dragons who fought for the pearl, and eventually the dragon of Longxing Mountain

### BAMBOO AND TOFU

Locally made bamboo baskets (竹篮) are famous for their leak-proof qualities and make good souvenirs. Zhangguying Village locals are also particularly fond of bean curd (豆腐), so most of the food here is made from beans.

won and got the pearl, ensuring that Zhangguying Village remains blessed and protected. The dragon which lost was the dragon of Changlong Mountain, which is now farmland.

Built in the Qianlong period of the Qing Dynasty (1735-1796), Wangjiaduan (王家塅) is the best preserved ancient building in the village. It was constructed under the command of Yun Pugong, a 16th generation descendant of the village founder . The roof is designed like the two giant open wings. There are two alleys on the sides of the main room, and they are regarded as the paths the dragons left behind when taking off.

The building known as the New House (上新屋) was built in the 13th year of the Jiaqing period (1808) in the Qing Dynasty. Located on the "tail" of Longxing Mountain, New House has 173 rooms, and was built in the style of an ancient manor from the Ming and Qing Dynasties. The house has splendid high walls and is mainly constructed from wood, together with black bricks and granite. Baibusan Bridge (百步三桥), built in the Jiaqing period of the Qing Dynasty (1796-1820), is located in the middle of the village's architectural complex. The ancient buildings on both sides of the river are said to resemble an amazing painting of folk life and guaranteed impress every visitor.

Beside the village flows Weixi River, which has been compared to a raging yellow dragon. A few metres from the river bank lies Long Life Well (长寿井), which possesses clean and clear water, a stark contrast to the turbid yellow water of the river and a reminder of the Chinese idiom "The well water does not mix with the river water" (井水不犯河水).

The village's folk museum (民俗展览馆) can be found inside a tall house on a long path beside the river. The exhibits are categorised into six aspects of folk culture — annual customs, age customs, marriages, families, funerals and agricultural activity. The 1,320 items on display include ancient production tools such as an old oil squeezing machine (榨油机) and a water mill powered by pedals. (脚踏水车).

Generations of village locals worshipped ancient Chinese philosophers Confucius and Mengzi, meaning they gave particular importance to education, filial piety, respecting the elderly and loving children. The villagers were proud of their academic achievements: during feudal times, reportedly more than 40 people earned honours in the imperial examinations.

The landscape of Zhangguying Village

# Gaoyi Village

## Tongjia Longevity Village

The residents of Gaoyi Village have kept their ancient customs for generations, and to this day they burn firewood and live in wooden houses. There are many elderly people in the village, giving it the nickname "Village of Longevity". Villagers like to entertain visitors with folk songs and guide them around the village.

### Getting there

Gaoyi Village, Gaoyi Town, Huitong District, Huaihua, Hunan Province.
Nearest City: Huaihua.
湖南省怀化市会同县高椅乡高椅村。
Take coach or train from Huaihua (怀化市)to Huitong County(会同县)( about 2hours).
From Huitong County take a bus to Gaoyi Village (RMB30 & about 3.5 hours).

Gaoyi Village formerly known as Duluntian, was a ferry crossing in ancient times. Later, because the village is backed by mountains, making it look as though it is sitting on a chair, it was renamed Gaoyi (literally "high chair") Village. Eighty-five percent of villagers have the surname Yang (杨) and belong to the Tongjia minority (侗族). It is said that they are the offspring of an ancient marquis from the Southern Song Dynasty (1127-1279) named Yang Siyuan.

There are 104 well-preserved residences from the Ming and Qing Dynasties in Gaoyi Village. With Wutong Temple (五通庙) in the middle, the residences stretch outward in the shape of a plum flower, divided into five clusters — Laowu Street (老屋街), Kanjiao (坎脚), Dawu Alley (大屋巷), Tiandun (田段) and Shangxia Stockade (上下寨). Laowu Street is in the west and contains houses built in the early Ming Dynasty. Folk residences in Tianduan, north of the village, are mainly architecture from the late Ming Dynasty. To the east is Dawu Alley, where all the folk residences were constructed in the early years of the Qing Dynasty. Tianduan is in the south, divided into upper and lower stockades, and the buildings here were built in the middle of the Qing Dynasty.

Gaoyi VIllage Resident

Walking through the black-bricked alleys lined by folk residences is like venturing into a giant maze. The high walls press in on the alleys from both sides, making them deep and dark. The house of every family has tiny yards conecting them to their neighbours,

Typical Ming Dynasty courtyard

Mountain setting

Tranquil Gaoyi Village

a typical feature seen in regions south of the Yangtze River. Paintings of animals or flowers adorn the walls of the houses, and through them, the identity of the host – whether he is a military officer or scholar or farmer – is often readily apparent.

The residences feature architectural styles from different eras. For example, the two-storey Mingchang Yunbing residence (民畅运滨) on Laowu Alley was built in the early Ming Dynasty. Typical of architecture from that time it has only one entrance with two rooms on each floor. Made from wood, the house is surrounded by high walls and the base of the wall is made from blocks of stone. The structure and design of the house is simple with plain-coloured columns. By contrast, Qing Dynasty houses are more elaborate, and usually have exquisite decorations and sculptures on the windows and furniture.

During the Jiaqing period of the Qing Dynasty (1796-1820), one of the sons of an honour student named Yang Sheng created a school. Later, his third son quit his government job and returned to the village, opening another school named "Qingbai Tang" (清白堂, Honesty College), also known as "Wenxue Guan" (Literary College). It is a two-storey wooden house with one entrance and three rooms, and remains well preserved to this day.

During the Tongzhi period of the Qing Dynasty (1856-1875), a wealthy man by the name of Fang Shen raised funds to build the "Drunken Moon Building" (醉月楼) which later became an entertainment and recreation venue for gathering scholars. In 1909, it was changed into a girls school where former candidates of imperial examinations from other towns

would be invited to be teachers.

Viewed from atop of the nearby mountains, the waters of Wu Shui flow across the mountains and down to the foot of Shantang Mountain. The shape of the flowing water apparently looks like the Chinese character"弓" (archer's bow). It is said even though locals were good at business and many had made fortunes elsewhere, they kept the local traditions of "ploughing and studying" through the generations. Since ancient times, there were few businesses or workshops based in the village, so it was a village of strong traditional agricultural and literary culture, "untainted" by commerce. According to Shen Jin Lu( 绅衿录) a book that records the candidates of imperial examinations, the total number of successful candidates from the village in feudal times was 293.

The customs of Gaoyi Village are rich and colourful. From the first day of the Chinese New Year to the Lantern Festival on the fiftheenth day (Chinese New Year usually falls in late January or early February), it is a traditional custom for the Tongjia people to peform the Dragon Lantern Dance (舞龙灯). After the Lantern Festival, there is a ritual to send the dragon back home, in which participants light fireworks or ignite firewood around the dragon lantern, ending the annual celebration with a great fire.

Tanxi (傩戏), also known as Gangpusa, is a kind of local opera performed by the Tongjia people of Gaoyi Village. This ancient and mysterious folk art has been passed from generation to generation through word of mouth. Most of the 30 or so plays are short but full of action. During the autumn and winter months, performers in their drama costumes can be seen performing on the village's theatre stage.

## OLD HOUSES

Lao Wu Street and Lao Wu alley have a long history, and 5 Ming architectures and 6 Qing architectures are still well preserved there. There are more folk houses in good condition in Da Wu Alley (大屋巷).



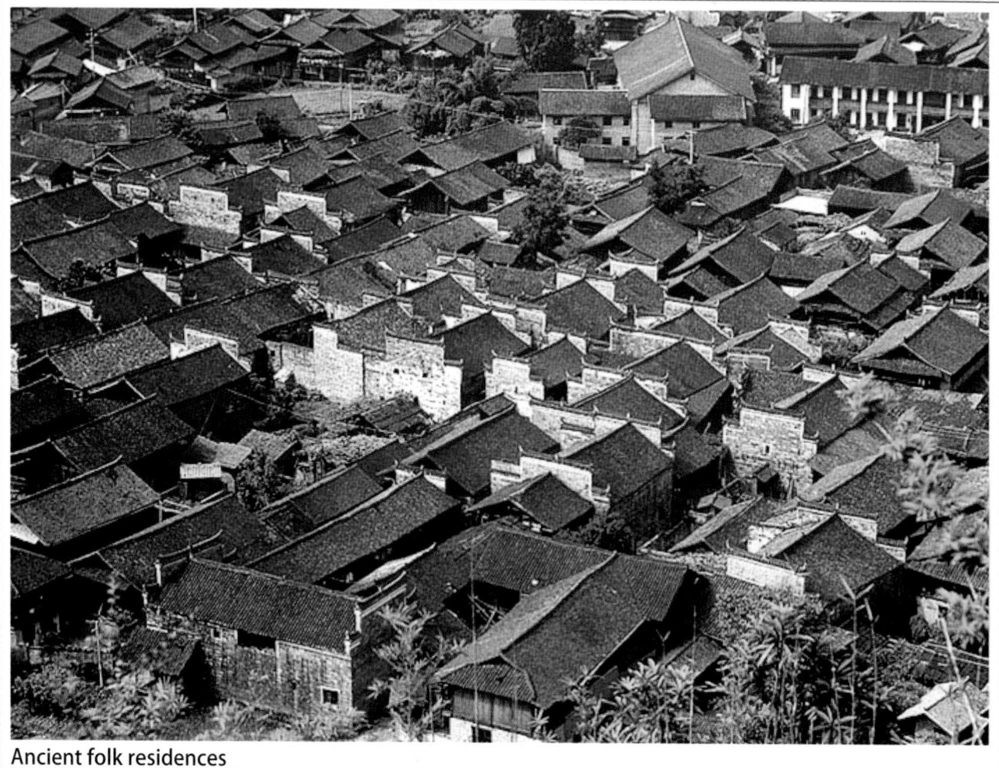

Ancient folk residences

# Ganyantou Village

## The Essence of South Hunan Dwellings

Ganyantou Village is full of houses with black tiles and white walls, built close together, with upturned eaves pointing straight to the sky. On sunny days, the blue sky, verdant hills and green waters complement the majestic elegancy of those ancient dwellings.



**Getting there**

Ganyantou Village, Fujiaqiao Town, Lingling district, Yongzhou, Hunan.
Nearest City: Yongzhou.
湖南省永州市零陵区富家桥镇干岩头村。
From Yongzhou airport take a bus to Lingling District（零陵区).In Lingling District, buses leave to Ganyantou Village from the Shuangpai Car Park (双牌停车场). Get off the bus at Najindu bridge(南津渡大桥) and then walk for 5 minutes to arrive at Ganyantou village.

The village's dwellings sit in the south and face the north, near waters and close to hills in the south, east and west. The Zhou Family Grand Courtyard (周家大院) is an community of ancient residential houses. It is known for the quality of its carvings and painting, abundance of history, richness of folk culture and breadth of content.

The Zhou Family Grand Courtyard was established during the Jingtai period of the Ming Dynasty (1450-1456), though construction was not complished until 1904. The Zhou family are the decendants of neo-confucianist Zhou Dunyi of the Song Dynasty. Feng shui-inspired architecture is abundantly represented in this grand courtyard. It is surrounded by hills on three sides, with a broad view and magnificent hills on either side. Two rivers converge in front of the coutyard, and there is a bridge with various decorations on the carved railings.

The grand courtyard comprises six smaller

Outside the wall of the Zhou Family Grand Courtyard

courtyards arranged in the shape of the Big Dipper. The six courtyards stand in a line and are connected by paths paved with pebbles. They are each separated by less than one hunded metres, standing alone but also harmoniously connected to each other. Inside the buildings are carving works of plants and figures, exhibiting a variety of fine skills which highlight the ingeniousness of the village' s ancient residents.

Every courtyard is constructed according to the gradient of the hill on which it lies, making them assessible and suitable for living. Moreover, ditches to drain off floodwater, gutters to discharge water, patios paved with bluestones and a fire brick paved interior, ensure that excess water and moisture is always discharged from the house. Holes in the walls were for observing and resisting the enemy. Every courtyard has a dooryard and patio, which were ideal places for family meetings and gatherings.

The Red Door Building (红门楼) was bulit by Minister Zhou Xisheng and it is regarded as the most attractive of the six courtyards. The mutiple-eave roof symbolises the unusual social status of its owner.

The most well-preserved courtyard is the former residence of Zhou Chongfu (周崇傅故居). The walls on the south and north sides have a length of 120 metres and the walls on the other two sides have a length of 100 metres. Some of the courtyard's houses are connected with corridors. Every house has two patios, one corridor, one central room and two wing rooms. Most of the windows are removable and the stones and wood are delicately carved and engraved. The well-preserved residential houses impart a typical sense of Confucian culture.

Zhou family's "new" courtyard

Other well-preserved architecture in the village include two private schools, confucian shrines, dormitories, gardens, and courtyards.

The Zhou family has produced many talents and experts, which is said to be attributable to its rigorous promotion of education and their respct for teachers and teachings.

Backyard of an ancient residence

### STIR-FRIED FROG

Santanyou is a good place to try such Hunan dishes as Lingling blood duck (零陵血鸭), rice flour meat (米粉肉), preseved egg (?? ??), duck with bamboo shoot (老鸭笋尖), river snails (嗝田螺), smoked ham (烟熏腊肉), stir-fried frog with peppers (尖椒爆田鸡), spicy salted duck (酱板鸭), boiled eels (水煮鳝鱼) and wild snakes (野味异蛇).

The natural wonders of Ganyantou Village are also extraordinary and also exemplify the Chinese genius for visual metaphor. At the back of the village there is a peculiar rock which is shaped like a huge umbrella, apparently large enough to shelter more than a hundred people in the rain. Unsurprisingly, locals call it "Umbrella Rock" (雨伞岩). Three are three huge stones west of the rock called "Hidden Master Rock" (隐师岩) which are interlocked with each other. From the north, "Umbrella Rock" and "Hidden Maseter Rock" appear as one, said to resemble a walking camel with heavy luggage. East of the village, there are two connected stones called "Buddhist Monk's Knife" (村人称其为戒刀岩) because of their shape. The stones have a number of names because they look like different things from different angles. For instance, from Songshuwan Village in the north, the stones are said to look like a whispering couple, lowering their heads and hugging with a child on their back, giving it the name "Couple's Peak". Behind the peak lies a huge rock. A temple used to rest on the top of the rock, so it is known as "Temple Rock" (寺院岩). From the exit of Songshuwan Village, the Couple Peak appears linked with Temple Rock to form the shape of a monkey. Accordingly, locals call this "Moon-gazing Monkey". From the east, Couple Peak and Temple Rock appear stacked on top each other, and so it is named "Golden Turtle Calling Out for A Companion" (金龟唤伴).

Overlooking Ganyantou Village

# Shanggantang Village

## Sweet Apple Village on the Old Post Road

Shanggantang Village possesses wonderful landscapes and a rich heritage of Hunan architecture, commerce, education and religion.

### Getting there

Shanggantang Village, Xiacengpu Town, Jiangyong County, Yongzhou, Hunan.Nearest City: Yongzhou.
湖南省永州市江永县夏层铺镇上甘棠村。
Buses depart from Yongzhou Long-distance Bus Station (永州长途汽车站) to Jiangyong County (江永县)(about 2.5hours). At Jiangyong County, transfer to a bus heading to Taochuan Town(桃川镇) (about 1/2 hr) and then get off at the entrance to the village.

Situated 25 km south-west of the county town, the village's original ancestors settled here during the Tang Dynasty, more than 1240 years ago. They named the village "Gantang" (甘棠) where "Gan" means sweet, while "Tang" refers to wild apples. However, the village's name also has an alternative explanation: "gantang" also originally meant a kind of giant tree, which was used as a commendatory term for praising officials with political achievements. This explanation suggests that the original ancestors of the village-founding Zhou family rendered outstanding service to the government.

Wenchang Pavilion was built in the Southern Song Dynasty and sits in the south of the village. It used to be the place where villagers to made sacrifices to the Daoist

Wenchang Pavilion

## TURTLE HILL

"Sunset on Turtle Hill" ((龟山夕照) is another of the original "Eight Sights" of Shanggantang which remain well-preserved. Turtle Hill is a 268-metre stone hill which is said to be shaped like a turtle. There used to be a pavilion on the top of the hill, and it remains a good place to enjoy panoramic views of the village.

immortal, Wenquxing (文曲星). It has been repaired several times, and currently has four floors with a total height of 16 metres. On its right, there is the Dragon and Phoenix Temple (龙凤庵), now rebuilt as a primary school. Built in the Qing Dynasty, 500 metres from Wenchang Pavilion, Shouxuan Pavilion (寿宣亭) is located on the ancient post road to Guangxi Province. It is constructed with stones and wood, and contains a stone stele carved with the lyrics of a Buddhist song intended to enlighten people.

There is a stone bridge from Wenchang Pavilion which enables visitors to enter the village proper. The bridge was named Bu Ying (Cross Ocean) Bridge (步瀛桥) and was built in 1126, but was regularly repaired throughout various dynasties for hundreds of years. It was used for connecting to the ancient post road (古驿道) in front of the village. Local legend says that every time a stone falls out from Bu Ying Bridge, one of the villagers will become an official of the government.

Behind Bu Ying Bridge is a stone hill named Yue Ang Hill (日昂山). Three hundred and twenty-eight metres tall and with verdant and luxuriantly green trees, it is regarded as one of the original "eight scenes" of Gantang Village. The other seven scenes were: Fishermen on the River, Reading in the Morning, Cultivating in Spring, Hermit in the Pavilion, Sunset on Turtle Hill, Fine Day on West Hill and the Good Chimes Temple. However Green Ang Hill and Sunset on Turtle Hill (龟山夕照) are the only two scenes which remain well-preserved.

Yuebei Pavilion (月陂亭) sits beside Xiemu River in the southeast of Shanggantang Village. It is the entry to the post roads to Guangdong and Guangxi Provinces. There is a stone wall which is about 200-300 metres long with 27 ancient stone inscriptions. According to research, one of the inscriptions dates back a thousand years. The inscriptions mainly express appreciation and praise for the wonderful landscapes of the village and the various contributions made by the Zhou family. They also extol merits and virtues, offer advice and suggestions, express thanks and gratitude, and refer to the history of the Song, Yuan, Ming and Qing

The delicate Bu Ying Bridge and magnificent Wenchang Pavilion

An idyllic setting

Dynasties. The inscriptions understandably are of great value to the study of the history of rural areas and folk customs during these times, especially in relation to native history, culture and religion.

After enjoying the inscriptions, visitors can enter the village through the south gate (南门). Pass the ancient gate tower and there will be a 500-metre-long anti-flood wall on the left, the Zhou Family Ancestral Hall (周氏祠堂) on the right, and a blue stone-paved street with a history of more than 1,200 years. That narrow street runs south to north through the whole village and connects the four gate towers. Some shops line the road, which is the center of the village' s commercial district and contains a rural market.

The village faces west with the the Pingfeng Moutains in the east. The front of the village is surrounded by Xiemu River, which is said to enhance the village' s feng shui. More than 200 ancient residences remain in the village. The huge fire walls orderly layout, symmetrical arrangement, large scale wall surfaces, gates and doors, and the "horse head" walls, all represent the typical characteristics of architecture in southern Hunan.

Along Xiemu River, out of the north gate, there is a bay festooned with weeping willows. A small stone bridge said to be built in the Han Dynasty lies across the river. Though the bridge is askew, the surface is still sound. Ducks on the green water complete an idyllic scene.

Shanggantang Village produced more than 100 government officials in ancient times. Post-1949, the village claims to have produced more than 40 engineers, school principals, teachers, doctors and other notable locals. Portaits of some of them are displayed within the hall at various times.

Villagers washing their clothes in the river.

# 北方古村
# North
## Stone Streets and Scholars' Houses

# Cuandixia Village

## A Thread of Sky

Cuandixia Village lies in the mountains, filled with fascinating cultural artifacts and often wreathed in curling smoke. The village's old doors, windows and mottled stonewalls evoke memories of this flourishing township during the Ming and Qing Dynasties.

### Getting there

Cuandixia Village, Zhaitang Town, Mentougou District, Beijing..
Nearest City: Beijing.
北京市门头沟区斋堂镇爨底下村。
Take Beijing's subway line 1 to the last stop, Pingguoyuan (苹果园站).Walk about 150m west of Exit D of Pinguoyuan station and take a #929 Cuandixia Line bus to Cuandixia Village(爨底下村) directly. There are only two direct buses at 7:30 and 12:40 every day and the journey takes about 2.5hours. At other times, the #829 bus goes to Zhaitang Town(斋堂镇) ( about 2.5hours), from where a taxi to Cuandixia Village takes about 1/2hour and costs RMB35.

Cuandixia Village was established during the Yongle period of the Ming Dynasty (1403-1424). The most common family name in the village is Han (韩). The village lies at the foot of the Cuanliankou strategic pass of the ancient Jingxi Road (京西明代 "爨里安口" 险隘谷), just 90 km from Beijing. Surrounded by mountains, the overall arrangement of the village is said to resemble a "shoe-shaped" gold ingot. The Chinese character "cuan" (爨) is an old word for "oven", and the founders of the village named it "Cuandixia", which connotes avoiding the cold. In 1958, the word was changed from "cuan" to "chuan" due to Communist-era place-name simplification.

A quiet and beautiful alley that winds from east to west through the village is paved with purple and blue stones. The vilage's ancient dwellings include 70 sets of exquisite Qing Dynasty quadrangle dwellings with a total of 500 rooms. The residences usually comprise a principal room,

Cuandixia Village

Quadrangle dwelling

a room opposite to the principal room and wing rooms on the left and right. Quadrangle dwellings have been categorised by experts into "mountain-style" (山地四合院), "double-shop" (双店式四合院) and "shop-style" (店铺式四合院). There are screen walls inside and outside the doors where are found hitching posts and mounting stones for horses. The number of nails in a door was said to reflect a family's status. Almost all courtyards have finely crafted carved beams and painted rafters. Both sides of the gatehouses feature delicate wall paintings.

Built in the early Qing Dynasty, Guangliang Courtyard (广亮院) lies atop the village's central axis. It has two main buildings in the south and north. The courtyard can be divided into three sections — east, middle and west. These three relatively independent courtyards form a large quadrangle courtyard residence with 45 rooms. The medium-sized gatehouse known as Ruyi Gate (如意门) has seven steps. The floor of the gatehouse is paved with two slabs, one of which is inscribed with "Tread on Clouds" (脚踏青云, meaning "a smooth career"), and the other "A Purple Breeze from the East" (紫气东来, meaning "an auspicious omen).

Nanpo Ridge (南坡梁) is a mountain ridge with beautiful views. The mountain top enables visitors to overlook the entire village, which has a natural landscape that has been described by locals with inventive visual metaphors such as as "golden toad looking at the moon", "tortoise roaring at the sky", and "bat offering blessings."

Cuandixia Village belongs to the Qingshui River Valley, with ample shade provided by its abundant green trees. Behind the village is an ancient path known as "A Thread of Sky" (一线天), which was the only route to Hebei and Shanxi Provinces and Inner Mongolia during the Ming and Qing Dynasties. Many films and TV series wth historical settings

Overlooking Cuandixia Village

Despite the passage of time, Cuandixia Village still exhibits the style of hundreds of years ago.

have been shot in the village over the years.

Cuandixia Village contains many temples such as the Temple of Lord Guan (关公庙), the Empress Temple (娘娘庙), where locals pray to be blessed with offspring, and a Goddess of Mercy Temple (观音庙), where villages pray to the Buddhist deity Guanyin for peace. The Temple of Lord Guan was built in the 54th year of the Kangxi period during Qing Dynasty (1715) and stands about halfway up the hill in the east of the village. This grand temple has the highest location of all the temples in the village and is famous for its lofty stylobate and exquisite architecture.

The lanes of Cuandixia Village

The folk customs of Cuandixia Village are particularly colourful. In front of the gate of each quadrangle courtyard is a shrine dedicated to the Door Gods. Featuring various decorative patterns, the shrine would be placed in the wall during construction of the gatehouse. The name of the Door Gods are written in ink. Lord Guan, a heroic figure from the Chinese classic "Romance of the Three Kingdoms" (水浒传) is the main deity for ritual offerings in the village, which are aimed at protecting the village and preventing illness and disasters. Merchants also come here to pray for safety and wealth, thus ensuring that incense and candles are always burning inside the temple.

## LOCAL PRODUCE

The specialities of Cuanxixia Village include various wild vegetables, melons and seasonal fruits, such as Chinese toon (香椿), sophora flowers (槐花), yellow apricots and tender corns. Visitors can also buy free-range eggs, brine-dried bean curd and many herbs all year round.

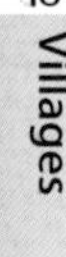

# Lingshui Village

## The Scholars' Village in West Beijing

In imperial times, Lingshui Village was known as the "Juren Village" of Jingxi County. The village's mottled houses, half-ruined temple walls and the branches and leaves of its thousand-year-old trees all contribute to its scholastic atmosphere.

### Getting there

Lingshui Village, Zhaitang Town, Mentougou District, Beijing.
Nearest City: :Beijing..
北京市门头沟区斋堂镇灵水村。
Take Beijing's subway line 1 to the last stop, Pingguoyuan (苹果园站).Walk about 150m west of Exit D of Pinguoyuan station and take a #929 bus to Junxiang Bus Station(军响乡站) ( about 2.5 hours), and then continue by taxi to Lingshui Village (RMB20 & 10mins).

Lingshui Village lies southwest of Miaofeng Mountain, 78 km from Beijing. It was founded back in the Han Dynasty and took shape during the Liao and Jin Dynasties. The village has a mass of courtyards with houses on three sides and quadrangle dwellings dating back to the Ming and Qing Dynasties. There are also many temple ruins, such as the South Sea Fire Dragon King Temple (南海火龙王庙), the Goddess Temple (天仙圣母庙), the White Clothes Temple (白衣庵), as well as the Shengquan Nunnery (胜泉庵).

Viewed from above, Lingshui village apparently

Many ancient dwellings in Linshui Village are situated in dense foliage.

resembles a tortoise. In Chinese mythology, the "black tortoise" (玄武) deity was in charge of the north. The tortoise is also a symbol for auspiciousness and longevity. The head of the "black tortoise" faces south, and its tail points north. Three east-west streets and three north-south lanes run through the village, which has a layout thought to resemble the Chinese character "Ling" (灵) (spiritual being), hence giving the village the first half of its name. The second character "Shui" means water and is a reference to the 72 wells in the village.

Much of the architecture of dwellings in Lingshui Village is an example of "the style of the officials" (仕者风范). Among the Juren (a title given to successful candidates in the imperial examinations at the provincial level) houses, the former residence of Liu Zengguang (刘增广的故居) is the most unique. Built during the Qing Dynasty, it is a courtyard residence, with an entrance screen wall at the gate of the house and a horse-tethering post at the back. The wood-carved screen in the north building is well preserved.

Residence number 78 (78号宅院), located in the middle of the village's main axis, is

The ancient dwellings of Lingshui Village

constructed from wood-like bricks to give the impression of a wooden building. The residence's massive walls were built with tightly laid bricks and its double-decker rafter roof have protruding eaves on both sides and feature exquisite carvings. It is said that the gatehouse is the only existing residential construction in the village to date back to the Yuan Dynasty. Under the eaves outside the upper part of the gatehouseare are bricks carved with fish patterns, symbolising "years of happiness".

At the foot of Lotus Mountain in the northwest of the village stands Shengquan Nunnery, built in the Han Dynasty. Lingquan Temple (灵泉寺), previously named Ruiling Temple, was the oldest temple in the village, but is now a primary school. There are two tall ginkgo trees at the far end of the yard inside the gate of the temple.

Others temples, including the South Sea Fire Dragon King Temple, Goddess Temple, Guanyin Temple (观音堂) and Erlang Temple (二郎庙) are closely adjacent to each other in the west of the village. The Fire Dragon Temple of Nanhai lies the in the centre of this architectural complex

## SCHOLAR'S FARE

Scholarly products of Linshui Village include the famous Juren congee (举人粥) and also Juren wine (举人酒). Other specialities are dried and fresh fruits such as walnuts, apricots, Chinese-dates and red apricots.

and is said to have been built in the Jin Dynasty and rebuilt in the 15th year of the Jiajing period of the Ming Dynasty (1536). Nowadays, the principal hall of the temple is no longer in existence.

In the yard, there are two giant thousand-year-old cypress trees. One of the trees planted in the Jin Dynasty has a 20-cm mulberry growing in the hole of its trunk. The other cypress tree has a 70-cm elm growing around its base.

The "Autumn Congee Holiday" (秋粥节) celebrated in Lingshui Village evey year, usually at the beginning of August, is to honour Magistrate Liu, who donated food to people stricken by disasters at the end of the Qing Dynasty. At the beginning of autumn, students preparing for the college entrance exams will rush here to taste "Juren congee", in the hope that they can emulate the success of the village ancestors.

The local small Bangzi Opera and the Chinese Yellow River Lantern Festival, which usually fall in February, are also well known.

The ruins of the Nanhai Fire Dragon Temple in Lingshui Village

# Yujia Village

## The Stone Village

Yujia Village is situated in the remote mountains and has a unique architectural beauty, long history and rich folklore. The village is truly a stone haven, with stone buildings, pavilions, houses, courtyards, streets, lanes, bridges, balustrades, girders, columns, gates, windows, vessels, tables, beds, niches, bells and boards...

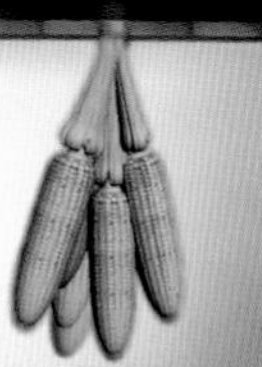

### Getting there

Yujia Village, Yujia Country, Jingxing County, Shijiazhuang City, Hebei Province.
Nearest City: Shijiazhuang.
河北省石家庄市井陉县于家乡于家村。
Take a bus from Shijiazhuang Railway Station(石家庄火车站) to Jingxing County(井陉县) (about 1.5hours),and then transfer to a taxi to Yujia Village (RMB20 & 1/2hour).

Yujia Village lies in the midwest of Jingxing County. Inside, Cool Pavilion (清凉阁) sits at the east gate and West Head Pavilion (西头阁) is at the west gate, while Goddess of Mercy Pavilion lies at the south gate (观音阁) and Dragon Sky Pavilion (龙天阁) lies at the north.

Yujia Village has a history of more than 500 years. Most of the villagers with the surname Yu (于) are descendants of Ming Dynasty general Yu Qian, who was killed during the political upheaval of the "Nangong Restoration" episode (1449-1457) during the Ming Dynasty. Yujia Village (literally "Yu Family Village') was established after Yu's descendants escaped to the Taihang Mountains in Jingxing County .

Due to a severe water shortage during the early stages of construction, the village founders paid particular attention

A historic building in Yujia VIllage

to preserving water and established strict water usage guidelines. The "Willow Pond Regulation" tablet ("柳池禁约" 碑) inscribed in the 39th year of the Qianlong period of the Qing Dynasty (1735-1795) sets out clear rules for pond management and pond water distribution, which played an important role in solving the water supply problem for people and animals in this drought-prone village. Another tablet with the title "Village Norms for Rectifying" (整饬村规" 碑) prohibits gambling and stipulates: "Those found running gambling houses will be made to write a drama and sing and dance for three days".

Despite being small and located in the remote mountains, Yujia Village contains 22 ancient temples, ancient pavilions and ancient theatrical stages, all built with stone. Three of the four village gates are temples, four of the six main village streets have pavillions, the four theatrical stages all have different shapes and the residential dwellings are all interconnected.

Yujia Village also has more than 400 dwellings, 4,000 stone buildings, 3,700 squared metres of stone streets, 1,000

Yujia Village's old stone houses still stand firm after hundreds of years.

stone well cellars, 2,000 acres of stone terraces, 2,000 stone tools and 10 old tablets.

The forefathers of Yujia Village had explicit norms for the layouts of houses and streets. Accordingly, the streets in the village run east to west, and the lanes south to north, and are linked by a series of alleys. The six streets, seven lanes and eighteen alleys form a criss-cross pattern, connecting every street and house in the village.

Also known as Immortals Pavilion, Cool (Qingliang) Pavilion is regarded as a symbol of Yujia Village. The pavillion was built in the 9th year of the Wanli period of the Ming Dynasty (1581) by Yu Qian's descendant Yu Xichun, who is said to have possessed tremendous strength. Qinglian Pavillion was initially supposed to have nine floors, but when construction had only reached second floor, Yu Xichun apparently broke his arms while hanging a banner, and later died before his vision could be realised. According to villagers, Yu Xichun's bloodstains can still be seen on the flagstones of the pavilion.

## BED AND BOARD

The mayor of Yujia Village is keen to develop ecologically responsible tourism. Several villagers offer simple accomodation - usually it is best to arrange this after arrival, so you can check out the room first. Most hosts will offer to prepare an evening meal for you ... one popular dish is handmade noodles made from sweet potato and wheat flour (红薯面与白面相揉合而成的于家村手擀面).

There are there are only three floors in Cool Pavillion, which features an ingenious design with carved beams and painted raffers, five roof ridges with six beasts, corbel brackets and double eaves. A fan-shaped gold-plated board is hung on the west gate, while a stone table hangs in the eastt.

Built in the late Ming Dynasty, Sihe Courtyard (四合楼院) is a towering brick building with stone foundations and an area of nearly one thousand square metres. The building is grand and lofty, simple yet elegant, spacious and open while remaining warm in winter and cool in summer. The upstairs reception room of the main building has thick beams and big columns but no partition, which make the room appear spacious and grand. A corridor runs past the reception room windows and offers a panoramic view of the scenery of Nanshan (South Mountain).

Yujia Village also has a stone museum which features a large quantity of ancient stone vessels and natural stone exhibits, as well as many farm tools and ancient utensils. There are altogether six exhibition rooms, while in the yard there is a collection of bizarrely shaped, colourful stones and plant fossils.

# Liuliqu Village

## The Hometown of Coloured Glaze

Liuliqu Village ("Coloured Glaze Ditch Village") is known as the "Hometown of Coloured Glaze" because of its high quality shale which can be processed into beautiful glaze products. The colourful glazed tiles produced here can be found on numerous temples and palaces dating from the Ming and Qing Dynasties. It has been said that, "Without Liuliqu VIllage, there would be no Forbidden City".

### Getting there

Liuliqu Village, Longquan Town, Longtougou District, Beijing..
Nearest City: Beijing.
北京市门头沟区龙泉镇琉璃渠村。
Take Beijing's subway line 1 to the last stop, Pingguoyuan (苹果园站) and then continue to Liuliqu village by a #829 bus (1hour); the bus stop is 150m West of Exit A of the Pinguoyuan subway station. Alternatively take a #890 bus from the south square of West Beijing Station(北京西站南广场) directly to Liuliqu Village (about 2 hours).

Liuliqu Village is backed by Nine Dragons Mountain (九龙山) and faces the Yongding River. The royal court first established coloured glaze factories in the village during the Yuan Dynasty, By the Qianlong period of the Qing Dynasty (1735-1796), Beijing's coloured glaze factory was relocated here, and a ditch was built, giving the village its current name. Liuliqu Village's well-preserved relics include the only yellow glaze roof overpass built in the Beijing region during the Qing Dynasty, Dragon King Temple (龙王庙) and Mountain Spirit Temple (山神庙).

The coloured glaze products from Liuliqu Village were used in vast quantities by the royal court in the Ming and Qing Dynasties, and even during the Communist era, when they were employed in building the Great Hall of the People and the Chairman Mao Memorial Hall, as well as the Diaoyutai State Guesthouse (used for entertaining foreign VIPs), and even Beijing West Station.

The Lantern Pavilion (灯阁), also known as the Three Officials Pavilion, was built in the 21st year of the Qianlong era in the Qing Dynasty (1756) and is located at the east

Quadrangle courtyard of an ancient coloured glaze factory

God of War Temple.

entrance of the village. Its base is built from bricks and stones, and is shaped like a stage. The pavilion faces east and has three main halls. There are colourful glazed flowers and glazed plaques under the roof. The one on the west side is translated to read "Three Officials Pavilion" (三官阁), while the one in the east implies that "people who live in this house will be prosperous" (文星高照). The front and back walls are decorated with hexagonal "turtle brocade" (龟背锦) glazed bricks.

The House of the Coloured Glaze Manufacturer (琉璃厂商宅院), is a courtyard residence with two entrances. It was the mansion of a glaze factory manager named Zhao (赵) in the Qing Dynasty. This family made colourful glaze for the imperial palace for more than 200 years.

The Deng Family Courtyard Residence (邓家大院) is located at the east entrance of Back Street (后街). Local legend says that it was built by an oil vendor. The residence has three entrances, and the unique overhanging arch facing the street is big enough to let horses and cars pass through. The serene front and back courtyards have corridors and doors with exquisite brick carvings.

Built in the Ming Dynasty, The God oF War Temple (关帝庙) is located at the west entrance of Liuliqu Village. The complex is an intact courtyard, sitting west to east, with three main halls. The coloured glaze base of the stage is exquisitely modelled, with statues of Zhou Cang (a famous general) and Lord Guan (of Chinese historical classic the "Three Kingdoms") standing on both sides. In front of the temple there are six inscriptions recording the temple's history of restorations and the names of benefactors.

Located in the north of the village, Virtue Tea House (善茶棚) is the biggest tea house on the path to Miaofeng Mountain. The teahouse has a large courtyard with six main halls and floors paved with bricks. In front of the courtyard are cedar wood doors and wooden fences.

"Ugly Son" Mountain Villa (丑儿岭山庄) is located on on a hill south of Liuliqu Village. More than 20,000 fruit trees are planted here, making it is a relaxing spot. There is also a small zoo featuring farm animals such as chickens, geese, sheep and cattle.

## CHERRY PICKING

The parklands around Liuliqu Village are abundant with cherries, thin shelled walnuts and grapes, as well as rare wild peaches, persimmon and mountain apricot, sweet corn, kidney beans, cushaw, black soya beans and mung beans. Every harvest season there is a fruit and vegetable picking festival (水果采摘季) which tourists may participate in.

# Ranzhuang Village

## Tunnel Warfare Relics

Ruanzhuang Village is filled with relics from the tunnel warfare which took place during the Sino-Japanese war in the Jizhong Plain (Central Hebei) region. Unsurprisingly, the village is a popular location for war movie shoots.

### Getting there

Ranzhuang Village, Ranzhuang Town,Qingyuan County, Baoding, Hebei.. Nearest City: Shijiazhuang.

河北省保定市清苑县冉庄镇冉庄村。

Take a train from Shijiazhuang (石家庄站) to Baoding (保定站)(about 1 hour), then walk 5minutes to Baoding's Jiangcheng bus station(保定江城客运站). At the bus station, board a bus heading to Yangcheng(阳城) and get off at Ranzhuang Village (about 1 hour). There is a RMB20 fee for entrance to the Ranzhuang Tunnel Warfare Site.

Ranzhuang Village is located on the Jizhong Plain, 30km southwest of Baoding City and within reach of Beijing and Tianjin. During the Sino-Japanese and Liberation Civil Wars, Ranzhuang's villagers used tunnel warfare to fight in secret against the enemy, causing the opposition to make a detour from Heifengkou rather than passing through the village directly.

The old pagoda trees and big bell at the village's entrance are symbols of the Ranzhuang Tunnel Warfare Site. Centered on, or rather below, Shizi Street (十字街), the tunnels have four main branches running east, west, south and north, which then extend into 20 more small branches. There are tunnels which connect to other villages: Dongsunzhuang in the west, Jiangzhuang in the northeast, and the Sui Family Tomb (隋家坟) in the southeast. The overall length of the tunnels is close to 30 km. Built around 2 metres underground, the tunnels are usually about 0.7-0.8 metres wide and 1-1.5 metres high. The tunnels are divided into two types: military use and civilian use.

Down in the tunnels there are headquarters, restrooms, granaries, signposts, oil lamps, underground arsenals and pit traps. The design and build of the passageways made them very difficult for the enemy to find. Further, connecting tunnels with village wells not only helped with ventilation, but also supplied water directly to people in tunnels. For convenience of surveillance and attack, several above-ground buildings and high points are

Sculptures in Ranzhuang Memorial Hall

connected with the tunnel system.

The main architectural features of the tunnels have been characterized by the list-crazy Chinese as the "Three Connects" (三通), "Three Combinations" (三交叉), and "Five Proofs" (五防). Three Connects refers to high buildings connected with each other, tunnels connected with each other, and fortresses connected with each other. Three Combinations refers to conspicuous loopholes combined with inconspicuous ones and firepower of the high buildings and the walls combined with the firepower of the fortresses. Five Proofs refers to being damage proof, lock proof, water proof, gas proof and fire proof.

During the Sino-Japanese and Liberation Civil Wars, Ranzhuang Villager residents apparently utilised these tunnels in 17 direct battles with the Japanese and Kuomintang armies, 55 ambushes and pursuits, as well as 85 battles fought outside the village. Five of the large scale tunnel battles resulted in the death of 163 enemies.

The Ranzhuang Tunnel Warfare Site (地道战遗址保护区) covers an area of 300,000 square metres. Three thousand metres of the original tunnels still exist and 1,200 metres are open to visitors. Ranzhuang Tunnel Warfare Memorial Hall (冉庄地道战纪念馆), built in 1959, is now open to visitors free of charge. It features an exhibition hall, tunnel sites and underground war facilities. The exhibition hall displays 431 revolutionary relics, which are combined with multimedia exhibits to help visitors to visualise the scenes of the past.

Records of Ranzhuang Village's Embroided Dragon Lantern Dance (绣球龙灯) have existed since the Wanli period of the Ming Dynasty (1572-1620). Meanwhile Hahaqiang (哈哈腔), also known as Liuzidiao, is a popular form of local opera found in Hebei and Shandong Provinces.

## DONKEY BURGERS

Baoding donkey burgers (驴肉火烧)are reasonably priced at RMB2 each! Other, perhaps more palatable, village snacks include vermicelli, strawberry and “resist Japan” cakes (?战饼). The village also sells local artworks and incense.

Ranzhuang Tunnel Warfare Memorial Hall

# Yingtan Village

## The Red Stone Castle

Yingtan Village is embraced by a river and green hills on three sides. Built entirely with red hill stones, the village is said to look like a red castle from a distance.





**Getting there**

Yingtan Village, Luluo Town, Xingtai County, Xingtai, Hebei province.
Nearest City: Shijiazhuang.
河北省邢台市邢台县路罗镇英谈村。
Take a train from Shijiazhaung Station to Xingtai Station（邢台站）(about 1hour). At Xingtai take another bus to Luluo County(路罗镇) (about 1.5hours) then get off at Yangzhuang(杨庄), and take a taxi for the final 1.5KM to Yingtan village.

Yingtan Village is located about 70 km from Beijing. There are two tales about the origin of its name. In the first, the insurrectionary army of General Huang Chao from the Tang Dynasty had encamped here and held a "conference of heroes" (英谈, "Yintan). In the second, the original village is said to be the remains of a barracks (营盘, "Yingpan") of an insurrectionary army during the Huangchao Rebellion in the late Tang Dynasty (875 AD).

Yingtan Village was built against a mountain and the streets extend upward with the slope. From the top of the village, visitors can see a deep river which locals call Back Ditch (后沟). There are 18 bridges on the river, with shapes which have been likened to the moon or a rainbow.

Yingtan Village is a world of stone with stone towers, caves, bridges, roads, mills, stoves and so forth. There are 67 dwellings dating back to the Ming and Qing Dynasties, making it one of the best-preserved stone villages in the province. Above the east gate (东城门) is a pavilion, and beside the city wall (城墙) is a water gate hidden amongst the green trees.

The stone buildings inside the village are usually two or three storeys high and built with local red sandstone. The roof is a large slate, rain and snow proof, cool in summer and warm in winter. The windows come in all shapes and sizes – square, round, half-round, long and peaked. Each house in the village is connected with all others and every courtyard has both a front gate and back door.

Sitang Stone Pavilion (四堂石楼) features a Qing Dynasty-style gate tower with wood carvings. Yingtan's villagers are said to be particularly rational in that they do not believe in ghosts or spirits, and hence the village has none of the shrines usually found in similar rural communities. However,

the four ancestor halls in the centre of the town are regarded as sacred by locals. At every festival and Chinese New Year, locals offer sacrifices to their ancestors and burn incense in the halls as a sign of respect. One legend is that the four halls are a legacy of the Huang Chao insurrectionary army, with each representing one of the four generals in the military camp.

Dehe Hall (德和堂), built during the Qianlong period of the Qing Dynasty (1735-1795), has 33 rooms. The hall is home to an apparently magical "Waterdrop Spirit Spring" (滴水神泉), whose water is said to never dry and never flood, merely producing one drop of water at a time. There is an old well (老井) inside the village with a two-storey stone house built over it. Although the river is dry, the spring water in this well is still plentiful. According to villagers, the water in this well will never dry and never freeze, even in winter.

Built with small stones, Small Stone Pavilion (小石楼) is the oldest architecture in the village with a history of nearly 600 years. Rulin Hall (汝霖堂) was built in the Qianlong period of the Qing Dynasty. During the Sino-Japanese War,

Village slope of dwellings

A stone mill in Yingtai Village.

Communist marshall Liu Bocheng stayed here when he passed through the village. Zhonghe Hall (中和堂), built during the Xianfeng period of the Qing Dynasty (1850-1861), is a courtyard-style building on a bridge. Inside the courtyard there are fruit trees which are thin at bottom and thick on top. Lu Zhonglin, the former chairman of Hehei Province, came to Yingtan Village in 1937, and this small Chinese-style courtyard became the government office of Hebei. The room on the right side was his bathroom and the stone bathtub he used once still remains.

An impressive Stone Screen Wall (石影壁) is located in an ordinary family courtyard. With a unique wave pattern on both sides, the wall is 2 metres high, 1.4 metres wide and 50 cm thick, and was discovered by villagers when escavating the mountain.

During the anti-Japanese years, this small village with only 100 families had 30-40 people serve in the resistance army, six of whom were sacrificed in battle, giving Yingtan Village its heroic reputation.

## TOOLS OF THE TRADE

Traditional tools like stone mortars, stone pestles and stone mills can be seen everywhere in Yingtan Village and are used by locals to mash beans, corn, make congee, bean curd and pancakes.

# Piancheng Village

## Mysterious Stockade in the Taihang Mountains

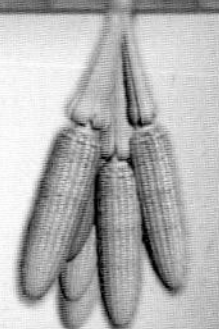

With records dating back to the Han Dynasty, Piancheng Village is located deep in the Taihang Mountains and is embraced on three sides by green hills.

### Getting there

Piancheng Village, Piancheng Town, Shexian County, Handan, Hebei..
Nearest City: Shijiazhuang.
河北省邯郸市涉县偏城镇偏城村。
Take a high-speed train from Shijiazhuang (石家庄站) to Handan (邯郸站)(about 1hour). Walk 5 minutes to Handan Bus Terminal (邯郸汽车客运总站) and then take a bus to She County(涉县) (about 1.5hours). At She County, transfer to a non-stop bus to Piancheng Village(偏城村) (about 45 mins).

The origin of the village's name is ambiguous, although the character "城" (Cheng) means "city." However, in the inscription on the north gate of the Liu Family Stockade located in the centre of the village, the upper right dot in the "城" is not in its usual position but outside the main body of the character. According to some theories, this deliberately symbolises that Piancheng is not a city, particularly because it has only three gates (north, south and east) rather than the usual four.

What is not disputed is that the Liu Family Stockade (刘家寨) was built by the Liu family. The family used green stone bricks and built a 10-metre high wall. The east gate was set as the main gate, with a plaque that reads "Eterrnal Peace Stockade"(永安寨) in Chinese characters hung above the gate

Liujiazhai Village was built around the end of the Song Dynasty and the beginning of the Yuan Dynasty. It is a typical example of quadrangle architecture in the north which has been enhanced by being built on a mountain, together with its many brick, stone and wood carvings from the subsequent Ming and Qing Dynasties.

There are 47 courtyards inside the stockade, covering an area of 16,600 square metres. Eighty percent of the existing buildings were built during the Qing Dynasty and the Republic of China periods. Nowadays, local villagers still live in them, although some of the older houses have been restored.

In front of the government offices of Piancheng County is a street that runs from east to west. One lane to the south is called the "Six Door Corridor" (六门圪廊). It was named after a 16th generation descendant of the Liu Family, Liu Rong, who was the sixth child of the family.

The General's Mansion (将军第), which is located south of the Six Door Corridor, was the site of the Piancheng County government. Built upon a steep mountain, the mansion' s courtyard has three entrances, and from the main hall to the gate there is an elevation difference of 9 metres. Both the General's Mansion and the Jinshi Mansion (进士府) opposite it are courtyards which belonged to Liu Rong, who was a successful candidate in the highest imperial examinations (ie. a "Jinshi") in the Xuantong period in the Qing Dynasty (1908-1912).

The plaques above both courtyards in the General's Mansion and Jinshi Mansion are well preserved. It is said that this is because during the Sino-Japanese war, a hero occupied the courtyard and his plaque, which reads "Hero of Slaying Enemies" (杀敌英雄) in Chinese, covered (and thus protected) the original "Jinshi Mansion" plaque.

## WOOD AND WELL

Piancheng Village locals still collect firewood from the surrounding hills and drink well water. Local snacks include Zhuai Noodle (拽面), a famous delicacy.



**The village's atmosphere is captured by the four Chinese characters "Zheng Qi Yan Su" ("Tidy and Serious") above the gate tower.**

# Jimingyi Village

## The Ancient Post Station

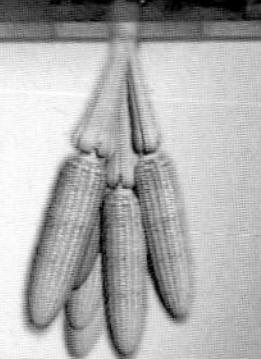

Jimingyi Village ("Cock-Crow Post Station") is home to the best-preserved ancient post station remaining in China. It possesses a very important position in the history of the postal service in China.



### Getting there

Jimingyi Village, Jiming Town, Huailai County, Zhangjiakou City, Hebei Province.
Nearest City: Beijing.
河北省张家口怀来县鸡鸣驿乡鸡鸣驿村。
Take a train from Beijing West Railway Station(北京西站) and get off at Xia Garden station(下花园站)(about 3 hours). Take a bus or taxi from Xia Garden station to Jimingyi Village Station (鸡鸣驿村)(5 km).

Jimingyi Village is also called Jiming Mountain Post Station. Situated 150 km from Beijing, the post station was initially built in the Yuan Dynasty and by 1420 had become the largest post station in the north capital area. Due to its unique strategic location, the post station itself is an independent town.

Clay walls were built around the village in 1472, and in 1570, the walls were reinforced with bricks. The whole post station is square in shape. The walls are as tall as 12 metres and apart from a collapsed section in the middle of the west wall, the other parts of the walls still stand today. Above the east and west gates there are gates with Chinese inscriptions

Overview of Jimingyi Village

which are translated to read "Jiming Mountain Station" (鸡鸣山驿) and "As Vigorous as the Big Dipper" (气冲斗牛). In 1738, the walls were renovated and a moat was built to the east of the town. Jiming Post Station remained in operation until the Northern Warlords Government began to shut down ancient post stations and set up a modern post office in 1913.

Two roads running north-south and three roads running east-west unevenly divide the town into three districts, nine parts and 12 sections. The main district extending east-west is mainly for military and political administration, and the west district stretching north-south contains core facilities of the post station. The exquisite grey-tiled houses and clay residences are said to be capable of weathering the effects of wind and sand.

There are postal official residences, storage buildings, guest rooms, stables, theatres and Buddhist and Taoist temples in the village, most of which are well preserved. The Official Guest House (公馆院) built in the Ming Dynasty sits

in the north of the post station and consists of three courtyards. It is where officials and courtiers dined and stayed over when they passed by. The partition boards feature exquisite carvings, with patterns of lyres, chess, lotus, bats and crickets.

The He Family Mansion (贺家大院) is the former command post and comprises five courtyards. The east gable wall contains a passage. It is where the Empress Dowager Cixi and Emperor Guangxu of the Qing Dynasty once stayed during their escape from the Eight-Nation Allied Forces's invasion into Beijing. The





Tower in Jimingyi Village

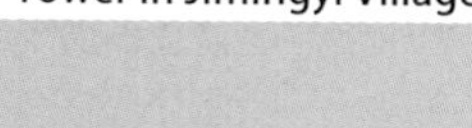

Pagoda in fields

Symbol of "Cock-Crow" Post Station

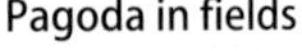

## POTATO FISH

Potato Fish is a well-known traditional delicacy of Zhangjiakou City. This is also a grape wine producing region of China. and home of China's best-known "Great Wall" label.

first courtyard contains a fine brick screen wall, and the gable of the second courtyard bears an inscription recording the stay of the Empress Dowager. The courtyards used to be connected together but are now independent halls.

There are eight ancient temples in the town, including a Temple of the Dragon King (龙王庙) and Temple of the God of Wealth (财神庙). Eternal Peace Temple (永宁寺i), with a history of more than 800 years, is the oldest building in the village. Mount Tai Temple (泰山庙) was built in 1651 during Emperor Shunzhi's reign in the Qing Dynasty (1643-1661). This was once a busy centre of public worship, and villagers frequently came here to pray for sons.

In the past, a grand temple fair was held in the village from the 13th to 18th day of the fourth month of lunar calendar. On the 15th day, devout men and women from Beijing, Tianjin, Shanxi Province and Inner Mongolia would make a pilgrimage here to offer incense and pray for fortune.

# Zhujiayu Village

## Village of the Holy Spring

The terrain of Zhujiayu Village ("Zhu Family Gorge Village") is like a ladder with winding paths intersecting the highest and lowest steps. There are around 200 ancient sites in the village with highlights including the Kangxi Double Bridge, a dual-lane ancient track, a God of War Temple and the Zhu Family Ancestral Hall.

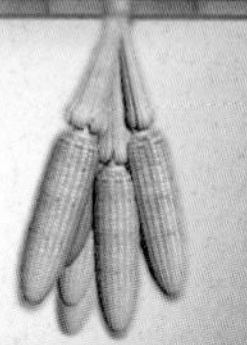

### Getting there

Zhujiayu Village, Guanzhuang County, Zhangqiu Town, Jinan City, Shandong Province.
Nearest City: Jinan.
山东省济南市章丘市官庄乡朱家峪村。
Take a bus from either Jinan East Bus Station(济南汽车东站) or Jinan Bus Station(济南汽车总站) to Mingshui City(明水市) (both services take about 1 hour). From Mingshui, transfer to a bus to Zhujiayu Village (RMB25 & 1/2 hour).

Zhujiayu Village is located at the northeast foot of Hu Mountain, 40 km from Jinan City. Zhujiayu Village gained its current name in the second year of Emperor Hongwu's reign in Ming Dynasty (1369) when the Zhu clan settled in the village - Zhu was then the family name of the emperor.

The "Holy Spring of Spirit Water" (圣水灵泉) was built in 1721 and is located in front of Holy Water Temple (圣水庙). A stone arch was built at the top of the well, with the inscription "Magic Spring of Holy Water". .It is said that the province was plagued by serious drought at the end of Emperor Kangxi's reign (1661-1722) in the Qing Dynasty. The Governor of

Ancient street in Zhujiayu Village

**MIGHTY TREE**

The Seven Arch Bridge (七孔桥) and Tan Well (坛井) are located at the southeast entrance of the old village. Not far from them is a giant cypress tree that is reputedly more than 3,000 years old. The crown of the cypress casts a shadow as large as 50 square metres.

Shandong Province, accompanied by Huang Bing, Magistrate of Haizhou Prefecture, came here to pray for rain and the prayer was answered. Hence the Governor ordered Huang Bing to commission the inscription for the spring.

Kangxi Double Bridge (康熙双桥) comprises two bridges standing about 10 metres apart. The east bridge was built in 1670 and the west one was built in 1688 but both are wide enough for both pedestrians and vehicles to go through. The bridges are made of bluestones and no plaster was used in their construction.

Wenchang Pavilion (文昌阁), built in 1838, is located between Yu Gate (圩门) and West Sentry Gate (西哨门). The main body has a pavilion on the top and an arched opening at the bottom. The ridge of the pavilion contains a Qing Dynasty carving of "two dragons playing with a pearl". Wenchang Pavilion faces south, standing opposite to Star Tower (魁星楼) at the peak of Wenfeng Mountain. The symbolism of "Star Tower" is to commemorate excellent scholastic achievement, while the "spirit" of Wenchang Pavilion is said to have overseen official career development, so these two buildings complement each other. During rainy and misty days in summer, clouds hang low over the the top of the pavilion and sometimes float through the arch opening.

Scenery at the entrance of the village

Layout of ancient buildings in Zhujiayu Village

To the west of Wenfeng mountain stands three parallel "Penholder Mountains" (笔架山), which were said to be where the celestial spirit of Star Tower (魁星) placed his pens. The pool to the east of the mountain is called "Ink-slab Pool" (魁星砚池). Legends say it is the ink-slab of the Star Tower spirit.

The village's God of War Temple (关帝庙) was built in the Ming Dynasty. Though small, it possesses a unique style, with lintels carved with "two dragons playing with a pearl" and stone pillars carved with flying dragons.

The Zhu Family Ancestral Hall (朱氏家祠) is located east of the north entrance. It was built in 1882 and comprises an inner court and an outer court. In the inner court there is an elegant and grand ancestral shrine made of big blue stones, bricks, wood beams, tiles, curved eaves and attached rooms. There used to be four precious trees in front of the shrine, but now only one remains.

Long Flow Spring (长流泉) is located at the foot of the east cliff. South Pool (南池) was built in the spring of 1898, and North Pool (北池) was built in March 1921. The stone dragon heads carved on the south wall and the north wall of South Pool face each other. During high tide, high quality spring water spouts from dragons' heads and into the square pool.

Ancient track in Zhujiayu Village

# Beifangcheng Village

## Village of Eight Hundred Castles

Despite a history of more than 430 years, Beifangcheng Village has managed to maintain its "丰" shaped layout which has remain unchanged since the Ming Dynasty. The village contains a well-preserved cluster of ancient buildings from the Ming, Qing Dynasties and Republic of China period, such as residences, theatres, temples and granaries.

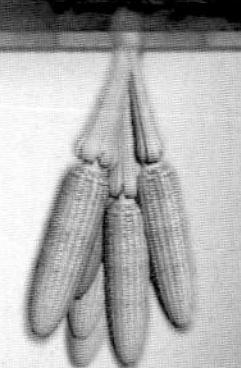

### Getting there

Beifangcheng Village, Yongquan, Wei County, Zhangjiakou City, Hebei Province.
Nearest City: Beijing.
河北省张家口市蔚县涌泉庄乡北方城村。
Take a train from Beijing West Railway Station(北京西站) and get off at Xia Garden station (下花园站)(about 3 hours). Take a long-distance coach from the nearby Xia Garden Bus Station(下花园汽车站to Wei County(蔚县)(about 2.5hours), and then transfer to a taxi to Beifangcheng Village (20mins).

Beifangcheng Village was established in 1567 and is located in a hilly area 8 km north of Weixian County, which is a fascinating mix of nomadic and Central Chinese culture. During the middle of the Ming Dynasty, castles were widely built in this region, earning it the nickname "Eight Hundred Castles" (which would serve as a literal translation of the village's name).

Since Beifangcheng Castle is square in shape, it is called "Square Castle". The layout of the castle is typically Chinese: six lanes structured around a main street on which lie a Wealth God Temple (财神庙) and Horse God Temple (马神庙.) Zhenwu Temple (真武庙), where Emperor Zhenwu (a Taoist deity) is enshrined, stands at the end of the street.

The "predecessor" of Beifangcheng Castle was a small castle in the present village's northeast, the ruins of which remain today. After the village's population grew, the small castle no longer met their needs, and as a result, Beifangcheng Castle was built on a new site. The road in

Beifangcheng Village has managed to maintain its unique simplicity despite modernisation

The solemn south gate of the ancient village

front of Beifangcheng Village is one of the Yanyun Ancient Tracks (云古道), an important network of roads during the Ming and Qing Dynasties. At the same time, it was the only passage to Congtai Temple (重台寺), the largest temple in Weixian County. In the past, throngs of caravans and camels came and went through this road, and Mongolian, Uygur and Han people have left their footprints here.

In ancient times, South Gate (南门) was the only entrance into Beifangcheng Castle. The fan-shaped plaque embedded above the arch bears an inscription with the Chinese characters for "Beifangcheng Castle."

Outside the gate is the only theatre in the village (戏台). The backstage area is separated by golden pillars and wooden partition boards with a coloured painting of pine and cypress trees. A door is set on the east wall, and Chinese characters which mean "Room of Contemplation" (清净室) are inscribed above it. The theatre is extremely busy during the first month of the lunar calendar, which usually covers late January and early February. Villagers are particularly fond of the Shanxi clapper opera (山西梆子) played by professional troupes.

The Dragon King Temple (龙王庙) is located east of the theater and contains three main halls. The inner gable of the main halls are decorated with painted murals which are bright in colour and elegant in style.

Goddess of Mercy Temple (观音庙) and "King of Hell" Hall (阎王殿) are located at the east and west sides of the gate opposite the theatre. They are surrounded by a fan-shaped brick wall half a metre high. When the play was on, women had to watch from behind the wall, while only men could stand in front of the stage to watch.

There are two temples about 100 metres north of the gate. The one in the east is the Wealth God Temple and the one in the west is Horse God Temple. A Buddhist Temple (佛殿) stands 50 metres further up north.

The Buddhist Temple directly faces Zhenwu Temple, which is built on a high platform. Everything that happens in the village can be seen from here. The temple's front hall is built underground and contains a small gate. A sequence of gold-plated murals on the east, west and north walls exhibit the life of Emperor Zhenwu, from his birth to when he supposedly became a deity.

### STICKY NOODLES

"Sticky noodles" (糊糊面) are a bean product developed by Weixian County locals. They are made of 12 kinds of beans such as wax bean, pea and horse beans. The beans are stir-fried until done and then ground, and are said to be of high nutritional value.

# Wudangzhao Village

## The Largest Lama Temple in China

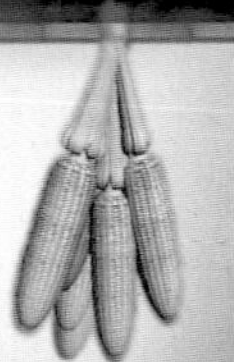

Wudangzhao Village lies in the Wudang Ravine area of the Yin Mountain, 70 km from Baotou City. The village's spectacular monastery is the biggest and most intact Tibetan lamasery in Inner Mongolia.



### Getting there

Wudangzhao Village, Wudangzhao Town, Shi Guai District, Bao Tou City, Inner Mongolia Autonomous Region..
Nearest City: Baotou.
内蒙古自治区包头市石拐区五当召镇五当召村。
Take a No. 7 bus from Baotou's Dong He District(东河区) to Shiguai District(石拐区) (RMB7 & 1 hour), then continue by taxi to Wudangzhao(五当召) (RMB 35 & 1/2hour).

Wudangzhao Village has different three names: in Mongolian, Chinese and Tibetan. "Wudang" in Mongolian means "The Willow Village", named for the thriving willows in its front valley. The village's Tibetan name is "Da Ge Er", which means "White Lotus", and its Chinese name of "Guangjue Temple" (兴旺) was bestowed by Emperor Qianlong during

Wudangszhao Village is built on a mountain and surrounded by streams

the 21st year of the his reign during the Qing Dynasty (1756).

Wudangzhao Temple (五当召寺) is one of the three most prestigious temples of Lamaism in China, along with the Potala Palace in Tibet and the Kumbum Monastery in Qinghai Province. The temple was first built in the Kangxi period of the Qing Dynasty (1654-1772), and grew to today's large scale after several periods of expansion. The monastery has 2,538 rooms which cover an area of 200 thousand square metres, and during its peak was said to have accommodated 1,200 lamas. The main buildings include six temples, three mansions, one hall and 94 lama dormitories, all in the traditional Tibetan style: flat roof, straight wall, small window and white in colour.

Inside the magnificent white temples of Wudangzhao Village, there are beautiful statues and murals. Every temple has distinctive features of its own, such as a 10-metre-high copper statue of Sakyamuni (释迦牟尼铜像), and a 9-metre-high copper statue of Tsongkhapa (宗喀巴铜像), the earliest ancestor of shamanism. According to statistics, there are more than 1,500 Buddha statues made of various materials including gold, silver, copper, wood and clay.

Wudangzhao Temple is still the location where lamas in the region gather to perform Buddhist rituals. From July 23rd to the first of August in the lunar calendar (usually mid-August in the Western calendar), the annual Mani Festival (嘛呢会) is held, creating colourful scenes as lamas walk around the monastery, holding prayer wheels, playing religious horns and beating sheepskin drums.

### MONGOLIAN FARE

The inexpensive restaurants around Wudangzhao Temple serve classic Mongolian cuisine such as hand grilled meat (手扒肉), Mongolian-style milk tea (奶茶), millet stir-fried in butter (炒米), steamed stuffed bun (蒙古包子), and fermented milk (奶酒).

# Meidaizhao Village

## Living with Buddha

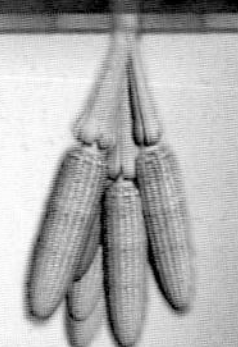

Meidaizhao Village was named after a "living Buddha" from the 17th century called Maidalihutuketu. The village is an important Dharma centre which helped Lamaism spread to Mongolia.

### Getting there

Meidaizhao Village Village, Meidaizhao Village Town, Tu Mo Te You Qi, Bao Tou City, Inner Mongolia Autonomous Region..
Nearest City: Baotou.
内蒙古自治区包头市土默特右旗美岱召镇美岱召村。
Several bus routes run directly from Baotou long-distance bus station (包头长途汽车站) to Meidaizhao Village (美岱召村) (about 1hour). Alternatively take a train from Baotou Station to Salaqi Station (萨拉齐站) (about 1hour). After exiting the train station, walk west for about 10mins to the intersection by the bridge, from where you can take a No.6 minibus to Meidaizhao Village (RMB5 & 40mins).

Taihe Gate of Meidaizhao Village

Meidaizhao Village was built in the Jiajing period of the Ming Dynasty and lies 100 km from the City of Hohhot. The village has a unique architectural style which imitates the style of buildings from the Han Dynasty while also mixing in Mongolian and Tibetan-styles. It is a fascinating lamasery which combines the functions of a village and temple.

In the Longqing period of the Ming Dynasty (1567-1572), the leader of the Tumet Mongolian tribe, Altan Khan (1507-1582), was conferred the title of "Lord of Shunyi District" (顺义王) by Emperor Longqing. Khan proceeded to build towns on the Tumo River, and in the third year of the Wanli period (1573-1620), the first completed town was named Fuhua Town (福化城). A western missionary by the name of Wallace came here to preach from Tibet in the 34th year of the Wanli period (1573-1620), and hence the village is also known as Wallace Temple.

The walls around Meidaizhao Village were built with earth and stones. At the four corners, there are 11-metre-high extended lookouts with turrets above. The gate tower is in the centre of the south wall, with a Ming Dynasty stone tablet which reads "Taihe Gate" (泰和门). Inside the village there are several courtyards where the Wang family of the Shunyi District once lived. There is also the famous Taihou Hall (太后殿), where the ashes of Altan Khan's wife Sangnianzi are stored in

Bird's-eye view of Meidaizhao Village

a sandalwood tower. The main halls of the temple are magnificent, with votive offerings to Buddhist and Bodhisattva statues, and murals with Buddhist stories. The murals in the Mahavira Hall describe the history of Sakyamuni and contain scenes of Mongolian noblemen worshiping the Buddhas. Among the Mongolian portraits, there is one of Altan Khan and his wife.

The Glass Palace (玻璃殿) is a triplex building where Altan Khan and Sanniangzi are still worshipped. The double-eave building in the northeast is called Empress Temple (太后庙) or Sanniangzi Temple. Sanniangzi, the third wife of the Altan Khan (Sanniangzi literally means "Third Lady") was known for her intelligence and beauty. According to legend, she convinced Altan Khan to adopt her idea of establishing friendly relations with China. After her husband's death, Sanniangzi continued the policy and maintained peace between the Tumet tribe and the Ming Dynasty for over 40 years.

In the 15th year of the Wanli period of the Ming Dynasty (1587), Sanniangzi was conferred the title of "Faithful Lady". A tablet on the gate of Meidaizhao Village is inscribed with 16 Chinese characters which can be translated to mean "The Peace of A Country and the Happiness of the People".

**FESTIVAL**

The temple fair (庙会) held in Meidaizhao Village every year on the 13th day of the fifth month of the lunar calendar (usually June) is one of the most famous cultural festivals in the west of Inner Mongolia.

Ancient architecture in the mountains

# Xiongyasuo Village

## The Last Ming Dynasty Stronghold

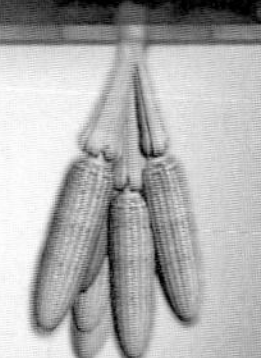

Xiongyasuo Village is the only remaining ancient coastal defense citadel on the east coast of China. The village is situated 44 km northeast of Jimo City, with the Huanghai Sea to the east. As there is a red cliff on White Horse Island in the northeast, the village is called "Xiongya", meaning "mighty cliff".

### Getting there

Xiongyasuo Village, Fengcheng Town, Jimo City, Qingdao City, Shandong Province.
Nearest City: Qingdao.
乘青岛至即墨的长途汽车到即墨汽车站，然后后乘班车至丰城，再包车前往（约10分钟车程）。
Take a bus from Qingdao City Bus Station (青岛市汽车站) to Jimo long-distance bus station (即墨长途客运站) (2hours). At Jimo transfer to a bus to FengCheng (丰城镇)(1 hour), then continue to Xiongyasuo Village by minibus (about 10 mins).

The Ancient Citadel of "Xiong (mighty) Cliff" (雄崖) was built in the 35th year of the Hongwu period of the Ming Dynasty (1402). It was a coastal defense castle that became one of the most important military fortresses in Shandong Province after its completion. In the 12th year of the Yongzheng period of the Qing Dynasty (1735), the citadel was largely ruined and the city abandoned. However, inside and around the citadel, there remain the City God Temple (城隍庙), Lord Guan Temple (关帝庙), and a Jade Emperor Temple (Y玉皇庙).

The Ancient Citadel of XIong Cliff is a square castle with earth walls covered by grey bricks. The rows of millstones on

Mythical creatures on the houses of Xiongyasuo Village

Ancient buildings of Xiongyasuo Village

the cross roads from west to east and south to north reflect the former prosperity of the village's grain and oil processing businesses. The south gate has been repaired several times. The eaves are short and undecorated, reflecting a tough military style. Though the west gate (西门) has collapsed, the frame can still be seen.

Standing on the south gate (南门) of Xiongyasuo Village, visitors will be able to see the Jade Emperor Temple. The temple has a highly unique hall built of stone with no beams. Built in the Hongwu period of the Ming Dynasty (1368-1398), the temple stands like a sentry atop the Jade Emperor Mountain southwest of the village. The inside room has a shrine and a statue of the Jade Emperor. The outside room has statues of other gods and murals on the interior walls. According to legend, the temple faces east because the builders were afraid of the mythical Dragon King (龙王), the lord of the seas, so they designed the gate to face the sea in order to show their respect.

On the left side within the south gate is a large Catholic church (天主教堂). According to records, German missionaries preached here in 1890 and the villagers made a note of seeing the priests riding on motorbikes. Now this church, which combines both Chinese and western styles, has become a warehouse.

In the west of Xiongyasuo Village there is an old well (老井) surrounded by 1.5-metre-long stone columns. The inscriptions on the interior wall of the well have been eroded by the water. Based to the remaining characters, the inscriptions appear to be the names of the donors of the well.

Magnificent gate tower of Xiongyasuo Village

## TEMPLE FAIR

A temple fair (庙会) is held in the village every year on the 9th day of the third month of the lunar calendar (usually the end of March). During the festival, the village will be crowded with daytrippers who have come to see the village's temples and gate towers.

# Dongchudao Village

## Silent Seaweed Cottages

Dongchudao Village is full of "silent seaweed houses". The weeds on the roof of seaweed cottages soften the hard rock and give the roofs of the houses a beautiful curve. These seaweed cottages have sheltered villagers from the wind and rain for over a hundred years.

### Getting there

Dongchudao Village Village, Ningjin sub district office, Rongcheng City, Weihai City, Shandong Province.
Nearest City: Weihai.
山东省威海市荣成市宁津街道办事处东楮岛村。
Take a long-distance bus from Weihai to Rongcheng City(荣成市) (about 1hour). At Rongcheng transfer to a bus to to Ningjin(宁津) (RMB6 & about 1 hour), then take another bus onto Dongchudao Village ( 30 yuan & 1hour).

First built in the Wanli period of the Ming Dynasty (1573-1620), Dongchudao Village is located in the easternmost part of of the Ningjin sub-district, north of the Shidaowan Provincial Tourist Resort (石岛湾省级旅游度假区). It is a small fishing village surrounded by the sea on three sides and famous for its large number of seaweed cottage (海草房) as well as its scenery, rich local culture, folklore, and sea products.

Dongchudao Village is supposedly shaped like a lotus. The south part of the village is filled with new red-tile houses and buildings, while the north part consists of the special seaweed cottages left by the ancient dwellers.

The village currently contains 144 seaweed houses with a total 650 rooms. Among them, the oldest one can be traced back to the Shunzhi period of the Qing Dynasty (1643-1661). Eighty-three of the seaweed houses (with 442 rooms) are

Seaweed cottages in Dongchudao Village

over a hundred years old, and these are mainly located in the center of the village.

The west side of the village is connected to the mainland, giving it nice views and pleasant weather. The famous seaweed houses are built with stone walls and have lively patterns inscribed on them. The triangular walls, square courtyards and thick seaweed on the roof tops are all special features of the houses. Normally there are some tiles or cement on the ridges in order to help the houses withstand strong winds. The houses are said to be warm in winter and cool in summer.

The seaweed used on the houses is a kind of wild algae which thrive at 5-10 metres below the surface of the sea. There are large amounts of salt and colloid in the seaweed. The mature seaweed is brought to shore by the current, and locals collect and dry them to build roof tops which are durable, leak proof and can absorb moisture. Villagers like to say that their seaweed cottages are the most unique eco houses in the world.

Walking down the stone alleys of the quiet old village is like passing through a time corridor. The rows of seaweed cottages are like old men, silently observing passers-by with indifference.

Dongchudao Village has a 7.5-km-long coastline with 5 km of high quality beaches which provide opportunities for swimming. There are 300 acres of beaches where people can gather seafood like sea slugs, crabs, scallops and oysters at low tide. Tourists can stay in the seaweed cottages, eat locally caught produce, and experience the culture of this fishing village up close.

Plants in front of the seaweed cottage

## MIRAGE

Yangjiazang Reef (杨家葬海礁) of Dongchudao Village is 1.5 km from land and is 13.3 metres high. It is said to look like a pen rack from the front, a warship from the southwest side, and a bridal sedan from the northeast. In the foggy times of early spring, locals have reported mirages of shapes like animals, plants or buildings.

# 西 部 古 村
# W E S T

## Drum Towers, Flower Bridges and Mosques

# Zengchong Village

## Hometown of Dong Culture

The beautiful Zengchong Village was laid out according to the philosophy of the Taoist Five Elements and Eight Diagrams – with a drum tower at its centre and three Fengyu (Wind and Rain) Bridges to unify the elements. Surrounded by mountains and streams, the village's fine structures are a typical representation of the culture of the Dong ethnic group from southern China.

### Getting there

Zengchong Village, Wangdong Town(往洞), Congjiang County(从江县), Qiandongnan Miao & Dong Autonomous County, Guizhou Province. Nearest City: Qiandongnan.
(黔东南苗族侗族自治州) 贵州省黔东南苗族侗族自治州从江县往洞乡增冲村。
Take a non-stop bus from Qiandongnan's Kaili Bus Station(凯里汽车站) to Congjiang Countyy's 从江县) Tingdong Bus Station(停洞车站)(3 hours). From Tingdong Bus Station, take a taxi or a bus onto Zengchong Village (about 1.5hours).

Located in the northwest of Jiangxian County, Zengchong Village lies in the region that borders the Guizhou, Hunan, and Guangxi Provinces. "Zengchong" originally meant "land of prosperity" and the village has a history of more than 600 years. A major draw is the 330-year-old Zengchong Drum Tower (增冲鼓楼), which is the oldest well-preserved Dong drum tower in the country. Other attractions include the Kangxi Wells (此外还有康熙井), Wind and Rain Bridge (风雨桥), yew trees, ancient tombs, and 24 residences with horse-head walls built during the reign of Qing Dynasty emperor Qianlong (1667-1772).

Mysterious and romantic, Zengchong Village is surrounded by a clean and clear stream and is occupied by numerous fire proofing ditches – which have apparently prevented the village from fire throughout history. The village provides an image of the serene and pleasant country life, with ancient residences and wooden diaojiaolou (吊脚木

Zengchong Drum Tower

Women of Zengchong Village washing clothes by a stream

楼, "hanging foot houses") built side by side, rustic scenes of women washing clothes by the stream, white geese paddling, carps in lakes, crowing cocks, barking dogs, and curls of smoke rising from kitchen chimneys. Quiet moss-covered blue brick lanes meander through the village and are adorned with delicate stone carvings

Built with layers piled upon layers, Zengchong Drum Tower has upswept eaves and shining red pillars, forming a magnificent view with another of the village' s main symbols – the three Wind and Rain (fengyu) Bridges.

Zengchong Drum Tower was built in the 11th year of the Kangxi period in the Qing Dynasty (1672). It is 26 metres tall and has 13 layers, with three gates and a calabash-shaped roof in the "double-eaves" style. The central structure contains four pillars, each 0.8 metres in diameter and 15 metres tall. The top two layers form the octagonal roof, which has been likened to two umbrellas cutting straight into the sky. On the tower's pavilion there is a large drum. The ridges

Narrow, simple, yet elegant ancient streets

Beautiful country lanes

of the tower are tiles bonded by a paste of kiwi stem jelly and lime, boasting upswept eaves and clay sculptures of different animals. On the boards of the eaves are colourful paintings of dragons, phoenixes, fish and grasshoppers, and under them are elegant wood carvings.

Zengchong Village is a place where locals love to dance and sing, especially Dong songs. As the Dong minority group have no formal written language, information about their history and knowledge were all recorded by songs. In Dong villages such as this one, traditional Dong songs are performed in celebrations of marriages, births, as well as funerals.

During festivals, locals will gather in the Drum Tower to perform "Caigetang" (踩歌堂), a traditional Dong group worship dance performed by two separate groups, one of men and the other of women. It is said that any person who takes part in the dance will be blessed by the gods.

## PARTY PEOPLE

Zengchong Village celebrates a bewildering variety of traditional festivals such as the Lantern Festival (正月十五), Spring-club Festival (春社节), Bullfighting Festival, (斗牛节), Qingming ("Tomb Sweeping") Festival (清明节), Black Rice Festival (乌米节), Rice Transplanting Festival (插秧节), Eating New Rice Festival (吃新米节), Mid-Autumn Festival (八月十五) and Lusheng (reed-pipe) Festival (芦笙节). During each celebration, the village will become extraordinarily bustling with people.

# Zhaoxingzhai Village

## Hometown of the Drum Tower

Surrounded by hills and mountains, Zhaoxingzhai Village is located in Liping County of Guizhou Province. The village has much to offer, including Dong-style "hanging foot'" buildings, tall wooden drum towers and beautiful landscapes.

### Getting there

Zhaoxingzhai Village, Zhaoxing County, Liping County, Qiandongnan Miao & Dong Autonomous County, Guizhou Province.. Nearest City: Qiandongnan.
贵州省黔东南苗族侗族自治州黎平县肇兴乡肇兴寨村
From Qiandongnan's Liping Airport(黎平机场),take a taxi to Liping Southern Bus Station(黎平汽车站) (about 1 hour). From Liping Southern Bus Station, you can take a bus to Zhaoxingzhai Village (RMB18 & 2 hours).

As the largest and oldest Dong village in China, the village has an important cultural and architectural heritage. The shape of the village, viewed from a mountain vantage point, has been compared to a boat.

Zhaoxingzhai Village is famous for its five drum towers, five flower bridges and five stages. A main street runs from east to west with the village government, schools and residences built on either side. The village features many wooden diaojiaolou (吊脚木楼, "hanging foot houses") in a state of picturesque disorder, providing a marvellous scene of flush gable roofs covered by blue tiles.

Visitors must enter Zhaoxingzhai Village through a "Wind and Rain" Bridge (风雨桥, also known as a "Flower Bridge"). According to local custom, each drum tower must be matched

Zhaoxingzhai Village is enclosed by hills and water

Overlooking the beautiful landscape of Zhaoxingzhai Village

by a wind and rain bridge, and a stage must be visible from each bridge. Distinctive features of these ancient bridges include their tiled roofs, which protect people from rain and snow, and long benches on either side for people to rest. After dusk, visitors will usually be able to see young village men and women singing on the bridges.

The village's drum towers (鼓楼) and flower bridges complement each other perfectly. The drum towers of the village are named after virtues, including benevolence, righteousness, courtesy, intelligence and fidelity. All drum towers are made of wood, with four big fir trees acting as the main pillars. The upper layers are joined by treenails without any iron nails. Drum towers were built as symbols of prosperity in Dong villages and are also places for entertainment and social activities, as well as welcoming guests, holding meetings and delivering messages or alerts.

During festivals or when welcoming guests, villagers will gather in drum towers to perform traditional Dong dances such as the "Caigetang" (踩歌堂). Dong songs are melodious and pleasant and boast a wide variety of styles, including wine songs, love songs, mountain songs, river songs and children's songs. Meanwhile the hill where Zhaoxing Middle School is located offers a panoramic view of the village.

Drum Tower of "Intelligence"

## REED PIPES

During the Mid-Autumn Festival (中秋节, usually in September) every second year, villagers will hold a "reed pipe" (芦笙) gathering during which hosts and guests sing along to the music of this traditional instrument.

# Longli Village

## Splendid Military Castle

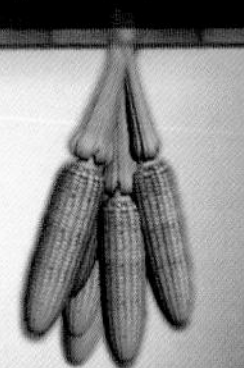

Longli Village is well known for its ancient streets, residences, bridges, wells, temples, tombs and memorial arches. The village was originally built in the Tang Dynasty and later became a vital military castle during the Ming Dynasty.



### Getting there

Longli Village, Longli County, Jingping County(锦屏县), Miao and Dong Autonomous Prefecture at Southeast Qian, Guizhou Province.
Nearest City: Qiandongnan.
贵州省黔东南苗族侗族自治州锦屏县隆里乡隆里村
Take a bus from Liping Bus Station(黎平汽车站) (a 1/2hour taxi ride from Liping Airport), to Aoshi((敖市) (RMB 6 & 1/2 hour). From Aoshi, take a taxi onto Longli Village(隆里村) (2 km).

Despite enduring more than 600 years of hardships, Longli remains the best-preserved ancient village castles in China's southern plateau area. Among the extant ancient residences of the village, the Tao Family Compound (陶家大院), Kejia Grand House (科甲第), Wuju Grand House (武举第) and the two Wang family temples (王氏宗祠) are the best preserved ones. Other interesting sites around the village include Wang Changling Temple (王昌龄祠), Zhuangyuan Bridge (状元桥) and Zhuangyuan Tomb (状元墓), which were all built to commemorate Tang Dynasty poet Wang Changling.

Built in 1359, the 19th year of Hongwu period of the Ming Dynasty, Longli Village was a military castle during the Ming Dynasty wars. The 4-metre-tall and 3-metre-wide ancient castle walls were made of earth and framed with cobble stones. Four gates were cleverly designed to leave potential adversaries guessing which one was real. According to locals, the east gate (东门) is the gate

Overlooking Longli Village

### SALTED FISH

Local snacks in Longli Village include Longli salted fish (隆里腌鱼), Chongyang wine (重阳酒), popcorn (米花), green vegetable cakes (菜粑粑), sticky cakes and fried chili (油炸辣椒).

A party escorts a bride to the groom's house

of fortune, the south gate (南门) the gate of happiness, the west gate (西门) the gate of water, and the north gate (北门) is known as the ghost gate. When a party is sent to escort a bride to her groom's home, or hold a funeral procession, they must go through the east gate and never the north gate. Inside the fortress, each street corner forms the Chinese character "丁" which symbolises the wish to have a flourishing population. There are 72 ancient wells in the village, one for each of the village's traditional family names.

Zhuangyuan Bridge (状元桥) was built in the 22nd year of the Wanli period of the Ming Dynasty (1594) in honour of Wang Changling, a poet from the Tang Dynasty Wang had achieved the status of "Zhuangyuan" awarded to those who enjoyed success in the Imperial examinations. Wang wrote many popular poems and he also established Longbiao College (龙标书院) to disseminate knowledge and develop customs. The college was later renovated during the Yongzheng period of the Qing Dynasty (1722-1735).

When Wang Changling was criticised for his poem "Lihua Ode" (黎花赋), his friend Li Bai, one of China's most legendary poets, wrote the following poem to Wang as a sign of support: "Cat-kin fall and cuckoo cry, I heard that you have arrived at Longbiao. I hope you can feel my heart just like the moon, being with you all the time".

Constructed in the Jiaqing period of the Qing Dynasty (1796-1820), the Tao Family Compound is the best preserved of the village's ancient residences. Located in the southeast, the residence has three halls and wing rooms on either side as well as tall horse-head walls. The courtyard is paved by blue stones, and on one side stands a delicate bluestone peace vase featuring carved dragons. In the halls, there are dainty carved wood windows and a square table made of superior rosewood and carved with two dragons, as well as "phoenix chairs" with "lion feet".

Longli Village has a colourful folk culture. The painted-face dragon play (花脸龙表演活), developed from Nuo Drama, is one unique local cultural highlight.. It is said that the play is based on a Song Dynasty folk story. During the performance, dancers performing the dragon dance will get their faces "painted" by the one holding the dragon's tail with mud or sticky rice. Legend says that anyone who is "painted" will enjoy good fortune.

# Loushang Village

## The Village at the Foot of Foding Mountain

Filled with ancient buildings, residences, lanes, bridges, wells, trees, tombs and books, Loushang village is located at the foot of the famous Buddhist mountain of Fodingshan, and is connected to the Provincial Foding Mountain Nature Reserve.



### Getting there

Loushang Village, Guorong County(国荣乡), Shixian County(石阡县), Tongren (铜仁区), Guizhou Province..
Nearest City: Tongren.
贵州省铜仁地区石阡县国荣乡楼上村。
Take a bus from Tongren（铜仁地区）to Shixian County (石阡县) (about 2 hours), and then transfer to a bus to Loushang Village (about 20 mins).

Built in the sixth year of the Hongzhi period in the Ming Dynasty (1494), Loushang Village was originally called "Zhaiji". The most prominent surname in the village is Zhou (周).

Loushang Village was established according to Chinese geomantic principles, with a "Green Dragon" (Liaoxian River) on the left, a "White Tiger" (a mountain peak) on the right, "Phoenix" (herons on ancient trees) at the front, a "Black Warrior" (Guishan Mountain) at the back, and the "Big Dipper" in the centre. The village was divided into four parts, of which the southeast part functioned as a production area, the southwest part as the residential district, the northwest part as a public place of entertainment, and the northeast part for tombs. The functional divisions were made according to the four quadrants created by the cross of Megrez, Phegda, Dubhe and Benetnasch in the Big Dipper.

Tall hundred-year-old trees can be seen everywhere in Loushang Village. Among them, the most magnificent are the seven ancient maple trees planted in front of Zitong Pavilion, (梓潼阁) which was constructed in the eighth year of the Yongli period of the Southern Ming Dynasty (1654). There are hundreds, perhaps thousands of white cranes nesting on the trees.

Nangui Bridge (南桂桥) was constructed in the second year of the Chongzhen period of the Ming Dynasty (1610-1644) from a single bluestone. It got its name from the nanmu and osmanthus trees in front of it, which are said to be like a unique gate through which visitors may enter the village. Inside, over 2,000 metres of ancient lanes were built in the shape of the Chinese character "寿" (meaning "longevity"). Residences are mostly wooden stone courtyard dwellings, facing south, backed by mountains and featuring

Scenery of Loushang Village

exquisite carvings from the Ming and Qing Dynasties.

Zhou Family Ancestral Hall (周氏宗祠) is one of the most magnificent ancient buildings in the village. Inside is a tablet on a crossbeam which records that the hall was built in the winter of the 19th year of Qing Dynasty's Guangxu period (1875-1908). Geliang Temple (葛凉寺) was constructed in the Qing Dynasty and was converted into a grain supply centre in the 1980s. Its structure is well preserved and contains three halls.

Tomb culture has a profound influence in the village, with many ancient tombs lying close to villagers' residences. The village has square stele tombs, nine "son tombs" and ten "Xiucai tombs" (commemorating those who passed the county level official examinations), and several tombs of officials.

Xiaotun Temple (小屯寺) is magnificent with elegant decorations. The main hall is well preserved and visitors can see tombs of monks, courtyards, stone steps, stone benches, stone drums and stone vats. Five of the monks' tombs are more than 200 years old.

The village-founding Zhou family appears to have been a studious lot, and over the years, more than 40 villagers with that name have succeeded in the imperials examinations.

The residents of Loushang Village still observe traditional customs such as the wedding celebration (哭嫁) and the funeral lament (哭丧), playing the so-na (唢呐, a kind of trumpet), embroidery, the "proposing a toast" song (敬酒歌) and the dragon dance.

### TWIN DRAGON HOLLOWS

Loushang Village has an intersting natural attraction called Twin Dragon Hollows (双龙洞.) Inside the hollows, visitors can view all kinds of strangely-shaped stalactites.

Dragon Dance, a folk custom of Loushang Village

# Matou Village

## Rebels' Stockade by the Qing River

Matou Village (literally "Horse Head Village") lies beside Qing River, halfway up the steep Mount Baihua. The village is a minority ethnic enclave inhabited predominantly by the Buyi people.



### Getting there

Matou Village, Hefeng Puyi and Miao village, Kaiyang County, Guiyang, Guizhou..
Nearest City: Guiyang.
贵州省贵阳市开阳县禾丰布依族苗族乡马头村
Take a bus from Guiyang Huaxi Bus Station (贵阳花溪汽车站(a 1/2hour taxi ride from Guiyang Longdongbao International Airport) to Hefeng Town(禾丰乡), (RMB10 & 2 hours), and then continue by taxi to Mayou Village (about 10 mins).

Fifty-eight kilometres east of Guiyang, Matou Village is located on the west bank of the Qinglong River, with the Qing River and Shenshui River embracing the north and east sides. The village is one of the largest Buyi villages in Guizhou Province and contains more than 90 buildings from the Ming and Qing Dynasties, a 50-metre stronghold wall, more than 1,000 metres of old streets, as well as temples, stone arch bridges and old wells.

Most of the village dwellings are wooden quandrangle buildings from the Ming and Qing Dynasties, with three-section stone courtyards and west-facing gates. The two main styles of village houses are "Triangle" courtyards (三角院), which have a main room plus a wing room, and"Yizi" courtyards (一字院), which only have the main room. Residences in both styles arre distributed around the village. The old wooden houses are stilt-style architectures with rails

Matou Village is embraced by tall mountains

An old lady carrying a bamboo basket

on both sides of the gates. The wood decorations contain deep cultural connotations with the most popular designs being those of dragons and phoenixes. Another commonly seen carving is the Chinese character "万" which the Buyi people consider to represent the crab flower, a symbol of their waterside living culture.

The Residence of Song Rongzong (宋荣宗宅), located in the village's northwest, is a three-section courtyard combined with a main room, wing rooms and screen wall. The stone courtyard and stone corridors are well preserved. There building has a wooden column, a green tile gablet roof, a main room with eight wing rooms, as well as carved gates and windows. In front of the gallery on the left wing is a column and gate with exquisite stone carvings on both sides. Red Army slogans can be seen on the wall.

The relics of the Song Family Mansion (宋氏的底窝紫江总管府) provide important evidence of the anti-Yuan Dynasty movement of family member Song Longji. The mansion possess more than 30 metres of stone screen walls, two courtyards, and a stone carving with the Chinese character" 寿" (which means "longevity"). It is the oldest existing site in Matou Village.

Song Longji was the most famous chief in the southwest area during the Yuan Dynasty. Song's tomb is located on Zuyang Stronghold, an ancestral grave mountain (宋氏祖坟).

The Sun Temple (朝阳寺) and the Prosperous Temple (兴隆寺) are testaments to the revived prosperity of Matou Village and the flourishing of Buddhism after the end of the Ming Dynasty. The Sun Temple was built in the second year of the Qianlong period of the Qing Dynasty (1737) and is located in the southeast corner of the village. The doors and windows are decorated with exquisite graphics of lotuses and auspicious words such as 福 (fortune), 禄, (wealth), 寿 (longevity) and 喜 (happiness). It is one of the oldest existing temples in the Guiyang region. After the Song Family Ancestral hall was rebuilt into a primary school, villagers moved three of Song Wanhua's wooden tablets into the rebuilt left wing room of Chaoyang Temple, where they

## ALL THAT'S RICE

Matou Village produce include popular local rice-based snacks such as New Year rice cakes (大年的两合米糕粑),glutinous rice dumplings (汤圆), sticky rice cakes (糯米粑), "fifth-month" (of the lunar calendar) rice dumplings (五月的粽粑) and "Qingming" (tomb-sweeping festival) rice dumplings (清明粑).

Dwellings in Matou Village

can still be seen today.

Prosperous Temple (兴隆寺) is located in the north of the village. It was built in the third year of the Shunzhi period in the Qing Dynasty (1646), but had to be rebuilt in the 1876 due to chaos and war during the Shunzhi (1643-1661) and Xianfeng (1850-1861) periods. Today, there are five existing halls and gates and the building still has windows decorated with wood carvings of lotuses, monkeys, flowers and plants.

On every sixth day of the sixth month in the lunar calendar (usually around mid-June), tens of thousands of Buyi people from the nearby areas will wear festival clothes and converge in Matou Village to hold the "June Six Singing Festival" (六月六"歌节).

Matou Village Lane

# Yunshantun Village

## Ming Dynasty Outpost

Yunshantun Village ("Cloud Mountain Outpost Village") is home to the Tunbao people. The village was founded in the Ming Dynasty as a military outpost.

### Getting there

Yunshantun Village, Qiyanqiao Town, Xixiu District, Anshun, Guizhou.
Nearest City: Guiyang.
贵州省安顺市西秀区七眼桥镇云山屯村
Take a long-distance bus from Guiyang Bus Station to Anshun City (about 1hour). From Anshun, tourist buses to Yungeng(云峰) pass Yunshantun Village (about 40mins).

Located inside a gorge in Vulture Mountain (Yunjiu Shan), Yunshantun Village was built in the 14th year of the reign of Emperor Hongwu during the Ming Dynasty (1381). All of the village's inhabitants are the descendants of the original inhabitants of the ancient military outpost, and are thus known in the area as "Outpost Descendants" (屯堡人).

Six hundred years ago, Hongwu Emperor Zhu Yuanzhang, founder of the Ming Dynasty (1328-1398) recruited soldiers in the Jiangzhe area (Jiangnan area and Zhejiang Province) and asked them to head to Guizhou Province with their families. The soldiers lived in the guard houses, fought in local wars, and reclaimed wastelands when idle. The number of military families reached several tens of thousands.

The village has only two gates. The gate in the front (前

The grand old village gate of Yunshantun Village

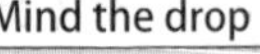

Mind the drop

屯门) was built with giant stones. The 1,000 metre city wall has a height of around 7-8 metres and a width of 1.5-2 metres. The wall is pockmarked with blast holes and crenels from battles over the years.

Through the front gate is a 600-metre-long street, which is surrounded by many lanes. Following an influx of merchants hundreds of years ago, commerce here was prosperous for a long time, and the village streets were filled with clothing stores, rice stores and drug stores.

Villagers of Yunshantun

Dwellings in Yunshantun Village are usually wooden structures with columns and suspended beams. The wooden walls, pillars, windows and gates of the houses have carvings of poems, or colourful representations of orchids, bamboos and chrysanthemums, as well as phoenix and cranes.

The rugged stone stairs along Vulture Mountain lead to Vulture Temple (云鹫寺). The temple was made in three stages – the earliest built (500 years ago) was Buddha Hall (大佛殿); the Jade Emperor Pavilion (玉皇阁) and Temple Of Lord Guan (关圣庙) were added during the Kangxi period of the Qing Dynasty (1654-1772), and Dailou Bridge (待漏桥) and the Paper Pagoda (化纸塔) were added in the early years of the Republic of China period.

In ancient times, the local Tunbao people (descendants

of Han soldiers from the Ming conquest of Yunnan) were called "phoenix heads" (凤头) because the married women of the village wore hair clasps in the shape of a phoenix head. Men in Yunshantun Village usually wrap a green cloth around their heads and wear long gowns, waistbands, straw sandals or cloth shoes. The village women wear kerchiefs, waistbands, embroidered soft boots and large robes decorated with lace. It is said that this kind of traditional dress dates back to the Ming Dynasty.

There are many unique festivals in Yunshantun Village. Among them, the Wang Gong Welcoming Festival (迎汪公) is perhaps the most fascinating. According to legend, Wang Gong was a local official in Huizhou Province during the Sui Dynasty who lent his support to the incoming Tang Dynasty. After his death, he was honoured as a martyr and buried on Mount Beilan in Qizhou City. Every year on the 16th of June in the lunar calendar, villagers of Yunshantun Village carry an icon of "Wang Gong" from the Wang Temple and put "him" into a red sedan for a parade through the village.

## NUO OPERA

Visitors to Yunshantun Village in mid-February or mid-August will be able to watch performances of the local form of Nuo Opera, which is at least 150 years old. Its main playlist includes performances of "The Eight Immortals Picture" (□仙图) and "The Case of Chen Shimei" (铡美案). The actors wear masks during the performances and the plays are mostly based on Chinese classics such as The Romance of the Three Kingdoms, meaning there are usually lots of fight scenes.

Landscape of Yunshantun Village

Ancient village dwellings

# Bingan Village

## Ancient Castle Hideout

Bingan Village is located on the old road from Sichuan Province to Guizhou Province, and is embraced on three sides by the Chishui River. The village has maintained its original appearance as a castle, with every ancient house, tile, wall and cornice marked by the vicissitudes of history.

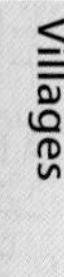

### Getting there

Bingan Village, Chishui, Zunyi, Guizhou..
Nearest City: Zunyi.
贵州省遵义市赤水市丙安乡丙安村。
There are direct buses from Chishui Bus Station (赤水客运站)in Zunyi City to Bingan County (丙安乡)(RMB 5 & 1/2 hour). Services generally depart only when a bus is full. Upon arrival at Bingan County take a boat (RMB1) across the river to Bingan Village.

Bingan Village's two ancient gates are well-preserved. Both are 2.1 metres wide and 7 metres tall, making them unusually dainty. The stairs in front of the gates are the only way into the village. There are two big white fig trees on either side of the gates, and many hanging houses are built on the cliff, usually hidden in the green bush and banana trees.

There is only one narrow stone street in the village. It is about 400 metres long and it has been an important trading place for villagers since ancient times. From the village gate, the street is not visible at first, but after a sharp turn, it opens up like a colourful vista.

Picturesque Bingan Village

Stepping onto this moss-covered stone street with its wooden walls and tile roofs is like slipping back into the Ming and Qing Dynasties. Bingan Village was historically a rest place for merchants, so there are many guest houses, restaurants, and tea houses, which have provided a steady living for villagers. Merchants from outside of the village also set up shop here, with people from the Hunan and Hubei Provinces reportedly having built the village's King Yu Palace (禹王宫).

After Chishui River was tamed during the Qianlong period of the Qing Dynasty (1735-1795), the village became a popular rest stop for passing merchants, making its markets even more prosperous. Nowadays, visitors can purchase handmade straw sandals and bamboo art wares in local stores, and witness the elderly playing card games inside their rooms.

Quiet neighbourhood

Bingan Village is situated 14 metres above the river bank, and with its steep terrain and the river bordering three sides, it is particularly easy to defend and difficult to attack by enemies. Despite this, the village was a frequent battleground. During the Taiping Rebellion (1851-1864), Shi Dakai, one

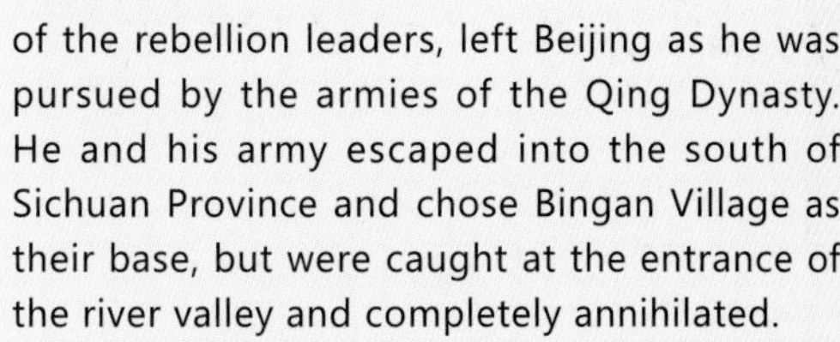

of the rebellion leaders, left Beijing as he was pursued by the armies of the Qing Dynasty. He and his army escaped into the south of Sichuan Province and chose Bingan Village as their base, but were caught at the entrance of the river valley and completely annihilated.

During their Long March of the 1930s, the Red Army crossed Chishui River four times, and a command post of the army was established in the village.

The mysterious Qingshi Bridge (清石桥) is 28 metres long and 1.4 metres wide. Its piers and deck are paved with giant stones, and how it was built remains a mystery to this day. There was once an exquisitely carved stone dragon and two stone lions on the bridge, but the lions were destroyed by flood, leaving only the dragon.

The natural landscape in Bingan Village is also an awesome sight. The magic Yingke

### BOATMEN OF BINGAN

The boatmen of Bingan Village usually leave early and return at dusk. As a local tradition, boat women fasten a red cloth on the sculls of their boats.

Waterfall (迎客瀑) is the biggest on Chishui River at 7 metres wide and 14 metres high. It pours from beneath the foot of a hundred-year-old banyan tree, said to be like a white dragon flying over the river.





Row of multi-floor village houses

# Moluo Village

## Kingdom of Women

Danba County is famous for its Jiarong Tibetan culture. Moluo Village, embraced by mountains on three sides, is a typical representative, with its many unique stone Tibetan blockhouses making it a valuable site for the study of Jiarong folk customs.

### Getting there

Moluo Village, Suopo Town, Danba County, Kardze Tibetan Autonomous Prefecture, Sichuan Province..
Nearest City: Chengdu..
四川省甘孜藏族自治州丹巴县梭坡乡莫洛村
There are 3 buses a day from Chengdu's Chadianzi Station (茶店子客运车站) to Danba County(丹巴县) (RMB61, about 6 hours). Time vary according to season, but the earliest bus generally leaves at about 6.30am. There are also 2 buses a day from Chengdu's Ximenzi Station(成都西门子车站) to Danba County.. Upon arrival at Danba, take a taxi to Moluo Village (RMB15 & about 2hours).

Facing the Dadu River, the terrain of the village slopes from northeast to south. The large numbers of stone blockhouses (碉楼) fuse the Tibetan village together, creating a living fossil of Tibetan stone architecture. Locals say that "Jiarong" (嘉绒) means "River Valley of the Queens", and in ancient times, the Jiarong region was the location of the Dong Nv Kingdom (东女国), whose culture was based around female worship.

According to records, in the ancient Dong Nv Kingdom, the ruler and officials were all women. Men were forbidden from entering politics and were restricted to the domains of battle and farming. Due to the relatively small number of women and their high social status, they practiced polyandry (a form of marriage where a woman has two or more husbands). At the time, there were more than 40,000 families living in this kingdom, distributed among the 80 villages

Ariel view of Moluo Village

## IT TAKES HANDS

If a Tibetan meets a friend following a long separation, they will put their hands on their faces. If they want to express respect, they will put their sleeves on their shoulders, bow and stretch their two arms or thumbs upward. Sticking out their tongues or helping another lead their horse are other ways to express respect.

in the valley. The populace lived below the sixth floor of the blockhouses, while the female king lived on the ninth floor.

There remain 343 blockhouses in Danba County today, and experts divde them into categories: blockhouses on key passes, beacon blockhouses, village blockhouses and family blockhouses. The majority are family and village blockhouses. Village blockhouses had a similar function in some ways to city gates, but were more flexible. Some blockhouses were built on key passes, many of them standing on steep cliffs, giving them a defensive function. Beacon blockhouses were used to pass on information but also had a defensive function as their walls are thick and stable and they tended to occupy commanding positions. If the enemy was far, villagers could shoot arrows from the blockhouse, or throw stones or wood if the enemy was closer.

Characteristics of Dong Nv culture include the powerful position of women, female worship, polyandry and various interesting marriage rituals. There were actually many different forms of marriage, such as one wife with one husband, one wife with many husbands, and one husband with many wives. These family formations all had the woman at their centre. However, Dong Nv Kingdom was a true "kingdom of women" rather than a matriarchal society.

One courtship ritual which expressed men's adoration of

Ancient architectures interspersed among green hills and trees

women was for a man to sing under a woman's blockhouse at night with his face covered by a cloak. Later in the night, the man would enter the room of the woman he liked, and if the woman reciprocated those feelings she would allow him to sleep with her. After their passions were spent, the man could spend the night in in the woman's home, but in the morning he would have to return to his mother's home.

Moluo Village is located in the west of Sichuan Province on the eastern border of the Qinghai Tibet Plateau. The Tibetan costume in this area has unique features and is called Kang costume. Women in this area often tie their hairs in a bun and wear longuettes.

Butter tea (油茶) is the most popular drink in any Tibetan area. Made of cheese, Tibetan tea and salt, the tea is consumed ubiquitously in the village. Receiving guests with tea is an ancient tradition of the Tibetan people and one which visitors will encounter when visiting herdsmen's tents or farmers' earth houses. Before a Tibetan goes far away from home, relatives and friends will offer him a Hadad (哈达), a long piece of silk used by Tibetan and Mongolian people as a greeting gift) and a cup of butter tea.

Locals singing and dancing in festival costumes

Another Tibetan drink, barley wine (青稞酒), is brewed with fermented barley. It is very popular in Tibet, especially during festival times. From April to August in the Tibetan calendar (usually from mid-April to mid-August), people will drink barley wine during festivals. Locals generally pitch a tent just for the dancing and drinking festivities.

# Yishala Village

## Village of the Yi Tribe

Yishala Village, which faces Jinsha River to the east, was built during the reign of the Hongwu Emperor during the Ming Dynasty (1368-1398). The ancient village is known as the "Great Southern Gate" of Panzhihua City in Sichuan Province. The village has always been a place where the cultures of the Han people and the Yi minority mixed together

### Getting there

Chishala Village, Pingdi Town, Renhe District, Panzhihua, Sichuan Province .
Nearest City: Panzhihua.
四川攀枝花市仁和区平地镇迤沙拉村。
Take bus from Panzhihua to Pingdi Town (平地镇)(about 1 hour) and then continue to Chishala village by taxi (10 mins).

The name "Yishala" comes from the language of the Yi (彝) minority ethnic group, and has an implied meaning of "the place where water leaks". Around 96% of the villagers belong to the Yi minority, making the village a core site for the study of Yi culture.

Yishala was an important point on a historic post road, located between the two of the biggest autonomic towns of the Yi minority. The Lazha Ferry crossing (拉乍渡口) of Jinsha (Golden Sand) River near the village was where legendary stateman Zhuge Liang reportedly crossed the river to the south more than 1,000 years ago. Zhuge Liang also frequently set up garrisons in the village on the way to Fang Mountain (where there are reputedly still many well-preserved relics from the Three Kingdoms period).

View of Yishala Village

Overlooking Yishala Village

The ancient Southern Post Road (驿道), which also constituted part of the west section of the southern Silk Road, began at Chengdu, passed Ya'an, Hanyuan, Xichang, and Laxha in Sichuan Province, then several cities in Yunnan Province, and eventually from Xiang Yun in Yunnan Province to Burma.

Yishala was the last stop before the Southern Post Road entered Yunnan from Lazha. It is said that once there was a big stone stele on the Lazha ferry inscribed with four Chinese letters which read "蜀滇交会" (meaning "the intersection of Sichuan and Yunnan"). Traces of the ancient riding track of the old Silk Road (南丝绸之路) may still be found in the village.

Even though they belong to the Yi minority, most of the people of Yishala Village have Han family names such as Mao (毛) and Zhang (张). Many Yi people in the village are the descendants of migrants from Jiangsu or Jiangxi Province, who were sent, often as soldiers, to the border regions during the Ming Dynasty. More than 600 years later, villagers still sing ballads about the departure of those people from their traditional hometowns. These days, however, almost all villagers have shared Han and Yi ancestry - ancestral tablet shrines can be found in many village houses.

The village residences are typically wooden structures with four buildings connected by five courtyards. The walls of the houses are white with black-bricked bases and delicate and exquisite sculptures can be found within the houses. The buildings here, to some extent, are similar to those often seen in the Jiangnan area (the region south of the Yangtze River).

## MEATY MEALS

There are many special foods in Yishala Village, such as roast whole lamb (烤全羊), baked beef (炕牛肉), pumpkin chicken (南瓜鸡), lamp hotpot (羊肉火锅) and lamb soup (羊肉汤).

The "Li Po Yi" (里泼彝人) is the unique name given to the community in Yishala Village. "Li" means women and "Po" means "men". The implied meaning of "Li Po" is the appreciation of the diligence and wisdom of women and the strength and courage of men. The history of Yishala Village is the history of the migration and integration of the Chinese nation and the sedimentary accretion of Chinese culture. The village is like a tiny window for visitors to view the thousand-year development of the integration of Han and Yi culture.

These days there is a booming folk culture tourist scene in Yishala which centres around the village's "10 scenic spots". The 10 include the likes of "Yi Minority Fortified Mountain Village Tourist Area" (彝族文化山寨区), "Ancient Post Road Tourist Zone" (古驿道旅游区), "Barrack of Zhuge Liang" - strategist and prime minister of the kingdom of Shu in the period of the Three Kingdoms (220-265) - (诸葛大营). and the "Pu Tao Gou Modern Agricultural Visitors Area" (葡萄沟现代观光农业区).

A small stream in front of the village

# Luobozhai Village

## Village of the Qiang

Luobozhai Village is occupied by around 1,000 people, making it one of the most densely populated villages in the Min River area. This is the only place where loess was used as as material for construction and it is the largest and oldest loess-constructed stockade of the Qiang ethnic minority.

### Getting there

Luobozhai,Yanmen Town, Wenchuan County, Ngawa Tibetan and Qiang Autonomous Prefecture, Sichuan Province.
Nearest City: Chengdu.
四川省阿坝藏族羌族自治州州汶川县雁门乡萝卜寨村
From Chengdu's Chadianzi Bus Station (成都茶店子汽车站), take one of the regular buses to Wenchuan County (汶川县)(about 3hours), then continue by minibus to Lobozhai Village (40 mins).

Luobozhai Village is about about 160 km from Chengdu, the capital of Sichuan Province, and lies on the route to the famous Jiuzhai Valley.

According to archeologists, human beings had existed in this area around 3000-4000 years ago. The name of the village has changed several times. Originally it was called "Phoenix Village" (凤凰寨) then 'Tiger Village" (老虎寨), before finally ending up with Luobozhai, which literally means "radish village".

Luobozhai Village sits between Feng Mountain and Huang Mountain. The names when combined mean "Phoenix" in Chinese, and together they have been likened to a giant phoenix spreading its wings. All villagers belong to the Qiang (羌) ethnic minority group. The stockaded village comprises numerous tiny streets and alleys made out of loess. The village was constructed for defense, and as such, almost all buildings are connected with each other, making the roofs appear conjoined. On the village gate there is a sun motif and a representation of Baishi (白石, literally meaning "white stone"), a religious symbol worshipped by the Qiang people. Designs representing other gods or holy spirits can also be seen on the roofs of houses.

The Dayu King Temple (大禹王庙) was built on a giant stone. Tourists can pray and make a wish in the temple, after which they will be given

a piece of red silk which can be taken home to relatives or friends as a blessing, or alternatively they can hang it on the village's holy tree. The white stones used during prayer can also be taken, or left on the dais by the altar. The pagoda now looks quite imposing with all the white stones accumulated over the years.

The Qiang minority has existed for thousands of years and has its own dialect but no official written language. Therefore, the history of Qiang has been transmitted through oral teachings and cultural practices. Qiang embroidery is one of the most important aspects of Qiang culture. Qiang minority women have cultivated a unique aesthetic taste which is expressed through the embroidery on their clothes and accessories. Qiang embroidery contains a wide range of themes, often about nature or natural creatures. In the past, all Qiang people wore long gowns made of flax. Men's garment were plain while women' s were colourful. The gowns of men were long enough the cover the knee and men would also wear leather coats and a waistband. Several items would hang on the waistband, including a leather cigarette case or a knife. Their feet would be covered by felt and they wore straw sandals or shoes made of bark or worn-out clothes. Shoes of children and the elderly were covered by a piece of cloud-shaped skin from a river deer. Most women wore shoes embroidered with flowers.

Village life is supported by agricultural production, supplemented by mixed farming. Local produce include Za wine (咂酒), which is made of highland barley, and Zheng Zheng wine (蒸蒸酒), which is made of corn. Many villagers smoke the local Orchid brand of cigarettes (兰花烟). Home-made preserved ham can be seen on the beams of every home, and may have been hung for years, resulting in a delicious flavor that is fatty but not greasy. The village is also known for some of its famous dishes, which include Chinese sauerkraut dumplings (酸菜搅), and steamed buns made of corn (玉米锅边馍馍).

Luobozhai Village was badly damaged by a violent earthquake which struck Wenchuan District of Sichuan province on 12 May 2008. The village has since been restored and most roads have been repaired. Since the restoration, locals finally gained access to tap water, finally ending their history of taking water from the top of the mountain.

## QIANG FESTIVALS

Qiang song and dance performances are regularly put on at night in Shalang Square (莎朗广场). Visitors might also see traditional physical trials such as"Tui Gan", a strength competition (推杆), "Bao Dan", a test of flexibility in reaction to force (抱蛋) and "Shi Kang". a test of balance (筛糠). Other highlights of Qiang festivals include eating roasted whole lamb (烤全羊), drinking local wine and singing folk songs.

Luobozhai Village as it was before the 2008 earthquake

# Baiwu Village

## The Copper Village

Baiwu Village has a history of more than 2,000 years and boasts an abundance of cultural and historic relics. Many officers and businessmen from different provinces settled in the village during the Ming and Qing Dynasties. Baiwu Village was first stop for copper transport from the mines to Beijing.

### Getting there

Baiwu Village, Nagu Town,Huize County, Qujing City, Yunnan Province..
Nearest City: Kunming .
云南省曲靖市会泽县娜姑镇白雾村
From Kunming Long-distance Bus Station (昆明汽车客运站),(a 10mins walk from Kunming Train Station(昆明站)), take a bus to Huize Bus Station(会泽客运站)(about 3hours). From Huize, direct buses cover the 32km to Baiwu Village in about 1/2 hour. The cost of the bus ticket is RMB19.

During the Ming and Qing dynasties, Baiwu village became prosperous from the copper mining business and many officials and traders from different provinces settled here. Most of the ancient architectures of the village are located on Baiwu Street (白雾街). The street is about 2 km long and runs east to west. On both sides of the street lie 24 ancient buildings from the Ming and Qing Dynasties, such as Shoufo Temple (寿佛寺), Zhangsheng Palace (张圣宫), Longevity Palace (万寿宫), the Palace of Three Sages (三圣宫) and God of Wealth Temple (财神庙). Other well-preserved

The landscape of Baiwu Village

residences, together with horse shops, post houses and other shops make for a rich assembly of interesting buildings.

The fortified wall of Baiwu Village was built during the 10th year of the Xianfeng period of the Qing Dynasty (1860). The length of the east wall is 317 metres, while the north wall is 300 metres, the south 350 metres and the west 273 metres. The walls are 5.8 metres in height with a thickness of 3 metres. The outside parts of the walls are paved by blocks filled with soil.

The structure of the Chen Family Mansion (陈氏住宅) is in the traditional "Sihe Wutianjing" style (consisting of four buildings and five courtyards). The floors of the courtyards were paved by stone bars into the Chinese characters "双喜" (meaning "double blessing" ). Despite this, shooting holes in the walls suggest that the villagers also knew less serene times.

The wealth earned by the village's copper business is reflected in its assembly halls. Most of the halls are located in places with beautiful natural views, near hills and brooks and can be regarded as a combination of temple and gardens. Some of the temples are simply used as assembly halls.

Saint Nouse Hall

Baiwu Village has lots of ancient water conservancy architectures. Most of the village' s bridges were constructed in the Qing Dynasty, such as Gather Bridge (长聚桥), Blessing Bridge 福来桥) and Victory Bridge (得胜桥). As old as they are, the bridges remain functional. Also worth visiting are the hills behind the village, which contain lots of ancient graves and steles.

Built during the reign of the Jiaqing Emperor of the Qing Dynasty (1796-1820), Culture Temple (文庙) is a place for villagers to worship three Chinese sages of antiquity – Confucius, Lord Guan (from the "Three Kingdoms" legends), and Wen Chang (the God of Learning) – and so the temple is also known as "Palace of Three Sages" (三圣宫). There is a memorial archway made of wood and stones which contains three doors and is bolstered by four columns. The shape of the roof looks like two open wings and the sculptures on it are exquisitely carved. The western and eastern attics closely support each other. Emperor Tower (天子台) makes the audience hall of the temple solemn and respectful. The ceiling of the hall has been dexterously decorated with paintings of Chinese classics such as "The Romance Of The Three Kingdoms", "Da Yu's Plough" and "Education Mencius Received from His Mother".

Since its establishment, Learning Temple has been the place for students of the village to study. One milestone in the village's cultural history was the collection and arrangement of an ancient Taoist book named "Dongjing ancient bell music" (圣谕宣讲).

## LONG AND WINDING ROAD

An ancient transportation route named Jinggu Road (京古道) is about 2 metres wide and 55 km long, stretching across the cliff and hills around Baiwu Village, with lots of twists and turns. The marks of horse hoofs are still visible on the bluestone road.

Built during the 21st year of the Guangxu period of the Qing Dynasty (1895), the theatre stage (戏台) is situated on the west of Baiwu Street opposite Yunnan Assembly Hall. In latter years of the Qing Dynasty, watching drama on the stage was an important village activity. The stage is formed by track-carrying beams and is bolstered by columns and a raised-beam. The roof has four snubby horns and is covered by dark-green tiles. The ground of the stage is a store and the first floor is the performance platform. On the right and left sides of the building are doors for entering into or getting out of the platform, and the names of the doors are "Chu Jiang" (出将) and "Ru Xiang" (入相). These four words combine to form a Chinese phrase which means "a person who has both civil and military abilities". The rice market (米市) in front of the stage can accommodate more than 2,000 people. Various Chinese opera genres including Peking Opera, Chuan Opera, Zhen Opera, Bang Zi, Hua Gu and Hua Deng are performed on this stage.

Baiwu Village was sustained throughout the years by the prosperity of its powerful copper business. Though its age-old prosperity has been worn away, its cultural and material legacy remains.

The Palace of Three Sages

# Nuodeng Village

## Bai Tribe Village

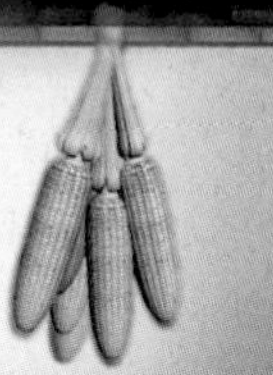

Nuodeng Village is located in the south of the natural heritage area bounded by three rivers (Yangtze River, Yellow River, Huai River). The village, whose current residents are an ethnic mix of the Bai minority and Han people. is said to have not changed much since the Tang Dynasty.

### Getting there

Nuodeng Village, Nuodeng Town, Yunlong County, Daili Autonomous Prefecture of Bai Nationality, Yunnan Province..
Nearest City: Lijiang.
云南省大理白族自治州云龙县诺邓镇诺邓村
Take a train from Lijiang to Dali Station(大理站) (about 2.5hours) and then continue from Dali Bus Station(大理客运站) to Yunlong County(云龙县) (RMB15 & 2.5hours). From Yunlong County, take an electric pedicab taxi to Nuodeng Village (RMB2 & 1 hour).

Nuodeng Village developed through its salt business and during feudal times was an important economic hub of west Yunnan Province. During the early years of the People's Republic of China, the village's traditional business declined. A house located at the entrance to the village was once the old centre of the salt business but is now a swampland of former salt wells.

There are about 300 to 400 families living in Nuodeng Village and from a distance, the Ming and Qing Dynasty folk residences in the village look like they were systematically arranged on the mountains, tier by tier. Resident families have raised horses in the village for centuries and the village's Guzong Lawn was the resting place for horses or cattle of Tibetans and the Hui minority in ancient times.

**FAMOUS HAM**

Nuodeng ham (诺邓火腿) is one of the "three famous hams" of Yunnan Province. The ham is soused in the locally produced "Guodi Salt". At the beginning of the Qing Dynasty, Nuodeng ham was one of the products traded to the countries of South and Southeastern Asia through the Southern Silk Road.

The ancient architecture in Nuodeng Village is well preserved and varied, with typical house designs favoured by the Bai minority ethnic group such as "siheyuans" (四合院, quadrangle-style architecture) and "sanfang yi zhaobi" (三坊一照壁), with a screen wall Another type of residence found in the village is the "siwo tianjing" (四合五天井), a house style of the Ming and Qing Dynasty periods with four buildings and five courtyards.

The village's architectural highlights include Jade Emperor Pavilion (玉皇阁), a Taoist construction built in the Ming Dynasty; The Star Gate (棂星门), the largest wooden memorial archway of the Qing Dynasty; and the Temple of Learning (文庙), built during the Kangxi period of the Qing Dynasty (1654-1772).

Longevity Palace (万寿宫), built in the Yuan Dynasty (1271-1368), is the oldest building in Nuodeng Village and was originally an assembly hall for receiving guests from other provinces. During the early days of the Ming Dynasty, the assembly hall was changed in to a temple called

Layers of ancient folk houses of Nuodeng Village

Longevity Temple (祝寿寺). A Ming Dynasty poem inscribed on the stele contains information about the temple.

Literary culture blossomed in Nuodeng Village. At the height of its flourishing the village produced many successful scholars such as Huang Gui, who is known as the "Great Confucius Scholar of the Yunnan Region".

The ancestors of the current Nuodeng villagers were Bai (白) people, but they were said to be from mainland China. Whatever their cultural origins, they were assimilated by the culture of the local Bai minority, creating a unique local culture. The village still preserves authentic Bai cultural features such as "Chui Chui Qiang" (吹吹腔), an ancient traditional Chinese opera form, Bai folk songs and an ancient music format called "Dongjing ancient bell music", (洞经古乐) which demonstrates the integration of Taoism and local beliefs.

Front gate of a Nuodeng Village residence

Scenic sites worth visiting around the village include Heavenly Pool (天池), the painting of supreme being Tai Ji (太极图), Taoist buildings on Hutou Mountain (虎头山道教建筑群), the Sanskrit Steles and Tombs of Cremation (顺荡梵文碑火葬墓群), as well as a group of ancient bridges. (古桥). Locals say that every kind of temple, memorial archway, assembly hall, ancestral hall, alley that can be seen across China can be found in Nuodeng Village.

# Zhengying Village

## Jiangnan in Yunnan

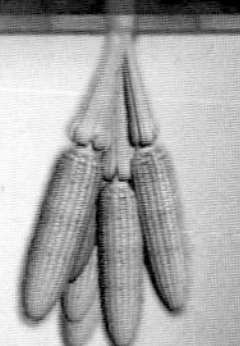

The ancestral temples, pavilions, schools and typical constructions of Zhengying Village combine architectural grandeur and the grace of ancient gardens, underpinning its claim to be the "First Village of Yunnan".

### Getting there

Zhengying village, Baoxiu town, Shiping County, Honghe Hani and Yi Autonomous Prefecture, Yunnan province.
Nearest City: Kunming.
云南省红河哈尼族彝族自治州石屏县宝秀镇郑营村
From Kunming Bus Station(昆明汽车站) take a bus to Honghe Shiping County(红河石屏县)(5 hours), and then transfer to a taxi or bus to Zhengying village (about 1/2 hour).

Zhengying Village faces Xiu Mountian in the west and Chirui lake in the north, making it a scenic spot. Originally "Pusheng Village", the name of the village was changed to "Zhengying" after it became dominated by people with the surname Zheng. By the late Ming Dynasty however, the village already had many other family names. At present, most villagers have Zheng, Wu, Chen or Li as their surnames and each family has their own ancestral temple.

Zhengying Village's landscape of farms and rivers is suggestive of the lush Jiangnan region (south of the Yangtze River) where many of the village ancestors allegedly came from. The village streets are paved by green stones, and most of the village houses face the north and have large courtyards. The village's ancestral temples, studies, yards and lanes also exhibit the delicacy of Jiangnan architecture.

In Zhengying Village culture, scholars were at the social pinnacle, which is why village lanes are filled with scholarly institutions such as Jinshi Residence (进士宅), Sima Mansion (司马第) and Hanlin House (翰林居).

Chen Family Ancestral Hall (陈氏宗祠) was built by Chen Heting (who once studied

The Chen Family Ancestral Hall

in Japan and became a businessman after quitting his offical job) in 1925 and boasts a memorial archway-style gate made from bricks. Along the central axis of the complex there is a stone bridge, the middle hall and the main hall. In each of the halls there is a yard flanked by two symmetrical pavilions. The stone bridge in front of the middle hall is a one-hole stone archbridge, on which there are stone carvings of the Chinese zodiac. The two-storey main hall has two rooms in the front and two rooms in the back and is built on a 1.2-metre-high stone base, under which are two 1.95-metre-high stone lions.

The Zheng Family Ancestral Hall (郑氏宗祠) was built in the Guangxu period of the Qing Dynasty (1875-1908), and is situated one hundred metres from the east of the Chen Family Ancestral Hall. The building is a courtyard with buildings on four side (siheyuan) made from earth, wood and stones and is adorned with beautiful carvings.

The house of Chen Zaidong (陈载东的住宅) lies in the middle of the village and is regarded as the most outstanding of all the village's folk residences. It is a siheyuan with three successive yards and features a large hall with delicate carvings and gold-plated doors and windows.

Zheying Village is currently populated by people from the Han (汉), Yi (彝), Dai (傣) and Hani (哈尼) ethnic groups, with the Han group representing the majority. The "Haicai qiang" (海菜腔) style of folk song and dance from Yi culture is quite unique and includes a famous dragon dance performed by women.

Stone carvings of the Chinese zodiac

### BAYBERRY WOOD

Near the village is a a large wood of red bayberries which visitors are free to pick from during the summer. Other local delicacies include Shiping Fried Fish (石屏煎鱼), Shiping Tofu (石屏豆腐) and Baojiang Tofu (包浆豆腐).

The delicate architectures of Zhengying Village

# Donglianhua Village

## Old Village of the Mabang

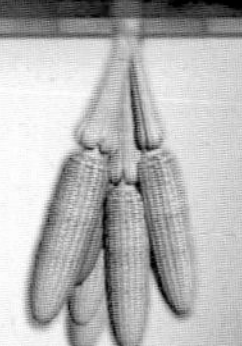

Donglianhua Village is a typical village of the Hui ethnic group. Seated on the bank of the Mitang River and with water on three sides, the village features a rich and varied folk culture and features more than 30 well-preserved buildings..

### Getting there

Donglianhua village, Yongjian town, Weishan County, Daili Autonomous Prefecture of Bai Nationality, Yunnan province..
Nearest City: Lijiang.
云南省大理白族自治州巍山县永建镇东莲花村
Take a train from Lijiang to Dali Station (大理站)(about 2.5hours), then continue by bus to Weishan County(巍山县) (about 1hour).

Donglianhua Village is situated in the northeast part of Weishan autonomous prefecture. The village is filled with verdant trees, rich fields, flowing rivers, twittering birds and fragrant flowers. The village streets are neat and clean, and every village family is said to plant trees and flowers as a symbol of their harmonic balance with nature.

As at the end of 2007, there were 1065 villagers in total, among which more than 100 were immigrants or relatives of immigrants from Burma and Thailand. Seven leaders from the Mabang tribe reportedly lived in the village during the Qing Dynasty.

Back in the Republic of China period, the Mabang (马帮) tribe of Wei Mountain consisted primarily of people from the Hui ethnic group. Leaders of the Mabang tribe built various houses and yards in the village during their time in Donglianhua Village. The village's five watchtowers, 28 old residences and many old buildings still represent the unique mix of Mabang culture and Hui style that has been preserved throughout history.

Maruji House (马如骥旧居) is famous for its unique architectural feature of containing "one tower, two yards, three doors, four pavilions, five halls and six courtyards". After passing through the heavy front gate you will encounter four Chinese characters etched on marble which can be translated to say: "Stay True to Islam for Life"

Donglianhua Mosque

(世守清真). After so many years the decorations of the house remain vivid. In particular, the colour paintings on the second floor are still extremely clear and beautiful. One highlight is an artwork entitled "View of Shanghai Streets" (上海街景) which expresses the open mindedness of Mabang merchants and their hopes for the future.

Donglianhua Mosque (东莲花清真寺0 is at the centre of local Hui culture. It was originally built in the early years of the Qing Dynasty and became a mosque in the 13th year of the Republic of China period (1924). The temple, exhibiting a mix of Chinese and Islamic beauty, is built with earth and wood, and in the main hall there is a tablet inscribed with Chinese words meaning"Honesty First" (诚一不二), written by Yang Shengqi, a major general from the Republic of China period.

Many aspects of Donglianhua Village retain an Islamic heritage. There are local scholars skilled in Persian and Arabian. Religious life here is solemn and steady, giving the village the nickname "Little Mecca". Traditional Islamic festivals are held every year and traditional Islamic foods, customs, dress and handicraft remain popular in the village.

Hui-style houses

The centre of local Hui culture

## ON THE TEA HORSE ROAD

The one-time patriarch of the local Ma clan, Ma Ruji, was said to have many influential friends in commerce, politics and the military. He allegedly led the Mabang tribe of Menghua County on trading missions along the Ancient Tea Horse Road. (茶马古道). The dam he built still benefits villagers even to this day.

# Nanchangtan Village

## Lost Village of the Western Xia

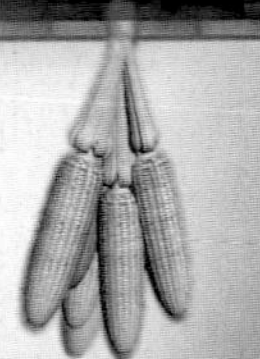

Separated from the rest of world by mountains, Nanchangtan Village is a mysterious old village on the middle bank of the Yellow River. Most of the villagers share the family name Tuo and are believed to be the descendants of inhabitants dating back to the Western Xia Dynasty.

### Getting there

Namchangtan Village, Xiangshan County, Zhongwei City, Ningxia Hui Autonomous Region..
Nearest City: Ningxia.
宁夏回族自治区中卫市香山乡南长滩村
From Ningxia Station (宁夏站) take a train to Zhongwei Station(中卫站) (about 1/2hour) then transfer to a bus to Hongquan Town (红泉乡)(1hour). At Hongquan Town, take a taxi to Nanchangtan Village (南长滩村) (RMB50 & 40 mins).

Nanchangtan Village rests at the border of Gansu and Ningxia Provinces. Each spring, the village's peach flowers are said to blossom like clouds, thus earning it the alternative name of "Pear Flower Village". Initially, it was believed that the village originated 700 years ago, when a group of descendants of the Western Xia regime came here to live a quiet life. However, the discovery of Qin and Han Dynasty ruins and relics suggests that the earliest villagers lived here some 2,000 years ago. Meanwhile, slogans from the Mao era still can be seen on the walls of the village's earth houses, which are lined up side by side in rows.

Scenery of Nanchangtan Village

Walking into Nanchangtan Village

Most villagers in Nanchangtan have the family name Tuo (拓). They believe they are the descendants of the Western Xia people and have a complete family tree of their own. In the 1980s, a scholar of the Western Xia regime, Li Fanwen, confirmed this to be true. In recent years, the relationship between Nanchangtan Village and the mysterious Western Xia Dynasty has become a hot draw for travellers.

In Nanchangtan Village, there's a rule that people with same family names shouldn't marry one another, which is why villagers tend to marry those with different family names from Gansu Province and and other villages in Ningxia Province.

Nowadays, more and more Nanchangtan residents want to leave the mountains to improve their fortunes in the outside world, ironically just as more and more people are arriving from all parts of the world to Nanchangtan Village to discover its amazing beauty.

### ANCIENT PEAR TREES

The village has 3,000 ancient pear trees along its river bank, among which the oldest is 400 years old. The top of the tree produces a shadow with a coverage of up to 300 square metres.

# Guomari Village

## Dragon Boat Festival Village

Guomari Village is a Tu ethnic group stockaded village in the Tongren area, with great significance for the study of ancient Chinese garrisons. Visitors are also drawn by the spectacular festivities of the Dragon Boat Festival (which usually falls in Mid-May).

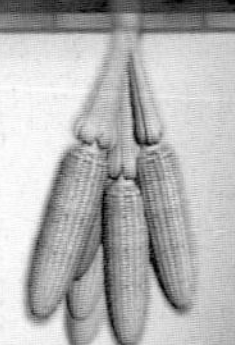

### Getting there

Guomari Village, Nianduhu Town, Tongren County, Huangnan Tibetan Autonomous Prefecture,Qinghai Province.
青海省黄南藏族自治州同仁县年都乎乡郭麻日村。
Nearest City: Xining
Buses from Xining City Bus Station(西宁市汽车站) to Tongren County (同仁县)will go by way of Guomari Village (RMB10 & 3 hours).

Originally buit up during the Ming and Qing Dynasty periods, the rampart of the Guomari Vllage walls was constructed by boards of rammed earth, with doors facing west, south and east. Some villagers still live in the fort, whose maze-like lanes are full of interesting details, such as the prayer wheel that is set on the top of every door. The houses are flat-roofed with decorations on the flying-rafters where pictures of flowers and algae are engraved. Most of the courtyards enclosed by buildings on all four sides.. and in their center there is usually a flagpole and a platform in typical Tibetan style for burning incense.

Guomari Temple (郭麻日寺), built in 1391, is the most popular of all the buildings in the village and the top of the temple provides a panoramic view of the village. Several buildings within the temple are open to the public, including the Sutra Chanting Hall 大经堂), Maitreya Palace （弥勒殿), Jianlong Granary (建隆务仓) and the Monks' Mansion (堪布仓昂欠). The three-storey Maitreya Palace was built by a Shiite "living buddha" who initiated the ceremonial practice of praying in the first month of the lunar year.

Twelve small pagodas embrace the main hall of Guomari Temple. The top floor of each pagoda is structured like a drum, and a chapel is set within. The base of the pagodas are surrounded by flat-roofed Tibetan-style cabins with prayer wheels inside.

Kalachakra Pagoda (时轮塔) is widely regarded as the greatest pagoda in the Tibetan areas of China. Designed in 1994, the round-based pagoda has five storeys and imitates the style of the Difo Pagoda where Sakyamuni first turned the Dharma-cakra. It took five years to construct and has a height of 33 metres and a base perimeter of 33 metres. Some clothes and personal effects of the 10th Penchen Lama are

The majestic Kalachakra Pagoda

stored in the core of the pagoda.

Guomari Village's Dragon Boat Festival (端午节) celebrations are legendary. The village residents tend to get up early in the mornings of the Festival. Before sunrise, family members will roll in the cornfields and wash their faces and bodies in the Longwu River. After sunrise, women fill all household utensils with water, and make buns with leek stuffing. On the morning of the festival, Family members will snip a few hairs from their horses and donkeys as a ritual to request safety and health for their domestic animals.

After the leek buns are steamed, some will be sent to relatives who have become monks while others are shared with daughters who are married. The monk is usually the "An Que" (安确), a person who directs the daily Buddhist ceremony for a household. Food is presented to the "An Que" as a sign of respect and reminding the "An Que" to pray for their ancestors. Villagers also present food to friends and relatives who have endured bereavements in the year. When all these rituals are completed, families will finally sit down to enjoy their buns. After breakfast, villagers will climb on Jidong Hill and go to the religious site of their own clan to burn incense. Afterwards, they will relax by the river - well-off families will camp there for the day.

Guomari VIllage Buddhist ceremony.

## BLOWING AWAY THE CLOUDS

After the Dragon Boat Festival, villagers will commence sacrificial rites to deter storms. Monks will first blow trumpets to ward off the bad weather. If that is ineffective, a special prayer wheel will be spun to blow the dark clouds away.

# Mazha Village

## China's Mecca

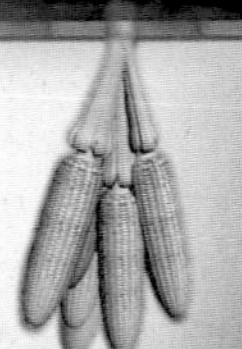

Located in an area with the lowest elevation and the hottest climate in China, Mazha Village, with 1,700 years of history behind it, is the oldest village belonging to the Uyghur ethnic minority and is one of the best preserved villages in Xinjiang Province.

### Getting there

Mazha Village, Guyugou Town, Shanshan County, Turpan, Xinjiang Uygur Autonomous Region..
Nearest City: Urumchi.
新疆维吾尔自治区吐鲁番地区鄯善县吐峪沟乡麻扎村。
From the Xinjiang capital of Urumchi, the quickest option is to fly from Urumchi Diwobao International Airport (乌鲁木齐地窝堡国际机场) to Turpan Jiaohe airport(吐鲁番交河机场). Take a bus from Turpan to Mazha Village (about 2.5 hours).

Mazha Village is located down in the Turpan Depression to the south of the Fire Mountain (Huoyanshan) of Xinjiang Province, about 47 km west of the city of Turpan. "Mazha", an Arabic transliteration of a Tibetan term meaning "holy" or "saint's tomb", is a reference to the old Islamic tombs of dignitaries. Mazha Village is a mysterious ancient village which is hidden amongst white poplar and mulberry trees. A narrow river rushes across the village from north to south, and along the river are several Uyghur dwellings. Their residents leave their homes to begin their work at sunrise

A mosque in Mazha Village

and don't return until sunset. Women in bright clothes can be seen washing clothes along the stream.

Mazha Village has the oldest vineyard (葡萄园) in Xinjiang Province, with vines that cover an area of 3 acres. Its villagers inherited the 2,000-year-old custom of building houses with yellow clay. The houses are connected with lanes, and their roofs are also used as a way to pass from home to home. The old dwellings are simple but embody a profound cultural tradition. Some of the architecture still hints at an ancient mix of Buddhism and Islamic cultures, with various wood carvings on the door frames such as flowers, geometric patterns and fruits. Patterns on the window frames encode information about the profession, hobby or status of the home owner.

One "mazha" (tomb) in Mazha Village called Al-Sahab Kahfi Mazha is one of the two famous mazhas in Xinjiang Province and one of the seven holy places of Islam. According to legend, in the seventh century, Muhammad's student Yemunaiha and four others went to China for missionary work. They walked east from Turpan and met a shepherd who became the first Moslem in China. Along with the other five, the shepherd and his dog then made their way to Tuyu Valley and lived in a cave. The six people and the shepherd's dog finally became saints and were buried there. Today, there are six soil tombs and one irregular stone shaped somewhat like a dog at the site. This holy tomb is regarded as the No. 1 Islamic holy place in China, giving it a reputation as "China's Mecca."

No modern vehicles can been seen in Mazha Village as villagers only travel by donkey cart. The village is generally quiet but on holidays, villagers can be seen wearing their most beautiful clothes and gathering on the streets, dancing the ancient Uyghur "Meshrep" and expressing their best wishes to each other.

Mazha Village at a glance

## THOUSAND BUDDHA CAVE

Not far west of Al-Sahab Kahfi Mazha is the Thousand Buddha Cave (千佛洞), one of the early sites where Buddhism was first introduced to China. It houses one of the top three Buddhist grottoes in Xinjiang Province and the earliest and largest existing grotto group built in the Gaochang Kingdom period (501-640) in Turpan. The grottoes and murals inside the cave are a valuable resource for studies of Chinese Buddhist culture, art and architectural history.

# Aletun Village

## The Land of Gold

Aletun Village village's Uyghur name is "Aletongleke", meaning "The Land of Gold". The village is the site of the ninth Hui king's tomb and palace and other constructions which not only reflect the Uyghur style, but also its absorption of the Han culture of Central China.

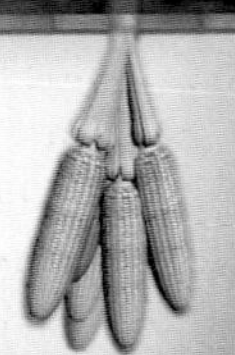



### Getting there

Aledun Village, Kumul City, Xinjiang Uigur Autonomous Region.
Nearest City: Urumchi.
新疆维吾尔自治区哈密市回城乡阿勒屯村
Take a short flight from Urumchi Diwobao International Airport(乌鲁木齐地窝堡堡国际机场) to Kumul Airport(哈密机场 ). From the airport, take a shuttle bus to the downtown area of Kumul city(哈密市), from where it is a 20 minute taxi ride to the mausoleum buildings of Aledun Village(阿勒屯村).

A panaromic view of Aledun Palace

The Kumul Royal Tomb (also known as the Hami imperial tombs) (哈密王陵) is the tomb building group for the royal family of the Kings of Kumul during the Qing Dynasty. The Uyghur ethnic group calls this place "Aledunleke" (阿勒屯勒克), which means "Golden Tomb". From 1697 to 1930, the Kumul power ruled through nine generations, the longest dynasty in Xinjiang Province. For more than two centuries, the ancient Kumul Kings of Hui played a role in building a stable Xinjiang, subduing rebellions and safeguarding national unity. The Kumul Khanate was nominated by the Qing government as the "head of eight regions in Xinjiang" (回疆八部之首). Ebeidula and his son followed the Kangxi Emperor on expeditions, put down a rebellion at Junggar, and received awards from a grateful Qing government. After the death of the seventh Kumul King of Hui Bohier, the Qing Dynasty granted him the title of "King Peace" and allocated funds to build this Kumul King Tomb, earmarking a site of about 1.3 hectares.

The mausoleum group comprises three parts: the Large Arch (大拱拜), pavilion-style architecture and Aitika Mosque. The 14 metre Large Arch is the tallest oneamong the mausoleum buildings and has a unique structure with strong Islamic overtones. The arch has a square bottom and round top, without beam support. Inside lies the mausoleum (陵墓) of the seventh Kumul King of Hui Bohier and his wives, and the eighth Kumul King of Hui Mohanned and his wife, all covered with yellow silk, a material that could only be used by the royal family. The internal walls and dome are affixed with white painted orchid tiles, making the mausoleum elegant and solemn.

Aitika Mosque (艾提卡清真寺), the largest mosque in Xinjiang Province, is located opposite the Large Arch. It is said that the fourth Kumul King of Hui Yusupu built the mosque in around 1760. It is 60 metres long and 36 metres wide, accounting for 2,300 square metres in area and is capable of accommodating up to 4,000 worshippers. The temple has nine rows of 108 wooden sculptured columns supporting the top. All columns are made from raw pines from the Tian Mountains and are so wide that they would need two people wrap their arms around each of them. The walls were painted with vivid and colourful flowers and inscribed with Arabic verses from the Koran. The floor is laid with black square bricks, and inside the door there is a screw ladder to the top of the mosque. In the morning of the Kurban Festival (古尔邦节, usually held around the beginning of December) and at the end of Ramadan, people climb to the top to recite the Koran, and it is said that the sound can be heard miles away.

A richly ornamented wooden pavilion was built in 1902 in an unusual style that combines the four ethnic architectural styles of the Manchu, Mongolian, Uyghur and Han nations. The burial system within is in the Uyghur-style, the outside top is in the Manchurian and Mongolian "helmet" style (盔顶式), while the corridors and eaves are in the traditional Han style. Buried here are the last Kumul King of Hui Shamuhutes and his wife, as well as the other kings of Uyghur.

The most legendary person from the ninth Kumul Dynasty (1882-1930) was Mailibaniu, the wife of seventh Kumul King Bohierand the only queen in the modern history of Kumul. After her husband was murdered by a peasant army, and succeeded by the ailing Mohammed, Mailibaniu helped to keep the ship of state on an even keel. Her name is still talked about today among the locals.

### PALACE REDUX

There used to be a Kumul Palace (哈密王宫) near the Kumul Tomb that was famous for its legendary beauty. Unfortunately, it was destroyed during a battle in 1931 and razed to the ground. The palace has now been rebuilt and is located beside the Kumul King Tomb.





The Aledun Tomb of Kumul King of Hui is solemn and dignified

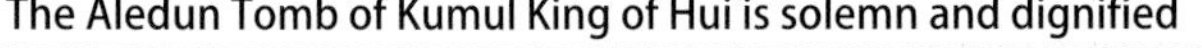

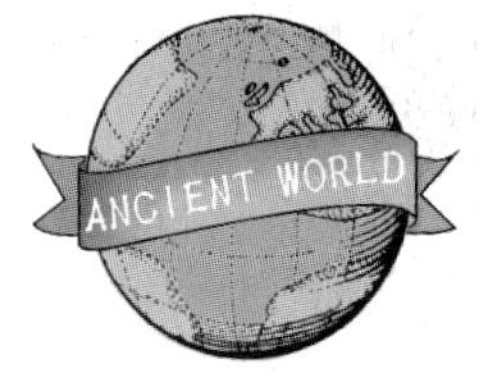


# Exploring the past

Ancient World is a new series of travel books with a unique focus on the legacy of the past. Every ancient village, town and city covered by our Ancient World guides bears the mark of an ancient way of life. Ancient World guides make this heritage accessible with detailed directions and information about culture and history.

---

Make-Do Publishing,
Hong Kong.


---



English edition first published 2012.
Editor: Howard Shi
Project Editor: Claire Liu
Art Editor: Gia Kei

---


ISBN 978-988-18419-8-8

# Dynasties

| Dynasty | Dates |
|---|---|
| Xia 夏朝 | B.C. 2070–B.C 1600 |
| Shang 商朝 | B.C. 1600–B.C 1046 |
| Zhou 周 | |
| Western Zhou 西周 | B.C. 1046–B.C 771 |
| Eastern Zhou 东周 | B.C. 770– B.C 256 |
| Spring and Autumn 春秋 | B.C. 770– B.C 476 |
| Warring States 战国 | B.C. 475–B.C 221 |
| Qin 秦朝 | B.C. 221–B.C 207 |
| Han 汉 | |
| Western Han 西汉 | B.C. 206– A.D 8 |
| Xin Chao 新朝 | A.D. 9 – 23 |
| East Han 东汉 | 25 – 220 |
| Three Kingdoms 三国 | |
| Wei 魏 | A.D. 220– 265 |
| Shu Han 蜀汉 | 221–263 |
| Wu 吴 | 222–280 |
| Jin 晋 | |
| Western Jin 西晋 | 265–316 |
| Eastern Jin 东晋 | 317–420 |
| Sixteen Kingdoms 十六国 | 304–439 |
| South 南朝 | |
| Song 宋 | 420 – 479 |
| Qi 齐 | 479 –502 |
| Liang 梁 | 502 –557 |
| Chen 陈 | 557 – 589 |

# Dynasties

| Dynasty | Dates |
|---|---|
| North 北朝 | |
| Northern Wei北魏 | 386 – 534 |
| WesternWei西魏 | 534 – 550 |
| Eastern Wei东魏 | 534 – 550 |
| Northern Qi 北齐 | 550 – 577 |
| Northern Zhou 北周 | 557 – 581 |
| Sui 隋 | 581 – 618 |
| Tang 唐 | 618 – 907 |
| Five Dynasties and Ten Kingdoms 五代十国 | 907 – 960 |
| Song 宋 | |
| Northern Song 北宋 | 960 – 1127 |
| Southern Song 南宋 | 1127 – 1279 |
| Liao 辽 | 907 – 1125 |
| Da Li 大理 | 937 – 1254 |
| Western Xia 西夏 | 1032 – 1227 |
| Jin 金 | 1115 – 1234 |
| Yuan 元 | 1206 – 1368 |
| Ming 明 | 1368 – 1644 |
| Qing 清 | 1616 – 1911 |
| Republic of China 中华民国 | 1912 – 1949 |
| People's Republic of China | 1949 – Now |

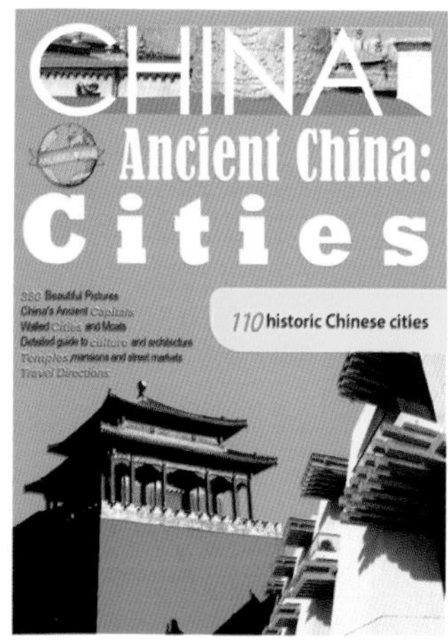


## Ancient China: Cities

**110 Ancient Chinese Cities.**

Ancient China: Cities has sections on ancient capitals, walled cities, and cities with a special significance in Chinese history. Ancient Chinese cities are differentiated from towns by their greater emphasis on political and military functions. Over 5,000 years of Chinese history, China has had numerous capitals, with one giving way to another as dynasties rose and fell.

·Ancient Chinese capitals.
·Centres of the ancient Chinese world.
·Unique urban architecture.
·Cities associated with China's revolutions.
·From opera to temple fairs.
·Full directions.
·Cultural treasures.

## Ancient China: Towns

**143 Ancient Chinese Towns.**

Ancient China: Towns introduces historic Chinese river towns, mountain towns, fortress towns and border towns. Ancient towns in China were founded primarily for trade purposes but their development was driven by many different forces. The architecture of ancient Chinese towns can be divided into private buildings (like courtyard residences and private gardens) and public buildings (like ancestral temples, colleges, opera towers, guild halls and bridges.)

·Lake towns with dreamlike settings.
·Gardens in the mountains.
·Culture and history.
·Towns with many tales to tell.
·Detailed travel directions.
·Architecture and art.
·Temples,  gates and walls.